D1265676

MEDIEVAL CHURCH AND SOCIETY

MEDIEVAL CHURCH AND SOCIETY

Collected Essays

CHRISTOPHER BROOKE

NEW YORK UNIVERSITY PRESS

First published 1971 in Great Britain
by Sidgwick and Jackson Limited

First published 1972 in
the United States of America

SBN.8147-0968-0

Library of Congress Catalog Card Number: 72-166506

Printed in Great Britain

Contents

List of Illustrations

Preface

The essays in this book were written at various times over the last fifteen years or so, and seven of them have been printed before. Errors have been corrected, and a few adjustments and revisions made to fit them to their present context; but a radical revision would have been contrary to the purpose of the book, and in some cases an arbitrary and meaningless task. Thus, Chapter 4 represents in considerable detail, on a number of points, the state of learning in 1956. If I were to compose it again now, in a number of ways the approach would be different, the annotation on a different basis. If I rewrote it, scholars who wished to refer to the paper would have two articles and not one to contend with; and one is nuisance enough. A few indications of new work or of new editions of texts have been inserted, somewhat arbitrarily, in the nature of the case; but it is hoped that they will be helpful and save confusion.

I owe far more debts than can be listed here. But any gathering of my creditors must include my wife, Dr Rosalind Brooke, who has improved all these papers by help and criticism, and done far more than that to several of them. Many years ago, I lent a hand in checking the notes to her *Early Franciscan Government*; a missing reference, and the happy accident that the French editions of Sabatier's *Life of St Francis* have no index, led me to re-read that masterpiece; of this, Chapter 10 is the fruit. It is an impertinent witness to my attempts to glean something from her Franciscan learning, as well as to an interest first roused by Professor Dom David Knowles's lectures – and to him my debt also appears in every chapter. Chapter 1, in particular, owes much to my brother, Professor Nicholas Brooke. Dr J. V. Fearns gave me much help in the preparation of Chapter 7; Dr R. A. Markus in Chapters 2 and 3. If Wolfram von Eschenbach appears like King Charles's head, in and out of context, the blame must partly fall on Mr Hugh Sacker, to whose thesis 'The Tolerance Idea in Wolfram's *Willehalm*' (Frankfurt-am-Main, 1955), and to whose book *An Introduction to Wolfram's Parzival* (Cambridge, 1963), I owe almost all of what I know of Wolfram, though I have had kind help in this field too from Dr Marianne Wynne.

To the editors and publishers of the original papers and lectures, I am much indebted for consent and approval for their reprinting here; and in particular to the Secretary of the Liverpool University Press and to the University of Liverpool (1); to Professor C. W. Dugmore (2); to Professor F. H. Hinsley, editor of the *Historical Journal,* formerly the *Cambridge Historical Journal* (4)[1]; to Dr Albert Hollaender, editor of the *Journal of the Society of Archivists* (5); to Professor A. G. Dickens, Director of the Institute of Historical Research and editor of the Institute's *Bulletin* (7); to Dr Frank Taylor, Librarian of the John Rylands Library and editor of its *Bulletin* (8); to the President, Secretary, and Council of the Royal Historical Society (11). Chapter 12 is a lecture from which an extract was printed in *The Layman in Christian History,* ed. S. C. Neill and H.-R. Weber (London, S.C.M. Press for the World Council of Churches, 1963), pp. 127 ff.; I am grateful to the editors and to Mr Martin Conway, Publications Secretary of the World Council of Churches, for their consent. It is based on Iris Origo's *Merchant of Prato* (Jonathan Cape, 1957; reprinted Penguin Books, 1963), and to the author and publishers we owe the kind permission to print extracts from this fascinating revelation of a fourteenth-century merchant and his world. My thanks are also due to Hodder and Stoughton Ltd for permission to quote from Sabatier's *Life of St Francis,* translated by L. S. Houghton.

For giving their consent to the reproduction of the illustrations, I am indebted for Plate I to the Trustees of the British Museum

[1] It has also previously appeared in *Change in Medieval Society*, ed. Sylvia Thrupp (New York, 1964), pp. 49–71.

(plate from Add. MS.49,598, fo.118v); for Plate II, Messrs T. Nelson and Sons Ltd and Messrs Elsevier of Amsterdam (plate from the *Atlas of the Early Christian World,* fig. 430); for Plate III, Mr Edwin Smith and Messrs Thames and Hudson Ltd (plate from G. Hutton, *English Parish Churches,* Pl. 114); and for Plate IV, the Delegates of the Oxford University Press (plate from A. W. Clapham, *English Romanesque Architecture after the Conquest,* fig. 16). My grateful thanks go to the Aberdeen University Press for providing the blocks for these illustrations.

Finally, I am particularly grateful to the directors and editors of Sidgwick and Jackson Ltd who suggested that the collection be made and helped very materially in making it – especially to Lord Longford, John Chancellor, William Armstrong, and Beth Williams.

C.N.L.B.

LIST OF ABBREVIATIONS

C.H.J.: *Cambridge Historical Journal.*

D.N.B.: *Dictionary of National Biography,* ed. L. Stephen and S. Lee, 66 vols., London, 1885–1901, repr. 22 vols., Oxford, 1921–2.

Eadmer, *Hist. Nov.*: Eadmer, *Historia Novorum in Anglia,* ed. M. Rule, Rolls Series, London, 1884.

E.H.R.: *English Historical Review.*

Hist. Ch. York: *The Historians of the Church of York and its Archbishops,* ed. J. Raine, 3 vols., Rolls Series, London, 1879–94.

JL.: *Regesta Pontificum Romanorum,* ed. P. Jaffé, Rev. G. Wattenbach, S. Loewenfeld, F. Kaltenbrunner, P. Ewald, 2 vols., Leipzig, 1885–8.

Journ. Theol. Studies: *Journal of Theological Studies*

Mandonnet-Vicaire: P. Mandonnet and M.-H. Vicaire, *Saint Dominique, l'idée, l'homme et l'oeuvre,* 2 vols., Paris, 1937.

MOPH: *Monumenta Ordinis Fratrum Praedicatorum Historica.*

PL: *Patrologiae cursus completus, series Latina,* ed. J. P. Migne, 221 vols., Paris, 1844–64.

QFD: *Quellen und Forschungen zur Geschichte des Dominikanerordens in Deutschland.*

TRHS, Trans. R. Hist. Soc.: *Transactions of the Royal Historical Society.*

Vicaire (1955): M.-H. Vicaire, *S. Dominique de Caleruega d'après les documents du XIIIe siècle,* Paris, 1955.

Vicaire (1964): M.-H. Vicaire, *Histoire de S. Dominique,* 2 vols., Paris, 1957, cited from English translation by K. Pond, London, 1964.

X: *Decretalium Gregorii pp. IX compilatio* in *Corpus Iuris Canonici,* ed. E. Friedberg, II, Leipzig, 1881.

Yorks. Arch. J.: *Yorkshire Archaeological Journal.*

LIST OF ABBREVIATIONS

Introduction

History is an imaginative subject. It is many other things besides: it can be a means to sharpen our analytical faculties; it can be used as a guide to the modern world. It has a range of educational purposes, and (if discreetly used) is of some direct practical value. But for the moment let us dwell on the relations of history and imagination. I am not speaking of fancy, either the idle fancy of the dreamer or the controlled fancy of the novelist; but the attempt to piece together an intelligible, credible picture of the world of the past – credible in so far as it conforms to the evidence which survives from that world, and also to our experience of human nature and the world in which we live. We are already in deep water. The psychologists tell us that human nature changes; and some will say that it is only by the controlled and discreet use of historical imagination that we can tell how much, and in what ways, it has changed. Yet so long as we take imagination to mean the faculty of understanding in a broad and deep sense, what we have said is neither absurd nor false to the practice of historians.

The grip, the fascination of the past – the yearning to find ways of uncovering it, can easily become a disease. The symptoms are total immersion in the past, an incapacity *not* to see the past in every tree and field and street corner, an ineradicable tendency when faced with anything to ask first 'how old is it?', a tendency to line the walls of every room one can lay hands on with books about the past, and never to be content unless the floor is also well covered. It can lead to all sorts of absurdities, including an insatiable desire to live in the past in a literal sense, to break through time's screen. From this, most historians are exempt: they are too much aware of the practical disadvantages of living even a hundred years ago, let alone a millennium, to be seriously tempted; and the condition of their science is that theories cannot be checked against direct experience: it would spoil our fun if we could be transported to the Middle Ages, and the assumption that we cannot do this is an essential presupposition of historical study. This is true even of very recent history. Living witnesses can be gathered in their multitudes; and as the archives slowly unfold, evidence is revealed beyond the medievalist's wildest dream. But evidence it remains, not different in fundamental character from that for the more distant past. We cannot check even the recent past by revisiting it.

The historian's preoccupation with what is dead and gone seems to many people to be involvement with what is, by definition, irrelevant and best forgotten. This book is not for them. Slightly more subtle is the heresy which reckons only recent history, or modern history (however defined), as relevant to the modern world. If this is simply a plea that more attention should be paid to contemporary history in schools and universities, I would support it wholeheartedly. When it involves a feeling that history syllabuses in the past have been excessively parochial, and that the drier aspects of the Middle Ages have commanded a disproportionate amount of attention, then I sympathize at the least. But the view that the Middle Ages are best forgotten, that history can be reckoned to start in 1900 or 1750 or 1500 – or else that medieval history is a harmless option for fanatics, but one which serious students of modern history should be spared – such a view must be sternly resisted. There are many social scientists to whom the study of history seems useless, since they are concerned with phenomena for which only living evidence is really useful – useful, that is, as a basis for a full understanding of social structure or for economic statistics of sufficient sophistication. Their views command a measure of respect. But as soon as it is admitted that study of the past has any value or relevance, then we have to face the real objections to history as a science: that the evidence is fragmentary and cannot be checked; that it can at best reveal to us what actually happened and not the choices and alternatives which were rejected or failed to materialize; and that the whole range of recorded time, so far, is unconscionably short, a tiny fragment of the human past, scarcely perceptible in the history of the world. Thus it seems to me a mockery that anyone should seriously engage in the study of the past, whether at school or at university, and have no conception of even so limited a range of time as the 5,000 years of the historical past. Of course, it can only be selective and fragmentary; but if the special function of history is to give a sense of depth and of time, then it must include some real experience of periods of history widely scattered, and that is one reason why I am a fervent believer in the value of contemporary history and of ancient history, as well as of the Middle Ages.

Relevance is a strangely ambiguous word. It can refer to practical utility, or to a whole range of values plunging deep into our civilization and to the depths of our consciousness. Let us start at the surface and then work deeper into the mine. It can be readily conceded that practical information from the recent past is often relevant in cases in which earlier history is not; but to suggest that this is always so is nonsense. If I buy a house, however old it may be, only a short part of its recent history is likely to be relevant (under current law) to its legal ownership; it would be absurd to suggest that the earlier history of an old house could have no relevance to its owner – absurd, even for understanding how it is constructed in order to keep it in repair. To understand the structure of a garden suburb, thirty or forty years of history may suffice; yet it would be foolish to suppose that earlier history was irrelevant in an ancient town nearby. There are many economic problems in the modern world which can be illuminated by a study of economic history since the Industrial Revolution, but hardly at all by anything which lay before. But equally, the history of developed, industrial economies is of doubtful relevance to the developing world. We must never expect to draw easy lessons from the past; but clearly some understanding of what happened when Western Europe began to convert itself – with only modest external help, without foreign aid, without OXFAM, without *Mater et Magistra* – from an underdeveloped into a developing world, has much to teach those who make the practical arrangements. Some knowledge of the economic history of Europe from 1000 to 1700 is of obvious utility to those who study the economics of underdeveloped countries; to the true understanding of the developing world the history of modern industrial Europe is as irrelevant as its economics.

We are often told that those who study the history of cities must understand what a city is, something of its nature as seen through the eyes of geographers, sociologists, and architects; it would seem equally true that an intimate knowledge of the history of a city is essential for those who re-plan and re-build it. It is obvious, and widely accepted. Yet we live in an age of paradoxes; and while there has never been so much fervour of research into the past, nor so great a public interest (as any well-publicized exhibition in a London museum or gallery bears witness), yet equally there has never been so much ignorant destruction of the past. In this case, knowledge is not just desirable; it is urgent. There are notable examples of an alliance between historical and archaeological expertise and well informed local fervour to ensure that the past is adequately recorded before new roads and new building sweep it away for ever; the activities of the Winchester Research Unit are an obvious example. The need for such alliances in every ancient town is now becoming evident. It is no substitute in itself for intelligent and imaginative planning; nor do I underestimate the planner's difficulties. It is simply obvious, and coming at last (though almost too late) to be widely accepted, that intelligent planning presupposes adequate historical knowledge.

When a man reads of the consequences of certain types of historical study on the notions of nationality and race and colour in the nineteenth and twentieth centuries, he may reasonably conclude that history is altogether too practical a subject, and should be banned. But if we agree to give it one more chance, it is now clear that we cannot hope to understand the historical roots of European prejudices on these topics unless we are deeply read in the medieval history of African slavery and of Judaism, or, to put it another way, unless we have penetrated into the world which lies behind *Othello* and the *Merchant of Venice*. Not that one can isolate the medieval history of slavery from its ancient roots or its modern consequences; several aspects of the history of Christian slavery are summed up in the striking phrase on the tomb of John Newton, slave-trader turned Evangelical Divine, in St Mary Woolnoth's Church in the heart of the City of London: 'servant of the slaves of Africa'. But the sharp edge in Shakespeare's plays, and in some events too recent to contemplate, can hardly be understood unless one looks back, far back.

We have now dug deep into the mine. The history of medieval slavery will hardly give us practical help in a chance encounter in Europe, Africa, or America in the 1970s; rather the reverse. Yet it helps us, whatever our ancestry or background may be, to understand; and understanding in a broader sense is the chief concern of all the human sciences. Study of the past feeds our comprehension, very often, not by direct lessons or by lines joining past to present, but rather by the attempt to see a society or a civilization in the past as an imaginative whole. The wholeness is a manner of speaking, needless to say; our vision of the past can only be fragmentary. We may fill in the fragments of our vision by reading, or by writing, historical novels; but they will only stimulate us to true understanding if we remember that they are novels, and in the end, however much we may have gained in insight and vision, reject what is fancy. An attempt to recreate the past imaginatively in a concrete way is a genuine and satisfying task; it is perhaps the most substantial educational justification for the study of history; and it feeds the illness whose symptoms I described at the outset.

The essays which follow attempt to penetrate a society in the past, to give concrete expression to its nature, aspirations, and history. They study the interaction between the Christian Church and medieval society; they all attempt, sooner or later, to look at some aspect of this common theme. They do other things besides. The first began its career as my Inaugural Lecture at Liverpool University, the second was a contribution to the launching of the Ecclesiastical History Society, the tenth an occasional lecture for historical societies; but each, owing to the occasion or the theme, expresses something of a historian's faith.

To some readers, this may appear wholly irrelevant; history, they think, should be an objective study, and the historian's personal beliefs must not obtrude; the less they appear, the more successful the history. I have emphasized sufficiently, I think, in the first two essays, that differences of belief and background are no barrier to common work and mutual understanding in the study of history; and it has never been my practice to allow them to be so, or my experience that they were. For this reason, it is merely tiresome if they become too obtrusive; equally, however high-minded, the historian who attempts to hide his beliefs altogether may deceive his audience. But as a teacher of history I am moved to say something of my faith by an even more urgent consideration. The historian treats topics of moment, sometimes of great present concern, always topics which deeply moved men and women in the past. Cool analysis will be needed if he and his audience are to gain any understanding; but if that is the end of the matter, if the whole exposition is detached and withdrawn, if no indication is given that the historian sees that great issues are at stake, then he will be convicted of cynicism and indifference. The charge may be utterly false; but his audience cannot know it, and they will judge by what they know. To some, this will appear wholly unfair; the historian's business is to explain, to analyse, not to involve his audience; why cannot they leave him alone, to work at his last, to do his own specific task, and leave to the philosophers and the theologians any thought of the ultimate significance of the themes he handles? This would be a reasonable defence if the historian worked in a compartment, in a cell, separated from his other human concerns; but this is not so.

Yet any revelation of one's own convictions is a delicate task: too obtrusive a parade is tedious, and may degenerate into propaganda, which in such a context should be the reverse of the intention. The temptation to preach to a captive audience is strong in us all, and every one of these essays started its career as a lecture. I am not perfectly certain that I have evaded it successfully; I know only that I have tried; that my aim has been to share some measure of common understanding, of imaginative reconstruction, yet never to hide my belief that living issues were involved.

Three major themes run through these essays. Chapters 1, 2, 4, and 12 are in part an attempt to penetrate the world of ideas in which love and marriage and celibacy moved in the central Middle Ages; Chapters 5, 7, and 8 tackle aspects of religious sentiment, the first (as we must think) an aberration in sentiment reflected in the golden age of medieval forgery, the second the sentiment of dissent and its relation to the Catholic tradition of the same period, the third, religious sentiment in its most visible expression, in church building; and Chapters 10 and 11 approach the two key figures in the history of the religious life in the thirteenth century, St Francis and St Dominic. In a sense all these topics relate to the history of ideas, but not to the history of thought as commonly understood; for it is in the main ordinary ideas and assumptions of men who were not themselves distinguished as theologians or philosophers that are discussed: popes like Gregory VII and Gregory IX, saints like Francis and Dominic, and laymen like Wolfram von Eschenbach and Francesco di Marco Datini.

The diversity of origin of these essays will be very apparent to the reader, and it would be pointless to disguise it. I have tried to make clear the circumstances in which they were first written; and the interest of such a book must lie, if anywhere, precisely in the way diversity of approach and method reveals a common theme and purpose. I have therefore deliberately mingled lectures intended to give basic guide-lines and instruction, with papers intended to advance knowledge and expound detailed research. Minute researches cannot be the heart of any human discipline; and yet they are a very vital part of the work of any scholar. I have tried to reveal something of what I imagine my trade to be by the variety of shades of these essays. It may be that they will be read by some not at all familiar with the history of the medieval Church; I certainly hope so. For them, Chapters 3, 6 and 9 have been particularly chosen as anchors or guide-lines; and for clarity, all but the first two have been placed in some sort of chronological sequence, though some are wide ranging and cannot be thus tied down.

I have said that the fascination of the past can become a disease; I have also tried, as we all must from time to time, to make some justification for my trade. But at the end of the day it is the illness which makes us historians, and it is for those who feel the temptation to be immersed in the past, and believe (with Oscar Wilde) that the right way to treat temptation is to yield to it, that these essays are published.

1

The Dullness of the Past

Inaugural Lecture, as Professor of Mediaeval History, University of Liverpool, delivered on 28 February 1957, and published by the Liverpool University Press (1957).

IN the third book of Pope's *Dunciad* the Son of Dullness, personified as Colley Cibber, descends, like Aeneas, into the shades; and there he meets his great precursor Settle, who provides him with a glorious vision of future Empire. The kingdom of Dullness is at hand, and one of the many signs of its approaching victory is the busy activity of a historian 'of sober face, with learned dust besprent'. He takes the form of Thomas Hearne, the eccentric Oxford non-juror, who dedicated his life to editing medieval texts with a rare accuracy, to controversies on the age of Oxford and Cambridge, and to other high matters. Settle apostrophizes his disciple:

> 'To future ages may thy dulness last,
> As thou preserv'st the dulness of the past.'

The association of historical scholarship and dullness has been a constant theme with poets and novelists. History 'tells me nothing that does not either vex or weary me', says Catherine Morland in *Northanger Abbey*. 'The quarrels of popes and kings, with wars or pestilences in every page; the men all so good for nothing, and hardly any women at all, it is very tiresome; and yet I often think it odd that it should be so dull, for a great deal of it must be invention.' In saying this she does but echo the loudest condemnation of all, from Sir Philip Sidney.

> 'The historian . . . loaden with old mouse-eaten records, authorising himselfe for the most part upon other histories, whose greatest authorities are built uppon the notable foundation heresay, having much ado to accord differing writers, and to prick truth out of partiality: better acquainted with a 1000. yeres ago, then with the present age, and yet better knowing how this world goeth, then how his owne wit runneth; curious for antiquities, and inquisitive of novelties; a wonder to yoong folkes, and a tyrant in table talke. . . .'[1]

These three passages make very salutary reading for us, and should be framed in every historian's study. Every historian who has any talent for making his subject intelligible and interesting to a wider public has a duty to spend a part of his time proving to the world that history is not dull. Most of us have little talent in that direction; but we all have the duty of making our findings lucid and intelligible, and so interesting those who wish to learn. Many dull books have been written on history; our consciences are not entirely clear. But we repudiate the notion that history is inherently dull, or the historian by professional incapacity a bore.

There are some to whom the study of the past makes no appeal; they are lost souls. To the great body of mankind, whose main interests lie elsewhere, history has an appeal like every subject which is rational, humane, and cultivated, and overlaps the boundary of thought and action. It affects them (I take it) as the study of evolution affects me: I recognize that it has a value more than merely academic, I admit that it is a vital extension to human knowledge, I am prepared to read about it if it is lucidly and rationally expounded, with a little sugar to coat the pill. Some technicalities of history or biology may for one reason or

[1] *Defence of Poesie* (ed. A. Feuillart, Cambridge, 1923, p. 12). I follow the first quarto (Ponsonby), but read 'goeth . . . runneth' for 'goes . . . runnes' with the second quarto (Olney) and the Penshurst MS.

another interest a wider circle than historians or biologists; but by and large technical history, *de fundo* scholarship, will only be read by the professionals or by those keenly interested in the subject. They would be dull to an outsider; but that only means that their audience (like that of Proust or Joyce) is limited, not that they are inherently dull. A powerful fascination drives every scholar or researcher through a thousand tedious hours in a cold, ill-lit muniment room or a smelly laboratory, to an abstruse conclusion intelligible only to a few; but a skilful expositor can communicate to his audience the inspiration of his tedious result. We are all specialists in the modern world, whatever our profession; and the exposition of our speciality to our own coterie is as much a piece of craftsmanship as the exposition of a broader theme to a wider audience. I do not mean that a historian's scribblings at any level commonly attain the standard of high art; what I do mean is that we should care about our manner of exposition, however obscure our subject. The article of a really great scholar can give, rather austerely perhaps, a thrill akin to that of the craftsmen in prose who have made our profession great in the eyes of the world. It may be going a bit far to say that Housman's footnotes to Manilius give the small circle who can read them a delight not dissimilar from the delight a much wider circle derives from his poetry; and I think it is better to call scholarship a craft rather than an art. But in my own field, I derive a pleasure from essays in liturgical history (most abstruse of subjects) by Edmund Bishop, or from the essays on legal history by F. W. Maitland, which is not wholly other than the pleasure of reading Gibbon's *Decline and Fall.* History is both a science and a craft; and I should say the same, though sometimes with misgivings, of any academic discipline worth its salt.

If we repudiate the notion that history is dull in the ordinary sense of the word, we have still not escaped the censure of Sidney and Pope. Dullness for Pope had a far richer meaning than mere tedium, just as Wisdom to the Hebrews meant more than being sagacious. 'I can understand,' he might say, 'that you find the trivial details of your subject fascinating; that you regard the mutterings of the learned world as things of beauty.

It is evident from everything you say that your whole sense of values is radically at fault, that you are the sort of person who mistakes a mouldering parchment for the *Mona Lisa,* an *apparatus criticus* for the Iliad. You are a fine example of the reversal of values which I portrayed in the *Dunciad*; and if you were not beneath my contempt I would find a place for you in my next edition.' Pope saw, or thought he saw, the world of culture overwhelmed by the unbalanced and the second-rate. Whatever we may think of his condemnations, there is no doubt that his own vision, of a world of integrated thought and art, liberal in the antique sense, was very fine. The educated man must have a balanced education, must see things whole; and it is this insistence on wholeness which makes Pope so bitter about specialists of whatever kind – whether scholars like Bentley and Hearne, or connoisseurs like the specialist in butterflies who was arraigned before the goddess by the specialist in flowers for spoiling a favourite bloom with his butterfly net. All specialists, says the poet, lack a sense of proportion.

This is an old complaint, akin to John of Salisbury's against Cornificius and to Erasmus's against the schoolmen. The charge of dullness in the obvious sense I was able to repudiate by mere bravado; by simply asserting that it was not so. The charge that the historian is too often a specialist with a lop-sided sense of proportion is not so easy to counter. In part it cannot and must not be countered. So immense has been the progress of human knowledge since the days of Erasmus and Pope that knowledge nowadays can only be advanced by specialists. The sense of truthfulness and the liberal values which Pope admired have many enemies in the modern world. Whether or not we agree with Housman's view that 'the faintest of all human passions is the love of truth', I am convinced that the instinct that truth is worth laying hold of with care and precision owes its survival and progress in the last two centuries as much as anything to the exacting demands of scholars and scientists. Much that is admirable in our civilization, and much more than we realize that is characteristic of it, is the product of this specialization which the sages so much deplored.

The coin has a reverse; and in our heart of hearts most of us feel that there is more truth in the charges against over-specialization than we dare admit. The dangers of too specialized an education are very obvious; but I am more concerned with the danger to scholarship itself. A specialism cut off from the larger world of knowledge grows stale, inbred, fanciful; life in a vacuum can make a discipline entirely mad, like some of the more eccentric kinds of biblical criticism. History has been afflicted by the disease of specialization in two especially pernicious ways. First, it has been flattered and cajoled by one school of philosophers into thinking that the reconstruction of the past is a special type of intellectual activity, different in kind from other modes of thought; perhaps (as Collingwood seems to have supposed at the end of his life) superior to other modes of thought. This doctrine has been heady wine for the historical world; but I think we have survived it. I am convinced that history enfolds not one but many different forms of thought. At one extreme historians amass and analyse evidence, very much like a descriptive science – and so gain an uneasy respectability from the kindlier logical positivists; at the other extreme we analyse the play of human personality and all the subtleties of the human mind, and so mingle with the literary critics. History is not a separate mode of thought, but the common home of many interests and techniques and traditions, devised by those who have dedicated their best energies to the study of the past. The opposite danger from taking history to be a separate compartment in the human mind is that of thinking that the widely differing ways of studying the past can be isolated one from another. Inspired by a succession of scholars of wide vision, and faced by the threat of bankruptcy to their subject, Anglo-Saxon scholars have grown accustomed to mingle archaeology, philology, and literature with what is rather strangely called 'straight historical material'. But alliances of this kind are still not so common as they should be, especially in fields where material is abundant.

The danger of division is very great. It is not so long since a distinguished scholar told us that 'the archivist is not and ought not to be an historian'. He need not; one has heard of cooks of rare genius who had no palate themselves; one has heard of librarians who never opened a book. But the view that any of the barriers which divide our little worlds is desirable in itself is a terrible notion. There is a difference between the professions of historian and archivist, as there is a difference between engine driver and fireman; but they are, after all, driving the same train.

Nothing in the past is alien to the historian; nor is the whole field of his study past. In so far as mankind is the theme of his study, the historian is surrounded with living evidence. The field is too wide; to make precise observations, to make real contributions to knowledge, the historian does and inevitably must concentrate on a small province, and make it his own. But if he never peers over the walls which surround his speciality, most of his opportunities to advance knowledge of his subject will elude him. The barriers of history and archaeology, of history and literature, philology, economics, and anthropology, have long been breached; but real progress in medieval studies will always depend not on isolated mining operations, but on constant siege warfare on the walls which surround our little castles.

What is the answer? The specialist cannot hope to be expert even in all the techniques which provide us with knowledge of England in the Middle Ages – a very small slice of the total of human knowledge. In part we can collaborate and pool our information, as we already do to some extent, and as is much more systematically done by our scientific colleagues. But that is not the whole answer. It is not sufficient to lay monograph on monograph, to pile brick on brick. We must be able within our own minds to see the context of our work, to contemplate and to compare; and to see how our techniques are used in other fields. My own work has often led me to the criticism of literary sources, and I am profoundly grateful that I was early made aware how intensively New Testament scholars had been studying analogous problems over several generations. In contrast, the recent school of Form Critics sometimes write of the origin of the Gospels as if no one else had ever studied the problems of oral transmission, and as if one could plan the investigation according to arbitrary rules established in the void. These are technical matters; but the same applies to the broader interpretation of men and events. There is no reason why we should not all be aware of our deficiencies, and of the possibility that our neighbour may be able to help us; the mere knowledge of our ignorance is something. More than that, our specialities are some of them so narrow that a man can be a specialist in a variety of subjects, overlapping our conventional barriers. And most of all, we can acquire some understanding which is more than superficial of other techniques without having great wildernesses of knowledge put in our way. We can acquire the flavour of many disciplines without being mere dilettantes.

To put this in another way: the good historian should be well and widely educated. But education is the vaguest of words, and my aim is to make my foggy and oracular perceptions more precise. And so, without more ado, I will ask you to come with me into the medieval world, and see my problem actually at work. The evidence to be inspected lies partly inside, partly outside the normal range of historical material; but the historian of the twelfth century is constantly tempted by his neighbour's game. In a word, this is a poaching expedition, although I am poaching, not simply for the fun of it, but because I have to; because my speciality is sterile if I do not.

From Clairvaux on the edge of the Champagne country one of the greatest of medieval monks organized the most considerable ascetic movement of the central Middle Ages. St Bernard was the inspiration, though not the founder, of the Cistercian order. Only a day's journey away from Clairvaux lies Troyes, the home of Marie Countess of Champagne, and traditionally the centre of the cult of courtly love in Northern France. Two more diverse expressions of the human spirit could hardly be imagined. The word 'love' was often on Bernard's lips, and his greatest work was his *Sermons on the Canticle,* alias the *Song of Solomon*. But his love was the love of God for man and of man for God, not the love of man for man, still less the love of man for woman.

The *Song of Solomon* is one of the world's great love songs. However the pundits may dispute its original meaning, it can undoubtedly be read as a sublime expression of human, sensual love. The medieval Church took it to have a purely allegorical meaning; and medieval churchmen saw no incongruity in applying the language of carnal love to the love of God. In part this represents the force of a tradition, and is with us still; but it is also a measure of St Bernard's repudiation of human pleasures and delights. He did not repudiate human love: he was capable of deep personal affection and he accepted (perhaps a little unwillingly) the existence of family ties and the necessity of marriage in the world. But the love of man for woman, in any romantic sense, meant nothing to him, partly because of the fervour of his asceticism, partly because the romantic attitude to woman was alien to the European tradition of his day.

When St Bernard died at Clairvaux in 1153, Marie of Champagne was a young princess in the court of her father, Louis VII, King of France. She thus belonged to a generation grown accustomed to the teaching of the Cistercians, and her father counted many leading churchmen among his friends. Her life was in no way secluded or obscure. She was the daughter of Louis VII and Eleanor of Aquitaine; and after their marriage had been dissolved on the ground of consanguinity, both her parents remarried, Eleanor taking Henry of Anjou, later Henry II of England, for her second husband. Marie could number two kings of England and a king of France among her half-brothers, and her nephews and nieces and closer relations became in course of time kings or queens of almost every kingdom from England to Jerusalem and even aspired to both the Western and the Eastern Empires. Divorce in the modern sense was not permitted by the medieval Church; but the law of marriage was so exceedingly confused in the mid twelfth century, irregular betrothals so frequent, and the grounds of annulment so many that broken marriages were by no means rare, and illegal marriages for the sake of political advantage were common, sometimes validated by papal dispensation, more often not. Marie's parents (in the medieval sense of the word) had been divorced. Her son Henry was betrothed at the age of five or six to a lady of two; he was subsequently betrothed to her younger sister; he eventually married the heiress of the kingdom of Jerusalem, and held the empty title of king from 1192 to 1197. The complexity of political marriages in high society helps to explain two things about the Countess of Champagne. Louis VII was her father, and also her brother-in-law; his son and successor Philip Augustus was her half-brother, her nephew by marriage, and her daughter's brother-in-law; Louis VIII was her nephew, her nephew by marriage, and her great-nephew by marriage – and it passes the wit of man to say in how many ways she was related to the great St Louis. It also helps to explain why she held the marriage bond in some contempt. There is a record of her solemn judgement in a court of Love, that love and marriage are incompatible.

So many elements went to make the twelfth-century conception of courtly love that it defies definition. It was natural that an emotion so sublime and yet so extremely common as love should find expression in a wide variety of ways; and the very novelty of romantic love, which is essentially what we mean by *amour courtois,* lent ambiguity to its appreciation and confusion to the doctrine of its devotees. Romantic love means giving a high value to womankind, or rather to a particular lady, since it implies a personal relationship, and involves a belief that the whole range of emotions cultivated between man and woman in love are good, and to be pursued for their own sakes; above all that the woman is not a chattel or a drudge or an animal, but a human person whom nature has set aside to be pursued and tamed and worshipped. Courtly love I will not try to define; but only to disentangle some of the roots from which it springs.

The romantic attitude to women was before the twelfth century wholly alien to Europe.[2] We find it neither with the Greeks nor the Romans – who thought, by and large, that man was born for love and friendship, while a woman was to be married or seduced. True, they knew something of the greatness

[2] My interest in the theme of the second half of the lecture was first aroused by reading Mr Christopher Dawson's 'The Origins of the Romantic Tradition' (most recently reprinted in *Medieval Essays*, London, 1953) and Professor C. S. Lewis's *Allegory of Love* (Oxford, 1936). A full statement of my debts is neither possible nor appropriate here. A brief general survey of the literature is given in my *Twelfth Century Renaissance* (London, 1970), pp. 206–7; a particularly useful survey of Chrétien's world is to be found in J. F. Benton, 'The Court of Champagne as a literary center', *Speculum*, XXXVI (1961), pp. 551–91.

of woman; but the tragedy of Medea or of Dido was not romantic. The same holds with Teutonic legend, in which the place of women is vital; but they are furies of passion and spite, and no one in his senses would have approached Gudrun or Brynhildr with the soft-spoken adoration of Tristan or Gawain. The men and women of the early twelfth century knew a very wide range of emotion, from animal passion to the deep devotion of long comradeship in marriage; but to the Church's eye all carnal *passion* was a sin, and the tradition of marriage was a political alliance designed also to preserve the race, to canalize human instincts, and to provide for comfort and good housekeeping. None of these benefits is negligible, but there is certainly nothing romantic about them.

The renaissance of classical studies in the eleventh and twelfth centuries brought to a host of students the knowledge of Cicero on friendship and Ovid on the art of love. Of the two, Ovid was probably the more widely read. 'The art of love' would more appropriately be called 'the pleasures and trials of seduction,' and when Abelard first met Heloise, he viewed her with Ovid's eyes, as an attractive victim.[3] But in Heloise Abelard and Ovid met their match; partly as a result of her own exceptional genius, partly as a result of her natural sympathy with the doctrines of Cicero and the Stoics. From Cicero she learnt – as St Bernard was to learn – that love and friendship, to be genuine, must be disinterested; and little by little she imparted even to the egoist Abelard something of what that meant. It would be nobler, she thought, to remain Abelard's mistress than to sacrifice his career and ruin his reputation as a cleric sworn to celibacy by marrying him. But in the end he insisted, and they were married – clandestinely, illegally, but validly. For most of the rest of their lives they lived apart; but in their letters the distinguished abbess, by her patient, half-pagan

[3] For what follows, see E. Gilson, *Héloïse and Abélard* (Eng. trans., London, 1953). There is a doubt about the extent to which Heloise was herself responsible for the letters which pass under her name in their present form; but I do not think the doubt sufficient to affect the statement in the text. See below, p. 74 and n.; and now also R. W. Southern in *Medieval Humanism and Other Studies* (Oxford, 1970), pp. 86–104.

Stoicism, elicited from Abelard, the Christian theologian, a lofty doctrine of Christian marriage. And after his death Abelard's abbot, Peter the Venerable, wrote in a famous letter to Heloise: 'God fosters him, my venerable dear sister in the Lord – him to whom you have been attached, first in carnal union, then in the stronger, higher bond of divine love; under whom you have long served the Lord – God fosters him, I say, in your place, as your other self *(ut te alteram)* in his bosom; and keeps him to be restored to you, by his grace, at God's trumpet call. . . .'[4]

St Paul likened the union of husband and wife to the mystical union of Christ and his Church, and the Church never quite lost the deep sense of the sacredness of married love which this implied. But Peter the Venerable's expression of it was quite exceptional; it was commoner for the Church to remember the less flattering comments of the Apostle on marriage, and to view woman as man's worst enemy – a tendency enhanced by a violent anti-feminism which had been a commonplace of clerical literature since the days of St Jerome, and strengthened by the growing power of the ascetic ideal.

In the story of Heloise and Abelard we see many of the elements in our problem – the influence of Ovid, which helped to make the pursuit of love fashionable among the younger scholars of the day; the influence of the Church, which would tend to divert carnal passions into the marriage bed when it did not forbid them altogether; and a range of emotion from mere lust to a love heroically disinterested which owes something to Ovid and Cicero, but whose origins in great measure cannot, and hardly need to be explained. But there is still one element in the tradition of courtly love not accounted for. Abelard made Heloise's name famous in the early days of their courtship by his love songs; and since these songs have entirely disappeared, we cannot tell whether they contained the echo of the new tradition growing at this time in the south of France, among the Troubadours of the Midi.

The first of the Troubadours was William IX, Duke of Aquitaine; and their influence was centred in his court at Poitiers,

[4] See p. 55.

and passed through his grand-daughter Queen Eleanor, who herself held courts of love at Poitiers, to her daughter Marie and the court of Troyes. At Troyes it mingled with and penetrated the growing fashion for Arthurian romance; and in the course of the second half of the twelfth century spread all across France and into England and Germany, achieving its highest expression in the early 1200s in the *Parzival* of Wolfram von Eschenbach.

The troubadour's theme itself is no simple thing: it found room for songs of romantic love and for savage satire. But its most characteristic subject is the hopeless quest of a lady, conceived of as remote and inaccessible, an object of worship and romantic adoration, whose lightest command is law to man, her slave. The platonic element may sometimes have been exaggerated; and it may well have been supported by a tradition that the actual subject of the songs, like the dark lady of the sonnets, should be imaginary. But in any case we find among the Troubadours, at once, at its most artificial and rarefied, a full statement of what we mean by romantic love. It has no counterpart in Europe; but we find its like in many corners of Islam, and nowhere more clearly than in the highly cultivated, sophisticated world of Moslem Spain in the tenth and eleventh centuries. How much the Provençal lyric owed to the Mozarab is highly controversial; how much its themes and metres owed to the passes of the Pyrenees has been the subject of many scholarly battles as fierce as Roncesvalles. Since I can read neither Arabic nor Provençal, I must refrain from joining the battle; but some influence there must have been, and in some sense the romantic tradition in Europe owes more to the poets and lovers of Islam than to Ovid or St Paul.

We must return to Troyes and to the 1160s and 1170s; for it was apparently then that the romantic tradition first fully established itself, in the courts of love of the Countess of Champagne, in the Arthurian romances of Chrétien of Troyes – tales of knightly prowess, of the lonely quest for glory in the service of a lady – and in the treatise of Andreas the Chaplain. The chief subject of Chrétien's later romances is the knightly quest; its object, love – not the platonic love of some of the troubadours, but a love at once romantic, sophisticated, and carnal. No coherent doctrine of courtly love can be deduced from the writings of either Chrétien or Andreas, for the simple reason that they often contradict themselves. Chrétien's contradictions have never been adequately explained; and his critics have accused him too lightly of pandering to his patron's whims. But Andreas is a simpler problem. He is a compiler; and in his opinions there is something of Ovid, something of Christian morality (which leads him to denounce the whole business before he has done), a kind of elephantine irony of his own devising, and a great deal of skilfully reported feminine logic. But the true devotees of the religion of love clearly regarded it as a thing to be pursued for its own sake; with the lady as a semi-divine figure to be served and even worshipped; a sophisticated cult, whose ends and rewards lay wholly in the present.

St Bernard expressed the ecstasy of divine love in the language of human affection; and Chrétien and his like often gave a religious setting for the devotees of courtly love. But no two religious systems could be more remote from one another. This fact is emphasized by Chrétien himself with delicate humour, in the passage in which he closes his description of the adultery of Lancelot and Guinevere. 'To his sorrow, day comes when he must leave his mistress' side. It cost him such pain to leave her that he suffered a real martyr's agony. . . . When he leaves the room, he bows and acts precisely as if he were before a shrine; then he goes with a heavy heart. . . .' This is no expression of revolt against the Christian God, but seems more likely a mildly blasphemous comment on the consequences of courtly love; at least, it underlines a problem which must have worried many men of good will in the twelfth century. Suppose we believe that the world is good, that God made its pleasures for man's enjoyment; how do we reconcile this with St Bernard's call to a life of pure asceticism, to the Church's reluctance to allow even married couples the full enjoyment of their love?

The God of love, Amor or Cupid, is the natural descendant of classical mythology; he is also the expression of the medieval love of symbol and allegory, in which attributes and feelings were described and analysed as if they were persons; above all,

Love owed his success to the medieval genius for parody. Sometimes the parody is purely frivolous, as in the *Council of Remiremont,* a court of love decked out as the chapter of faults in a convent of nuns; or frivolity taken seriously as in the judgement of the countess of Champagne that marriage and love are incompatible, a document deriving its form (among other things) from a papal decretal. But the quality which makes medieval parody most foreign to us is the frequency with which it appears in a serious context. The crude parody from everyday life which accompanies a fifteenth-century nativity play may be shocking to our taste; but it does serve to emphasize, with remarkable force, both our common humanity with Christ and the gulf which separates our sinfulness from him; the angels of the thirteenth-century choir of Lincoln Cathedral carry our worship heavenwards, but the imp in their midst reminds us that our thoughts have stayed below, reminds us too of the presence of hell. And Chrétien's poem in the twelfth century shocks us by a sudden crack of the whip into seeing that the most sublime of carnal experiences can be a blasphemous parody of true religion.

Whether I am right about Chrétien or not, there can be no question that in spite of the artificial levity of the courts of love, the problem they raised provoked serious questions in the minds of a number of men. There are hints in Chrétien that love and marriage are not incompatible; that the marriage bond may square, if not fully reconcile the ecclesiastical authorities. As we read him we feel that any profound reconciliation is impossible; and yet the Church had not slammed all the doors. The attitude which permitted such a reconciliation has been well expressed by a modern theologian. 'If we . . . attempt to trace a . . . pattern in the love which is God's own nature, it will be in the faith common to St Augustine and St Thomas, that his invisible things are understood through the things that are made, that there is a relation not of identity but of analogy between the natural and the supernatural, between the changing and the changeless Good.'[5] In other words, it is no accident that we express love human and

[5] J. Burnaby, *Amor Dei: a study of the religion of St Augustine* (London, 1938), p. 305.

divine in the same kind of language. The secret marriage of the celibate Abelard and his mistress elicited from the Abbot of Cluny a sublime statement of the eternity of human wedlock. But a full reconciliation of St Paul's vision of mystical union and the doctrines of *Minne,* or courtly love, though hinted at before, is first seriously propounded in Wolfram von Eschenbach.[6] It is most improbable that Wolfram knew the writings of St Bernard directly; nor can we analyse with any assurance the degree of self-consciousness of his doctrines. But he certainly knew that the theologians of the twelfth century had laid a new emphasis on the individual's quest for God and on the analogy of divine and human love. Though he boasts of being no clerk and knowing no Latin, he was in his way a theologian as well as a knight and a poet: he had the theologian's capacity to analyse problems, the layman's capacity to believe in the world he lived in. His *Parzival* is an exceedingly long and complex poem, a moral quest in whose pursuit the whole range of knightly qualities is deployed and tested. Human love plays a part, though not a dominant part; and many of its problems are worked out in the loves of the lesser characters. But no doubt is left that the highest earthly reward of the knight, after he has acquired possession of the Grail, is the love of his wife, at bed and board.

Wolfram tamed the fever of courtly love in a way which was not acceptable to his contemporaries, and accepted the carnal pleasures of marriage to an extent which the Church has been slow to welcome. Marriage by arrangement and romantic love have been at war ever since; and it is impossible to say that the romantic attitude, much as it has done to raise the lot of womankind and foster qualities in our civilization which we cherish, has not carried with it a store of hazards and suffering. It is of the nature of the real qualities of civilization that they may carry us to the gates of hell as well as to heaven.

This story, and the social milieu which it so profoundly affected, is of more than merely historical interest. As a Christian I cannot be indifferent to the vital, if sometimes ambiguous role which the Church played in it; as a layman, it gives me much private pleasure that it was a layman, Wolfram, who justified

[6] See pp. 150 ff.

the ways of God to man; as a husband I regard it as one of the happiest events in European history. But my purpose in telling the story is to reveal the fearful predicament of the historian in the modern world who tries to view the past clearly, and to see it whole.

The wholeness I talk of is no philosophic concept, no notion of a 'totality of human experience' or of a whole civilization as the unit of research. Whatever we study we study more precisely and more fruitfully if the context in which we study it is broad and deep; and whatever we study, we study as human beings, with the wide and intense personal interests inherent in our human nature. By neither standard would the historian of twelfth-century society wish to neglect the story of which I have given so brief an outline; but if he treats of it, he must be an amateur in many studies, in Moslem culture, Provençal and middle French literature, in the German Minnesinger, in ethnology, and perhaps in psychology, and an amateur in no superficial sense of the word. I state an ideal which I have not attained. But although I remain an unrepentant specialist, my ideal gives a place for a vision of human understanding not so far removed from Pope's; at least as near, I fancy, as sense and the progress of knowledge will permit.

'The word amateur', wrote Jacob Burckhardt in his *Reflections,* 'owes its evil reputation to the arts. An artist must be a master or nothing. . . . In learning, on the other hand, a man can only be a master in one particular field, namely as a specialist, and in some field he *should* be a specialist. But if he is not to forfeit his capacity for taking general views or even his respect for general views, he should be an amateur at as many points as possible. . . . Otherwise he will remain ignorant in any field lying outside his own speciality and perhaps, as a man, a barbarian.'[7]

[7] *Reflections*, introd., quoted by A. Dru, *The Letters of Jacob Burckhardt* (Routledge and Kegan Paul, London, 1955), p. 20.

2

Problems of the Church Historian[1]

A lecture delivered to the Ecclesiastical History Society at its first winter meeting in January 1962, and first printed in Studies in Church History, *I (London: Nelson, 1964), ed. C. W. Dugmore and C. Duggan, pp. 1–19.*

PARADOXICALLY, the study of Church history, as we know it, is a characteristic product, in the first instance, of the scientific revolution of the seventeenth century. In that age, investigation of the Church's history, from within, did more than anything else to lay the foundations for the critical study of historical sources, most notably in the work of Mabillon and the Maurists. The study of the Church's history, and most particularly the history of its founder, rocked the world in the nineteenth century,

[1] This lecture was written for an occasion, and I have made no attempt to alter its character or to provide it with more than a skeleton of footnotes. Some historians dedicate almost the whole of their scholarly effort to the study of the Church; but I do not wish to confine the label 'Church historian' to these, nor would I count myself among them. By 'Church historian' I simply mean a historian who has more than a passing interest in the problems raised by the history of the Church. To some of these my selection of problems will appear arbitrary. I have certainly made no attempt to catalogue problems; and there are many scarcely touched on here, such as the problems of miracles and of the supernatural, on which large books can be (and have been) written.

Among recent general discussions, I have found special interest in the late Norman Sykes's *Man as Churchman* (Cambridge, 1960), ch 1.

and played a large part in providing the intellectual grounds both for modern belief and for modern disbelief. The Church's history has, in the past, provided the *locus classicus* of the problem of historical bias: is it possible, the question has been asked times out of number, for historians of different persuasions to agree in the study of the early Church, or of the Reformation? The question is a real one; we cannot confidently say more than that they can, without much difficulty, talk the same language; that true scholars nowadays will not think of not talking the same language. And this fact reveals the extraordinary power of reconciliation which the study of the Church's history has had. It does not always reconcile; the common pursuit of truth did little to foster good relations between Coulton and Gasquet. But this spirit of reconciliation is clearly a feature of our age. It is part of a much larger movement, of which we are all witnesses. I have seen with my own eyes a Jesuit father give a public lecture in Winchester College; I have not seen, but millions of my fellow-countrymen have, Catholic and Anglican metropolitans sitting side by side in cosy amity in a television studio. We all know how limited, in terms of visible reunion, is the significance of these events; but the movement towards reunion among Protestant churches and towards better relations among all the sane branches of the Christian family is one of the striking historical phenomena of our age; and a movement (if I may strike a personal note) of hope and joy. Beyond doubt the study of the Church's history and the dominance of the historical outlook over the last century and a half have much to do with this.

The Church historian, then, works in a great tradition, inherits a discipline which has profoundly influenced the intellectual world in which we live, has proved itself capable of wielding both the axe and the olive branch. It is an old subject, and for this reason there are not wanting those who feel that it has had its day, and is ripe for Christian burial. There has been a reaction – in some circles a violent reaction – against the dominance of history over the study of theology.

Two of the most influential historical studies published in the generation before I was born were Albert Schweitzer's *Quest of the Historical Jesus,* published in 1906, and Paul Sabatier's *Life of St Francis of Assisi,* published, according to the title page of the first edition, in 1894, according to the bibliographers, in 1893;[2] and from these I take the following extracts. Schweitzer wrote:

'It was not only each epoch that found its reflection in Jesus; each individual created Him in accordance with his own character. There is no historical task which so reveals a man's true self as the writing of a Life of Jesus. No vital force comes into the figure unless a man breathes into it all the hate or all the love of which he is capable. The stronger the love, or the stronger the hate, the more life-like is the figure which is produced. For hate as well as love can write a Life of Jesus, and the greatest of them are written with hate: that of Reimarus, the Wolfenbüttel Fragmentist, and that of David Friedrich Strauss. It was not so much hate of the Person of Jesus as of the supernatural nimbus with which it was so easy to surround Him, and with which He had in fact been surrounded. They were eager to picture Him as truly and purely human, to strip from Him the robes of splendour with which He had been apparelled, and clothe Him once more with the coarse garments in which He had walked in Galilee.

And their hate sharpened their historical insight. They advanced the study of the subject more than all the others put together.'[3]

Schweitzer was born in Alsace, a German subject because of the Franco-Prussian war. Sabatier became a pastor in Strasbourg, and so an Alsatian by adoption; but his refusal to assume German nationality compelled him to spend most of his earlier career in his native Cevennes. In his Introduction, in the midst of a passage quoted at length on another page (pp. 200–1), he wrote:

Francis's official historians . . . have done him in general ill-service. Their embellishments have hidden the real St Francis, who was, in fact, infinitely nobler than they have made him out to be. . . .

It is, then, a work of piety to seek behind the legend for the history. Is it presumptuous to ask our readers to try to under-

[2] See below, p. 197.

[3] English translation by W. Montgomery, 2nd ed. (London, 1911), pp. 4 f.

> stand the thirteenth century and love St Francis? They will be amply rewarded for the effort, and will soon find an unexpected charm in these too meagre landscapes, these souls without bodies, these sick imaginations which will pass before their eyes. Love is the true key to history.[4]

We shall not, now, agree wholeheartedly with either statement; but in three ways these passages will help to introduce us to our theme. They remind us that the study of history is not something we can divorce from our own concerns and personalities; they remind us, none the less, of how much we may have in common in the study of history which is independent of our religious differences; and they remind us that not all historians brought up in the late nineteenth century agreed with Acton and Bury that the historian is a judge or history a science, no less and no more.

If we ask, what is it which sets the Church historian's field apart from that of other historians; and further, what is it which separates history from all other branches of knowledge; what is the nature of the walls this subject can build round its world? – then the first, the strict answer to these questions is a very simple one: nothing. History is not a separate compartment in the intellectual mansion, nor an independent constellation in the academic firmament; nor is it a form of experience divorced from all others. Nor can we build any walls round our own particular province. The history of the Church is somehow related to the history of the Christian religion; but it is a religion which repudiates water-tight compartments, which claims to be concerned in all fields of human life, and in the world as a whole. Mr Christopher Hill has taught us that we cannot understand the English Church in the sixteenth and seventeenth centuries unless we study feoffees and impropriators.[5] St Francis not only insisted on poverty in his Order, but forbade his friars to handle coins, except in extreme emergency. How can we hope to understand this unless we know what money meant to a merchant's son in

[4] English translation by L. S. Houghton, London, 1926 edn., pp. xxiii–xxxiv (slightly adapted).

[5] C. Hill, *Economic Problems of the Church from Archbishop Whitgift to the Long Parliament* (Oxford, 1956).

thirteenth-century Italy? The early heresies have their counterpart in the economic, social, and political history of their time. All this is well known; so well known that we have seen a reaction, that we have in recent years been forcibly (and needfully) reminded that heresy is also an intellectual thing. Franciscan poverty is as unintelligible without the Gospels as it is without twelfth-century heresies and thirteenth-century trade; even the Anglican Church in the seventeenth century thought of other things than tithes and the road to promotion.

There are, then, no compartments in the study of Church history; and this raises the first of my problems. Church historians have a good record for avoiding parochialism, anyway parochialism in time; and this good record many of them still sustain. To take one example from many, the ease with which Professor Owen Chadwick passes from Cassian, via Bossuet, to Newman is a constant source of astonishment to me, and an example to us all. It is growing increasingly difficult: the periods of history and its various aspects grow increasingly specialized, and specialization is to be welcomed as the condition of growth. Yet it must remain possible for the different specialities to fertilize one another. We cannot hope to be specialists in many fields, but we must at least be able to have a sympathetic understanding of what they are at, and what we may hope to learn from them.

This problem, acute enough in itself, is closely related to the wider problem of the relation of Church history to the whole world of academic disciplines, above all to theology, and to the personal beliefs of Church historians. On this issue both Sabatier and Schweitzer were quite specific: the historian cannot be divorced from his personal beliefs; the true interest, the true value of his work, will be lost if he is. This is not a *carte blanche* for prejudice and bias. In Sabatier the critical spirit mingled with the romantic, as in his master Renan; in Strauss the critical and scientific spirit mingled with the philosophy of Hegel. A passionate desire to strip Our Lord or St Francis of the fog of conventional hagiography was a vital inspiration, which helped them both to be so drastic and so effective, and sustained Strauss in the pursuit of truth as he saw it, through a lifetime of bitterness and persecution. Sabatier lived in happier times. His book was put upon the Index, indeed; but he lived to enjoy in some measure the fruits of his own desire for reconciliation; he lived to proclaim that the originality of St Francis lay in his catholicism – not perhaps quite the catholicism of the Pope who canonized him, but the word was not thoughtlessly used;[6] he lived to have friends and disciples of many communions and of none. It is wrong, and useless, to divorce our work as historians from our beliefs; if we try to do so, we deceive ourselves.

The study of Church history depends for its success on men and women of widely different personality and belief finding in it a common interest, a sense of common purpose. It is not only that it is open equally to the Catholic, the Protestant, the Jew, and the Agnostic – but the study of the Church's history would be less respectable, less valuable, less fruitful than it has been if it had not been so diverse in the past. Sabatier's love expresses very forcibly the need for the historian to sympathize with the subject he is studying; Strauss's hate the need for him not to swallow it whole. That measure of scepticism which is the condition of all scientific enquiry must be mingled with other more human qualities, of love and hate, of like and dislike, before a balanced view of the past can be produced. All this sounds very personal, very subjective; yet it is this mingling of attitudes which is needed to give a cutting edge to our judgements, to enable us to penetrate to the heart of the problems we study. And it is the dialectic set up by this mingling of qualities and attitudes which has provided historians of widely different outlook with a sense that there is a common language which they can talk, common ground on which they can meet. In this sense the study of history, and of the Church's history, are distinct slices of human experience; not because they are separated from other kinds of experience by impenetrable barriers, but because they provide a meeting place, a space within which it is possible for scholars of very different outlooks – not to reconstruct a certain and irrefutable account of the past – but, quite simply, to agree.

This area of agreement is by no means a confined space. The historian's field is the whole of the past; nothing in it is alien to

[6] See pp. 203 ff. P. Sabatier, 'L'originalité de S. François d'Assise', in *Franciscan Essays*, British Society of Franciscan Studies, I (1912), pp. 1–17.

him. Yet what he sees as significant in it, what he chooses to study, must depend on his present interests. It is these which often give direction, actuality to his studies; it is often a sense of relation between past and present which gives history its constant, chronic excitement. I say 'often' because it is quite false to confine interest in the past into any single channel; and the only quality which we should regard as wholly necessary is the pursuit of historical truth. Without that, history as we understand the term could not exist at all; without a lively sense of its present actuality, of its relevance, as the cant phrase has it, it would, for most of us, be only partly living.

We are sometimes told that all historians in the late nineteenth century believed history to be a science, a fact-grubbing empirical science, with objective criteria, aiming to eliminate bias and diversity of view. It is true that notions akin to this were widely held; true too, that in their naïve form they no longer command wide assent. Yet one pillar of this doctrine is still very widely accepted; and this bland generalization about nineteenth-century historians is itself an example of it. Historians still feel a deep urge, an inescapable urge, to generalize; they feel it their duty, even in circumstances which are hardly congenial to generalization. Is it or is it not true that religious changes and the rise of capitalism were closely connected? Was the fourteenth or the fifteenth or the eighteenth century less religious than those which had gone before? Do we ourselves live in a materialistic age? It is no doubt true that in this crude form most scholars have lost the temptation to generalize; that the discussion of the relations between religion and the rise of capitalism has passed out of this realm. But in less crude forms the idea that our main business is to make general statements is still very powerful. A generalization is normally a judgement of quantity; it is obviously appropriate to certain aspects of social and economic history, where we have something like statistical information, and where quantitative analysis is valuable and interesting. Even in economic history, generalization alone can never be the aim; in Church history its place must commonly be peripheral. Questions like the ones I asked just now are quite devoid of meaning.

Sabatier and Schweitzer may serve to remind us, then, that not all nineteenth-century historians believed history to be an objective science. They managed to be both profound students of advanced critical method and profoundly personal in their approach. And the same can be said of some of the greatest scholars of the age. A medievalist may be forgiven for citing the names of Maitland and Edmund Bishop.[7] Both were fascinated by the technical achievements, especially of German scholarship. But Maitland's scholarship was intensely personal, constantly inspired by a vision of the human mind, the concrete situation in which the absurdities of English law had lived and moved and had their being. Bishop was a great technician; one might even call him the Housman of medieval liturgical texts – and that analogy will serve to remind us that just as the editor of Manilius was also the author of the *Shropshire Lad,* so the religious quest of Edmund Bishop, often frustrated and always tortuous, lay behind the precise language and the rare technical subtlety of the great studies collected in *Liturgica Historica.*[8] Bishop had his faults; yet he remains one of the immortals; and it is his capacity to penetrate a religious situation, to see liturgical texts as the expression of a whole civilization without fog and without sentimentality, as much as his technical skill, which earned him this immortality.

The Church historian of the future, studying the roots of good feeling between the Christians of different communions, and especially among Christian intellectuals in the mid twentieth century, will find the study of these four scholars of absorbing interest. He will see how the work of agnostics like Maitland, of liberal Protestants like Schweitzer and Sabatier, and Catholics like Bishop, combined to create the atmosphere of mid-twentieth-century scholarship; and he will see that Bishop's theological views, and his insistence that Catholic liturgical scholars must not ignore non-Catholic liturgies, and, even more specifically, Sabatier's passionate desire to subdue Protestant and Catholic feuds, were not irrelevant to their place in this movement (even if he has also to recall that Bishop was an *eminence grise* in the

[7] Maitland was not, of course, a Church historian in any narrow sense of the term, but clearly falls within my definition, above, p. 39.

[8] Oxford, 1918; cf. N. Abercrombie, *The life and work of Edmund Bishop* (London, 1959; with a Foreword by Professor Knowles).

condemnation of Anglican orders). It is the historian's task to generalize where he can; but he is often more concerned to analyse trends and ideas; especially the possible range of ideas. The fourteenth-century *Modus Tenendi Parliamentum*[9] propounded a view of the function of the Commons in Parliament which would have been thought quite daring in the early seventeenth century. On this account some historians have written it off as hopelessly eccentric and of no significance. What is significant is that such views could be held in the fourteenth century. How widely they were held we have no means of knowing. Their practical influence was small. But the historian can too easily be enslaved by practical consequences: he only knows what happened, not what might have happened; and it is this enslavement which makes the range of opinion held by thinking men in any age so interesting. We are sometimes told that agnosticism and atheism (in the modern sense) were unknown in the Middle Ages; that all men believed, even if their beliefs were not orthodox. But Wolfram von Eschenbach in the early thirteenth century wrote a large poem, the *Parzival,* one of whose central themes is loss of faith – and his poem was widely read. He went on, furthermore, to write his *Willehalm,* in which he analysed, in trenchant fashion, the problem of the good heathen, his place in God's providence and his chances of salvation. He made it abundantly clear that the good heathen (in his view) has his place in God's providence. He never finished the poem, probably because his story had got to the point where one of his best heathens, Rennewart, was in danger of baptism. Wolfram was a Christian, and would have liked to see Rennewart baptized – but his baptism would have weakened the force of the problem: what difference would baptism make to a good heathen?[10] The attitudes here revealed were not perhaps common ones, but they are none the less interesting for that. They serve to remind us how wide intellectual horizons can be; how much more interesting it often is to analyse the variety of human thought and opinion than to amass generalizations of dubious validity.

[9] See V. H. Galbraith, *Journal of the Warburg and Courtauld Institutes,* XVI (1953), pp. 81–99.

[10] See pp. 151–2.

Sabatier and Schweitzer introduced us to a variety of problems and difficulties on which the Church historian needs constantly to reflect. They have now, I think, served their turn, and I propose to make these problems somewhat more concrete by an exercise in historical fiction. State the case that a historian has it in mind to write a history of Christian marriage. He would find that he had many predecessors in the field, and that much important work had been done on many aspects of it;[11] yet he would also find that he had started a project of profound interest and relevance, and of almost insurmountable difficulty. The interest and the relevance need no underlining. In no age has the ideal of Christian marriage been so widely studied, or – within countries once Christian – so widely attacked. The Churches have asserted their views with much firmness, diversity, and heat; and sometimes with charity too. There can be no doubt, to my mind, that charity is what is needed above all – charity towards one another's differences, and towards the non-Christian point of view. Nor can the study of the history of Christian marriage fail to arouse in the theologian or the lawyer a sense of humility, a realization of the Church's failings and inadequacies. We need not take this too seriously: the Churches are young. Two thousand years may seem a long time in relation to recorded human history, but as a slice of the world's history, and of human experience, it is extremely short. None the less it is sufficiently long for us to learn many lessons from it, and not least the difficulty, the prevarication, the constant ambiguity of the Church's attitude to marriage. And if this teaches

[11] The literature on the theology and law of marriage is especially copious; for the period with which I am here particularly concerned, see especially A. Esmein, *Le mariage en droit canonique,* 2 vols., revised ed. by R. Génestal (Paris, 1929–35); J. Dauvillier, *Le mariage dans le droit classique de l'Eglise* (Paris, 1933); and, more generally, A. L. Smith, *Church and State in the Middle Ages* (Oxford, 1913), pp. 57–100; provisional bibliographies may be found in the ecclesiastical and theological dictionaries. The only general survey of the whole subject in English known to me is G. H. Joyce, *Christian Marriage* (London, 1933). From the point of view of social history, a particularly interesting example of recent studies is L. Stone's investigation of marriage in the English upper classes in the sixteenth and seventeenth centuries: 'Marriage among the English Nobility in the sixteenth and seventeenth centuries', in *Comparative Studies in Society and History,* III (1961), pp. 182–206.

our theologians that the problems are not so easy as some of them think, it will have done good.

Study of the history of marriage is exceedingly difficult. It can never be divorced from current prejudice; it cannot, it should not, be written without love or hate; it is no task for the Laodicean. Yet it is a task of extreme delicacy. The sacrament is performed by the parties themselves; in what it consists has never been clearly defined – and a theologian who tries to do so is guilty of interfering in matters which are not his concern. 'Those whom God hath joined together let no man put asunder' is a proposition to which most Christians would say heartily, Amen; but no Church has ever claimed to know, when man had witnessed a ceremony of marriage, whether in every case God had joined the couple. This may seem at first sight mere casuistry, but a little reading in the case-law of the medieval Church (to take no other example) quickly shows that it is not. More important, no Christian has ever been able to evade St Paul's elaborate insistence that the union of husband and wife was the symbol of the union of Christ and his Church; an inspiration and a terror to those for whom the doctrine of Christian marriage lies near the centre of their faith. But that is not all that St Paul said on the subject. In the same passage in Ephesians he gave the husband Christ's role in the union, which has been taken by male commentators to imply male superiority; and in 1 Corinthians ch. 7 he shows a more ambiguous attitude to marriage, twisting and turning between a lofty view and one not so lofty in an attempt (if I have understood recent commentators aright) to save the institution in a chaos of conflicting opinions in the Corinthian Church.

The historian of marriage would have to understand what biblical scholarship has to say about these and many other passages, and in every epoch which he studied the current interpretation of the Bible would have to be one of the starting points of his enquiry. Church history divorced from the Bible is meaningless. We all know, to give only one example, how the New Testament has ambushed the Churches time and time again – and broken the even flow of historical development – and in the history of marriage it is St Paul, in both moods, who has been particularly influential in directing the Church's course.

There is indeed a sense in which the history could be written as a commentary on 1 Corinthians ch. 7 and Ephesians ch. 5. But there is always a danger, if this is attempted, that the historian will discover the link between his own views and St Paul's, and assume that their common ground existed throughout the story. These passages have been open to the inspection of every Christian since the Epistles first circulated in the Church. But ideas on marriage have been as much influenced by the social background of the people and peoples who have been converted to Christianity as by St Paul, or Our Lord himself. Here we must return to our paradox. A living interest in the subject is vital if the history of marriage is to be a living work. But the historian will have from time to time quite self-consciously to un-think the present and to un-think St Paul. To help him, he has the copious literature on the Roman law of marriage, on Jewish ideas of marriage, and the more conjectural, but no less important, Germanic marriage customs.

This context, indeed, should be widened by comparative study of the rich, almost fantastic, diversity of marriage customs and notions revealed by the social anthropologists. In his earlier passages, this will be primarily of comparative value to him, to stir his imagination and fertilize his ideas; but, later on, as the Christian Churches expand over the whole known world, it becomes directly relevant. In a word, our historian has passed from being a biblical critic and expert in the history of exegesis to being an anthropologist. Nor is there any visible limit to the number of disciplines he must encounter. Marriage is related to theology and canon law, and he will need to use patristic scholarship, to understand the techniques of the scholastics, to capture the thought of the reformers, and so forth – and all this without becoming buried under the mountain of their works, or drowned in the rivers of ink which have flowed in their interpretation. When that is done, he will have some understanding of the idea of marriage; and history without ideas is a twilight subject. But marriage does not live wholly in the realm of theory; it is lived out in practice, in the dialectic, or, as some would say, in the Armageddon, of daily life. And it is here that the problem of method becomes most acute; and to lend some precision to what

I wish to say, I propose to concentrate now on the period from the eleventh to the thirteenth centuries.

First of all, there is, needless to say, no sharp division between theory and practice; one of the most interesting realms is that which lies poised between – the realm of common assumptions, of ordinary attitudes, and of gossip; for this provides the link between the two. Here, then, is Walter Map, the late-twelfth-century satirist:

> 'Pacuvius, weeping, said to his neighbour Arrius: "Friend, I have a disastrous tree in my garden: my first wife hung herself on it, so did my second later on, and now my third has done the same." Said Arrius: "I wonder that after so many strokes of luck you find it in you to weep." And again: "Good gods, what expenses has that tree suspended for you!" And a third time: "Friend, give me some cuttings of that tree to plant." '[12]

Map was a man of great learning, and this little story is a pastiche from Cicero, Quintilian, and Aulus Gellius – improved, be it said, by a brilliant story-teller. He was writing in a well-worn tradition; his little tract, which pretends to dissuade a benighted friend who is engaged to be married from taking the fatal step, was very popular, and so skilful is its anti-feminine satire that in due course it was attributed to St Jerome.

This satire is still in the world of learned humour, and it reminds us how difficult it is to get in touch with the notions of married folk in an age when the majority of those who have left us a memorial, the educated clergy, were celibate, and the majority of the married laity illiterate. To make contact with the lady's point of view is even more difficult, if not impossible. We must start, as must every medievalist, with a confession of ignorance: the acreage of our ignorance enormously exceeds, and will always exceed, the area of possible knowledge.

What we can do, first of all, is to study the practice of marriage in high society from narratives in the chronicles, from the case-

[12] *De nugis curialium*, IV, 3, trans. M. R. James (Cymmrodorion Record Series, 1923), p. 166.

law, by constructing genealogies; and, so far as high society is concerned, we are comparatively well served by the evidence, because the pursuit of good marriages for their childen was a favourite sport for the lay upper classes of Europe – perhaps after hunting and hawking, the most favoured sport of all. Kings like our own Henry II were well aware that a well-planned marriage conquered territory more effectively than armies, and the marriage game was played for the highest stakes.[13] Children unborn were married off in imagination, babies betrothed in fact; and widows sometimes paid heavy fines to stay single or have a say in their own disposal. The one thing which seems rarely to have been considered was the happiness of the partners.

We should be wrong, however, to take this evidence entirely at its face value, just as we should be wrong to assume from the strictness of the law that marriage was a more stable institution in that age than in ours. The law of marriage was, indeed, in a somewhat chaotic state, though rapidly being developed in the twelfth century; annulment was common, death even commoner. Since the men's occupation was war, which was not without its dangers even then, it was no uncommon thing for an eligible lady to have three husbands. Since the lady's occupation was bearing children, which was not much less dangerous than war, it was no uncommon thing for a man to have two wives.[14] Few men were quite so ruthless in disposing of their wives as Henry VIII was later to be, but eleventh-century Celts and Vikings were still unused to monogamy; and the Church had the greatest difficulty in restricting divorce.

Yet we should be quite wrong to think that the upper classes of Europe in this age viewed marriage cynically. Great men might

[13] See pp. 30–1.

[14] As a sample, a rough count of the twelfth-century marriages recorded in vols. X, XI, XII (pts. 1 and 2) of the revised ed. of the *Complete Peerage* produced the following figures: cases in which husband and wife are only known to have married once, 63; cases in which husband or wife or both are known to have married more than once, 55. In these 55 cases 18 husbands had two wives each, and one three; 31 wives had two husbands, 4 wives had three husbands and one four. The information relates solely to the baronial class; and even so, it is based on scanty indications, so that the number of second and third marriages may be seriously under-estimated.

often be unfaithful to the marriage bed, but inheritance, in most legal systems, was strictly confined to legitimate heirs. William the Conqueror was a bastard; one of the very few to win a duchy, let alone a kingdom; he knew what bastardy meant, and was faithful to his wife. Among Henry I's comparatively few known acts of generosity was the acknowledgement of upwards of twenty illegitimate children – but it was his nephew who succeeded him.

If we wish to go further than this in penetrating the lay view, we can observe something of the detailed practices by reconstructing genealogical trees and tables of succession; above all, we can observe the close lien between marriage and property in every class. We can occasionally tell the story of a marriage in some detail. What we lack entirely is the sort of intimate picture of married life which sources from the seventeenth century onwards provide so copiously. I do not know of any case history which is really revealing between the ancient world and the fourteenth century, save that of Heloise and Abelard.

In the down-to-earth letters of the Merchant of Prato and his wife we see a fourteenth-century marriage revealed with something of the subtlety and ambivalence of Shakespeare and the actuality of Tolstoy.[15] The marriage was not a happy one, though it grew warmer in later years; but that makes it all the more revealing of the strains and dangerous assumptions and ultimate strength of medieval marriage; and one would give much to have more such case histories for earlier centuries. In their absence one has to rely, for the atmosphere of marriage, on the stray comments of chroniclers and letter writers and the gossip of satirists; and, above all, on the assumptions, ideals, and aspirations revealed in secular literature. The twelfth century saw the rise of the romantic ideal, of the cult of courtly love. Whatever its origins it had from the first a religious and an irreligious element in it, just as it had a moral and an immoral face. It sanctified adultery; it also did much to humanize marriage. There is no world of experience in this period in which it is more dangerous to generalize, more necessary to analyse. It is a very delicate matter, inevitably, to decide how much relation there was between the world of courtly

[15] See pp. 235 ff., and Iris Origo, *The Merchant of Prato* (London, 1957).

ideal and the world of courtly practice.[16] The difficulty is made substantially worse by the difficulty of interpreting the vernacular French literature of the twelfth century. There has been a singular reluctance among the literary critics until quite recently to treat the romances as serious works of literature.[17] This is especially true of the French critics. The Germans have served us better. We can at least be sure that Wolfram's fierce attack on courtly love as currently understood, his elaborate analysis of many kinds of love and friendship, and his idealization of married love were meant to be taken seriously. How seriously they were taken by others we can never hope to know. But we shall be wise, on the one hand, not to wax too romantic about the code of chivalry, and, on the other hand, to take the vernacular literature of this age seriously: it is our one real contact with the minds of laymen.

The Church succeeded, by and large, in retaining control over the law of marriage and even extended the area of its control. Its law was ambiguous. In the Church's eyes marriage was tossed between the two traditions which had inspired the eleventh-century reformers – the development of sacramental doctrine, which enhanced the religious prestige of marriage, and the development of the ascetic and celibate ideal, which made the married life seem to many fervent churchmen a second best, the life suitable for weaker vessels, the view expressed in 1 Corinthians: 'It is better to marry than to burn.' The ascetic ideal was in tune with many of the strongest forces in the Church of the time and made the twelfth century a golden age in the history of medieval monasticism. But it also provided fertile soil for one of the most dramatic developments of the age: the rise of the Cathar heresy in the mid

[16] It is, indeed, difficult to see any substantial effect of the romantic ideal on marriage customs before the nineteenth century, and on this ground it has been denied that marriage was affected at all by it in the Middle Ages. This is unduly sceptical, just as it is unduly sceptical to deny that medieval romances have something to teach us about medieval marriage. They have much to tell us, so long as we do not erect general theories out of them, and so long as we do not read them in the light of twentieth-century notions of romance; just as *Romeo and Juliet* has much to tell us of sixteenth-century notions of love and marriage, so long as we remember the same provisos.

[17] Cf. H. Sacker, *Germanic Review*, XXXVI (1961), pp. 25 f.

and late twelfth century. With a suddenness very difficult to explain, the Cathar Churches, with an organized episcopate in France and Northern Italy, were able to challenge the monopoly of the Catholic Church in the west;[18] and it was the first time that the challenge had been really dangerous since the barbarian tribes had abandoned Arianism. The Cathars were dualists; they repudiated the world; they abominated procreation, which imprisoned more spirit in the evil world of matter. The Cathar *perfecti* maintained (on the whole) a very high standard of asceticism; their adherents lived more normal lives. But there is some evidence (though this has been disputed) that the Cathars preferred casual liaisons to marriage, which they regarded as organized vice.

But the Church did not forget its sacramental teaching. Already in the early twelfth century one voice had been raised to show the woman's point of view. It was a very personal, very striking viewpoint: but it was Heloise's own view of the secret and illegal match which had united her, fleetingly, to Abelard, which elicited from the warm heart and the courtly pen of Peter the Venerable of Cluny one of the very few descriptions of marriage from this age which seem to measure up to the standard set in Ephesians v.[19] The Church responded to the challenge of the Cathars by Crusade and Inquisition. But it was not persecution alone which destroyed the Cathar Church. The Catholic Church was recovering from the repudiation of man and the world which had threatened its doctrine in earlier centuries; its theology was becoming more humane; St Francis himself combined an extreme personal asceticism with a passionate delight in the world as God's world. It has been said that Francis's interest in animals was derived from the Cathar doctrine that animals had souls.[20] The connection is the exact reverse: to the Cathars the material world was the symbol of Satan; to Francis it was the symbol of God. His delight in the world was not due to nature mysticism; he preached to the

[18] See pp. 140 ff.; A. Borst, *Die Katharer* (Stuttgart, 1953), especially pp. 208–13, 231–9.

[19] See above, p. 33; Peter the Venerable, *Ep.* 4:21 (*PL*, CLXXXIX, cols. 346–53, esp. 352); on the marriage, cf. below, pp. 74–5 and n.

[20] Sir Steven Runciman, *The Medieval Manichee* (London, 1947), pp. 129, 174.

birds and called the sun, moon, fire, water, and even death his brothers and sisters, to emphasize to his hearers that all these things were of God's making, and in their nature good. To the history of marriage Francis contributed little directly, but his notions could not fail to fertilize the soil for the growth of an ideal which incorporated the idea of two human beings dedicating themselves to one another in perfect obedience, and in the hope (if they are so fortunate) that they may be able to share in God's creative work.

Between the eleventh and thirteenth centuries our material forbids us to make generalizations.[21] But it allows us to observe something of the range of ideas, and of the range of practices – not to produce average ages of marriage, or to deduce shifts in size of family, but examples to illustrate and illuminate the forces at work. There is much analysis that remains to be done; and from it the historian of society would learn a great deal of which he is profoundly ignorant at present; the historian of politics, of kings, and courts, would learn something, too, of the forces at work behind the marriage game. The historian of marriage cuts as it were a section through the other historical approaches and reveals much that is familiar in an unfamiliar light. He proceeds by analysis, not by generalization; he never ceases to confess his ignorance; but in these two ways he is only doing what every medievalist must do. His worst headache is that he must make some acquaintance with every historical discipline, and with some which are not normally thought of as historical. He cannot be an expert, a specialist, in all; what he needs is imaginative sympathy and understanding of what each can do, and a friend in each who is an expert to help him on his way. This is the essential nature of historical collaboration. Some tasks can be done by teams and seminars; many can not. We need to devise a type of co-operation in which we understand each other's problems and can help in them, while remaining specialists in our own particular fields.

[21] L. Stone, art. cit., is an interesting example of what can be done in a period for which some generalization is beginning to be possible, i.e. the sixteenth and seventeenth centuries.

3

Hildebrand[1]

IT happened one day in the late 1060s or early 1070s that the Cardinal Archdeacon of the Holy See was travelling on the Pope's business in Savoy with his friend, the Abbot of Cluny, perhaps the greatest of all the monastic leaders of western Europe. Cardinal Hildebrand was an unimpressive figure: short, undignified, with a weak voice, in a Europe growing increasingly conscious of birth and inheritance, this son of obscure parents could hardly hope to cut a figure. In contrast, St Hugh was one of a succession of young noblemen who had been placed early in the saddle at the great abbey. Like his predecessors he used his noble connections to protect his haven of peace in a violent age, and, in the course of a long life, revealed gifts of pastoral care and direction which earned him the reputation of sanctity. Two Abbots of Cluny spanned the whole eleventh century, and Hugh was still a comparatively young man at this time: he was to live till 1109,

[1] An introductory survey of books on Hildebrand and his world is given in my Historical Association Pamphlet *The Investiture Disputes* (1958, repr. 1966); much of the recent literature is in *Studi Gregoriani* (8 vols. so far, ed. G. B. Borino, Rome, 1947–60). The story of Hildebrand and the Abbot of Cluny was made famous by R. W. Southern, *Making of the Middle Ages* (London, 1953), p. 139; the version used here is that ed. R. W. Southern and F. S. Schmitt, *Memorials of St Anselm* (London, 1969), pp. 211–12. The major sources for his pontificate are his *Registrum,* ed. E. Caspar (*Mon. Germ. Hist., Epistolae Selectae,* Berlin, 1920–3; a selection in translation is in E. Emerton, *The Correspondence of Pope Gregory VII,* New York, 1932), and *Epistolae Vagantes* (ed. and trans. H. E. J. Cowdrey, Oxford Medieval Texts, forthcoming). See A. Murray, 'Pope Gregory VII and his letters', *Traditio,* XXII (1966), pp. 149–202.

and to see well under way the great third church of Cluny, the chief wonder of the western world in architecture and decoration of its age. Between Hildebrand and Hugh there came to be a close friendship based on opposing temperaments: the one dedicated, inspired, fanatical; the other, calm, majestic, wise. Hildebrand was in many ways very unwise, and it is largely his unwisdom which has given him immortal fame.

Their friendship was not won without misunderstanding. On this occasion the Cardinal and the Abbot were riding together when a throng of noblemen gathered round to pay respects to the Pope's legate. Hugh pricked his horse and went on a little; and watched the great men paying court to the insignificant Papal Archdeacon with a quizzical eye. 'Good God,' he thought, 'what pride must grow in this man's breast, to be smiled on and served, as it were by the whole world.' Then Hildebrand suddenly burst from the crowd and confronted the Abbot. 'I don't, Lord Abbot, I don't,' he cried out. 'What don't you do?' 'I'm not puffed up as you think in your heart of hearts. The honour they do is not to me, but to God and St Peter the Apostle, whose legate I am.' To us, the story reveals how impulsive Hildebrand was, how dependent on his small circle of true friends, how insecure he always felt in spite of the lofty offices he held. But the Abbot was there, and he evidently felt, too, the compulsive force behind the words, the deep sincerity of Hildebrand's devotion to the Apostle. And so in later years he edified monks and visitors at Cluny by telling the story.

Hildebrand was born about 1020, when the Papacy counted for little, in spite of all the mystique that surrounded the papal office, the solemnity of the worship in the great basilicas and innumerable lesser churches at Rome, and the popularity of Rome as a centre of pilgrimage. Almost all his life he was an official of the Curia. But the papal Court was not a large bureaucracy: since even the Pope had quite a small staff about him, it was possible for a young man of humble origin in the Pope's service to acquire a personal relation to the leading men of Rome, and to feel a strong personal relation to the presiding saint whose representative the Pope himself was thought to be. At this date the Papacy was degraded by scandals, and as a government meant little outside the papal states in central Italy. The very handwriting of most papal letters was illegible outside Italy. In this little world the tomb of St Peter seemed the centre of the universe. God and St Peter were as real, living persons in the Roman basilicas as were their human inhabitants; a great deal more real than the potentates of northern Europe.

In 1046, Hildebrand's elderly patron, Pope Gregory VI, an honourable Roman who had bought the Papacy in the hope of clearing away some of the scandals, was deposed by a synod inspired by the King of Germany and western Emperor, Henry III, and went into exile to Germany, taking with him his young protégé. Somehow, knowledge of Hildebrand's ability and devotion came to the ears of the eminent German bishop whom Henry eventually sent in 1048–9 (after two earlier candidates had died) to fill the Holy See as Pope Leo IX and reform it. Leo took Hildebrand back to Rome and made him one of the small group of powerful, brilliant, often incompatible personalities that set to work to reform the Church and the Papacy. To Leo, the German, the Papacy was God's instrument for the reform of the Church at large; in his short term of office (1049–54) he travelled much in Italy and north of the Alps, preaching reform and holding councils. But he also sent messengers all over Europe and to Constantinople; and for this he needed strong and able supporters who could act effectively as papal representatives. Hildebrand went on many such missions for Leo and his successors – and it was on one of these that he travelled with Hugh of Cluny. But Rome was always the centre of his world; even other parts of Italy were exile to him.

What did reform mean? What was wrong with the Church? The zealous have always thought the Church corrupt; saints and rebels in every age have denounced its abuses in such terms that the unwary historian cannot imagine how it has survived a century, let alone nearly 2,000 years. The diagnosis, however, and the prescription, have varied much in different ages. What was then thought to be wrong by the men who gathered round Leo was that the Church was being secularized: sacred offices bought and sold for money, clergy melting into the crowd and sharing the way of life and the vices of the ordinary layfolk, including under this head the vice (as some of the reformers undoubtedly saw it) of marriage. The prescription was that the clergy and all clerical offices should be increasingly independent of, and separate from, secular men. Many of the reformers were monks and were inclined to think that all clergy should live in monasteries or quasi-monastic institutions. Most of the reformers wished to see less lay interference in clerical appointments; several shuddered to think of the deeds of the Emperor Henry III – not for the result, which they welcomed, but that an Emperor should have presumed to do such things. In Rome in the eleventh century the Emperor was a distant potentate, St Peter very close at hand; Roman emperors might be tolerated if they did their proper job, to rule the barbarous peoples north of the Alps and protect the Holy See when it was threatened; but if they tried to rule in Rome they were likely to seem about as useful to the Church's cause as the Emperor Nero, who had been responsible for St Peter's death.

For over twenty years Hildebrand remained the devoted servant of Peter and his earthly vicars: helping to organize the new Curia (still a fairly elementary organ), helping to spread the word of reform round Europe, promulgating the monastic virtues. He had himself been a monk for a while, a stage in his life which made an impression on him out of all proportion to the time he had lived the regular life. He became increasingly identified with all that Rome and the new Papacy stood for; and like many men with no practical experience of warfare, increasingly convinced that men of war had been sent into the world to do God's work. Because of this belief, he urged the Pope to give his blessing to the Norman Conquest of England in 1066 and, in doing so, helped to bring a load of sorrow, in the name of moral and religious principle, on a country with which he had no first-hand acquaintance. It was in such adventures that the idea of the Crusades was born, perhaps the most damnable of all the inheritances of the eleventh-century Papacy.

Hildebrand may seem to us from this distance of time a harmless fanatic, a dedicated reformer, or even a man of spiritual insight and intense vision; of his devotion and sincerity it seems to me that there can be little doubt. But on 22 April 1073, the day when the people of Rome acclaimed St Peter's most devoted and distinguished servant as Pope, when Hildebrand became Gregory VII, a new and revolutionary view of the papal office was enthroned in the Holy See; and that is why the interpretation of Gregory VII and what he stood for is still a burning issue in the Roman Catholic Church. In a recent book,[2] two Roman Catholic historians, Robert Markus and Eric John, have made Gregory VII the author of a tragedy from which they reckon the Church to be only just emerging. Whatever view one takes of papal authority, it is clear that a great issue is at stake in the events of the 1070s and 1080s, an issue whose echoes can be clearly heard today.

To Pope Leo, the German, the Papacy was an instrument of reform; in the process of making it such his own vigour and the ability of his helpers revived every point of past doctrine which gave prestige and authority to the Pope. To Gregory, St Peter's authority was the one thing in the world that was wholly real; and it had all fallen on his shoulders. Seven years after his election, in 1080, not for the first time, he called on Peter (together with his chief colleague among the Roman martyrs, St Paul) to avenge him on his bitterest enemy, the Emperor Henry IV. He reminded the Apostles that he had been brought under their wing; but also how reluctantly he had accepted the various steps in his career. At first sight it seems hard to believe what he says: clearly he was in some sense an ambitious, pushful man; was he really so reluctant to be ordained, to be promoted, to become Pope? It is impossible to believe it wholeheartedly; yet equally, I am convinced that what he said so solemnly to his mentors was sincere: in 1074, a year after his election, he wrote to Hugh of Cluny, his greatest friend:

> 'We are weak, and the burden is more than mind and body can bear, yet we carry alone at this fearful time a mighty load not only of spiritual but of temporal business. Our circumstance, our overwhelming burden, frightens us daily; we can find no help, no support at all in this world.'[3]

[2] *Papacy and Hierarchy* (London, 1969), esp. pp. 63 ff.

[3] *Registrum*, I, 62 (ed. Caspar, I, p. 91). The quotations which follow are from VII, 149, III, 6* (II, p. 483, I, p. 254).On Gregory and St Hugh, see H. E. J. Cowdrey, *The Cluniacs and the Gregorian Reform* (Oxford, 1970).

For as his apostrophe proceeds, one feels the intense loneliness and isolation of the man whom the Apostles have ordered on to a mountain peak to denounce the world's sins and put everything to rights. And what was the result?

> 'The Devil's limbs have risen against me; they have dared to set hands on me even to blood.'

'Blood' was a word often on his lips; and his dearest ambition was to lead a Crusade; yet in his heart he knew he was no soldier. None the less, when enemies rose against the Church and the Pope, they had to be answered – even to blood.

Gregory was happiest, we may suppose, living in Rome, worshipping at the Apostles' tombs – still one of the Pope's main functions – sending out his messengers, and writing to bishops and kings in every corner of Christendom. His letters were his characteristic instrument; and we know a great deal about them, because his *Register,* the book which contains copies of a fair proportion, though not nearly all, of the letters he sent, still survives. The most surprising thing about it is how small it is. The creation of the papal monarchy – a system of government interfering all over western Christendom in spiritual matters and in politics where moral issues were involved – was well under way before Gregory came to the throne; but he gave the papal revolution in government a new twist. It was not, however, in any sense, a bureaucratic twist. It has been calculated that on average his chancery issued no more than two letters a week, and in his last year, when he was driven out of Rome, and his government in chaos, even less.[4]

Gregory strenuously denied that there was anything new in his claims or his actions. Once again, like many revolutionaries, he seems sincerely to have thought himself a mere restorer. He thought he was doing nothing for which precedent could not be found; as Pope he took the name Gregory – with a bow to his former patron, the disgraced Gregory VI – after the most influential of all the early popes, Gregory I (590–604), Gregory the Great. The resemblance, however, is superficial. In principle,

[4] See Murray, art. cit., esp. p. 164.

the essence of the doctrine of papal primacy, theological and judicial, over the whole of Christendom, had been asserted long before Gregory I.[5] In practice Gregory I had felt obliged to engage in a correspondence far more copious than Gregory VII's to do all his duties as Peter's heir, as heir to too many of the obligations of the Roman Empire in western Europe. But he treated bishops and kings as equals, at least in courtesy; for he was a courtly Roman from the last generations of the ancient world. Gregory VII, however, treated them like servants, sometimes like naughty children; and although he had been in some sense a diplomat for many years, he lacked the most elementary understanding of diplomatic tact.

St Peter's chief rival in northern Italy was St Ambrose: the church of Milan always felt itself almost the equal of the Holy See. Shortly before Gregory became Pope, war broke out between two factions in the church of Milan, one *ancien régime* and aristocratic, supported by the Emperors, the other reforming and revolutionary, supported by the Papacy. The Emperor Henry IV had already proved himself a tiresome young man of uncertain temper, not at all inclined, like his father, Henry III, to be a patron of the Holy See. Gregory was the world's worst judge of character, and as his view of his office was that he should sit in Rome and receive the world's homage by messenger and letter, he rarely (in later life) met either his friends or his enemies from north of the Alps. He tended to take the simple view that those who opposed him were either wholly depraved or temporarily inspired by the devil; those who supported him could do no wrong. Soon after his accession the young Henry IV allowed Gregory to have his way over Milan and sent the Pope a cordial letter freely admitting his faults. Whatever Henry lacked, he could show charm, and some of this communicated itself to the Pope even at that distance. For a brief spell Henry was his favourite son, great schemes were hatched in the Pope's fertile brain; a glorious vision of a partnership to rule the whole of Christendom dominated his thoughts.

In fact, Henry's submissiveness merely reflected his need for allies to deal with enemies at home. As soon as his civil war seemed

[5] See esp. W. Ullmann, *The Growth of Papal Government* (London, 1955).

to be concluded, he showed his teeth once again by accepting another candidate for the archbishopric of Milan, and investing him with the symbols of office. This act of 'investiture' with ring and staff was the symbol of lay interference in spiritual offices and appointments, and as such had just been denounced by Gregory. It was only one element in a thoroughly dangerous situation, but an element which was to rankle increasingly as time went on, so that the great battle between Empire and Papacy which lasted from 1075 until the end of 'lay investiture' in 1122, together with some attendant skirmishes in other kingdoms, has come to be known as the Investiture Dispute.

As soon as Gregory heard the news of Henry's *volte face,* he threatened Henry with excommunication: the scales fell from his eyes, and he could never see Henry in a favourable light again. Early the next year, in 1076, a group of German bishops met and sent an offensive letter to the Pope, interpreting his career in somewhat scurrilous terms and announcing his deposition. The letter was delivered as Gregory presided over a council in Rome. In the first of his magnificent apostrophes, he solemnly called on St Peter to avenge his faithful servant,

> 'that the nations may know and acknowledge that you are Peter and on your rock the son of the living God has built his Church and the gates of Hell shall not prevail against it.'

It soon became obvious that Henry had acted too precipitately. Rebellion flared again; some of the German bishops hastened to change sides. Henry was assured by a meeting of German leaders that if he did not receive absolution from the Pope by 22 February 1077 – exactly one year after the papal sentence – he would be deposed. There was a pause, and the Pope prepared for the one great journey of his pontificate: he promised the German princes to join them in sitting in judgement on the Emperor. He moved slowly north, escorted by his most constant lay supporter, the Countess Matilda of Tuscany. Then, without warning, came the appalling news that Henry, supposed many hundred miles away in his German kingdom, had crossed the Alps and was rapidly advancing to meet the Pope. Matilda took Gregory aside into one of her strongest castles, the castle of Canossa, and at Canossa was played the most famous drama of the eleventh century.

There proved to be no ground for fear: Henry came with peacer ful intentions. He had crossed the Mont Cenis pass in mid-winte- under most uncomfortable conditions, to come to the Pope as a suppliant for absolution. Henry gathered round the Pope a distinguished group of moderate folk who were likely to urge peaceful measures. In their midst was St Hugh of Cluny, one of the few men to whom Gregory sometimes listened. Canossa was strongly fortified, with a triple wall surrounding it; within the second wall Henry waited barefoot, for three days, a penitent, yet an insurgent too, besieging a stronger fortress than the castle. For three days Gregory held out, resisting the suppliant at the gate and the persuasions to mercy of St Hugh, who was also Henry's godfather, and the Countess Matilda, who had been won round by Henry to plead for mercy. Gregory saw clearly that, politically, Henry had trapped him. If he gave the King absolution he would be letting the German princes down, giving away the best advantage he could ever hope to have. Nor did he trust Henry's word. But he was also a Pope and a bishop, a Christian pastor responsible for Henry's soul; servant of the slaves of a God (as he declared himself in all his letters) who was thought of as a God of mercy as well as the supreme Judge. He was responsible for Henry's soul at the judgement seat; nothing could be more repugnant to his spiritual office than to reject a penitent sinner. Excommunication was a powerful weapon. But Gregory knew well that Henry, like many men of his day, would have been little bothered by it (when not actually troubled by thoughts of death) if it had not carried political penalties with it. If he refused to absolve the King, he would bring his office and his ban into derision; if he granted it, the political advantage would melt away. Henry paraded in the courtyard a dramatic symbol of humiliation in an age which fervently believed in symbols; but the humiliation even then was greater for the Pope within the castle.

In the end Gregory gave way: Henry swore a solemn oath to submit to the Pope's judgement on the dispute between himself and the German princes, and promised him a safe-conduct should he come north of the Alps. But Gregory never came: the plan to sit in judgement on Henry had collapsed. Gregory's German allies felt deserted; the more determined of them, however, proceeded to declare Henry deposed and to elect one of their own number, Rudolf of Rheinfelden, as his successor. For three years there were two kings in Germany, and Gregory was compelled to stand by in impotent misery observing the effect of his surrender at Canossa. He was bound to permit Henry a proper judicial hearing before he accepted his deposition; and, unlike Henry, he was bound by his conscience. His heart and mind were with Rudolf. Finally, in 1080, he declared Henry contumacious: it was evident that the trial would never take place. With a solemnity even greater than in 1076 he called on St Paul as well as St Peter to vindicate their cause; Henry had lapsed, was excommunicate, his subjects could not, should not, obey him further.

At every turn, Gregory's career shows the conflict which occurs when spiritual and temporal authority are confused. In theory, Gregory could have expounded the distinction; in the subtler minds of later popes, especially of a man like Innocent III (1198–1216), the distinction was perfectly clear. But he felt himself to be in a general sense God's instrument for the execution of His will here and now, visibly and effectively. He seems to have been more at home in the Old Testament than in the New, and like many eminent medieval churchmen, he could not believe that the God who had so constantly directed events to his own ends in the Books of Kings would not do so for his faithful children still. Hitherto, Peter and Paul had mysteriously allowed King Henry to go unchastised: it could only mean that they were keeping him for a worse fate. And so the Pope came to make his famous prophecy that within a few months Henry would be defeated or dead.

The story is full of irony. The prophecy was made in 1080; Henry died in 1106, surviving the Pope by over twenty years. But he died excommunicate and deserted by most of his followers, amid the ruins of all he had striven to do. His failure was fully as pronounced as Gregory's. Indeed, by 1106, after the brilliant pontificate of Gregory's more statesmanlike successor, Urban II (1088–99), the prestige of the Papacy stood high, that of the

Empire very low. The chief instrument of this reversal had been the preaching of the First Crusade. From this enterprise Henry was excluded, and his prestige suffered for it; unlike later Crusades, it was successful in its chief aim, to recover Jerusalem, and the prestige of the Pope who launched it was correspondingly enhanced. To us the Crusades involved a confusion between spiritual and temporal even more devastating than Gregory's; but at the time many felt, reasonably enough, that if the Papacy had to preach war, it was better that it preach it outside Christendom rather than foment civil war in Christian kingdoms. The fact remained that the Papacy had taken a fearful decision. Before the eleventh century, responsible churchmen commonly thought of war as an evil only occasionally justified, where self-defence or a cause of special justice and urgency was involved. It had never been entirely forgotten that Christianity was a religion of peace. The consecration of the idea of the Crusade in the eleventh century saddled the Church's hierarchy for centuries to come with a doctrine which in ignorant minds amounted to Holy War – to offensive war in God's cause. In the long run Gregory was to enjoy a posthumous triumph of a most unhappy kind.

The immediate circumstances of 1080, however, seemed to portend total disaster for the Papacy. It was Rudolf, not Henry, who died that year; and the effective opportunity to depose Henry died with him. Henry, meanwhile, had gathered once again an assembly of clergy and laity who declared Gregory himself deposed. This time they proceeded further, and elected a successor, who took the name of Clement III. The anti-Pope came, in due course, to command a considerable measure of support, from kings like William I of England, who were glad of an excuse to play one Pope off against the other and so be relieved for a time of the necessity to take any notice of the instructions of either. It is true that William only showed serious interest in Clement after Gregory's death, and then only as an excuse to recognize no Pope at all for a while. More immediately serious was that Gregory's own combination of personal tactlessness and wild prophecy had alienated many of his supporters. The majority of the cardinals deserted to Clement in 1080–1; from 1081 Gregory had to face what he had feared so long, the physical presence at the gates of Rome of Henry IV at the head of an army. In 1084 Henry finally captured the city; Clement crowned him Emperor and established his court in Rome itself; Gregory, in the Castel Sant'Angelo, was encircled by his enemies. In this crisis he turned to a new ally, the leader of the new Norman principalities in southern Italy, Robert Guiscard. Robert came, and recaptured Rome; his army gave the city one of the worst ravagings in its recorded history, and Gregory had to go south into exile with Guiscard, who was now his only protector.

The 44th Psalm[6] was always reckoned in the Middle Ages a marriage song for the mystical union of Christ and the Church. Christ and his Bride were apostrophized in turn, and the Bride's greatest moment was when it was said to her:

> 'Thou hast loved righteousness, and hated iniquity: wherefore God, even thy God, hath anointed thee with the oil of gladness above thy fellows.'

Of that Bride, the Church, Gregory was the earthly head; and he had always looked for an earthly as well as a heavenly return for his labours. As he lay dying on 25 May 1085 in Salerno, in his misery he is said to have cried:

> 'I have loved righteousness and hated iniquity: and therefore I die in exile.'

[6] 44th in the Vulgate; Psalm 45 in the *Book of Common Prayer*.

4

Gregorian Reform in Action: Clerical Marriage in England, 1050–1200[1]

A paper read at the Anglo-American Conference of Historians on 8 July 1955; first printed in Cambridge Historical Journal (C.H.J.), XII, *i (1956), pp. 1–21; reprinted in* Change in Medieval Society, *ed. Sylvia Thrupp (New York, 1964), pp. 49–71. An appendix to the original article,* C.H.J., XII, *ii (1956), pp. 187–8, is here omitted.*

FEW men have ever shown a more sublime faith in the divine origin of their mission than the papal reformers of the eleventh century. They set to work with a 'modest proposal' to destroy two of the most intimate and powerful foundations of clerical society: they aimed to abolish simony and, with it, the lay control of patronage; they tried to destroy the family life of the clergy. From one point of view they were doing only what every policeman does – they were trying to enforce the established law. From

[1] No systematic revision has been attempted. Further study has reinforced the view that clerical 'marriage' lasted long among the lower clergy – perhaps never died out – and has shown that marriage or at least paternity among the higher clergy was somewhat commoner in the late twelfth and thirteenth centuries than was here suggested (see esp. M. G. Cheney in *E.H.R.*, LXXXII (1967), p. 761.

Further studies of the St Paul's evidence are to be found in *A History of St Paul's Cathedral*, ed. W. R. Matthews and W. M. Atkins (London, 1957), chap. I (C.N.L. Brooke); A. Morey and Brooke, *Gilbert Foliot and his Letters* (Cambridge, 1965), chap. X and App. IV; J. Le Neve, *Fasti Ecclesiae Anglicanae, 1066–1300*, I, ed. D. E. Greenway (London, 1968).

another point of view their platform was a devastating social revolution. If we may admire the high idealism of Leo IX, Humbert, Hildebrand, and Peter Damian, we must also concede that their work had many victims; the legislation of the eleventh-century Popes on clerical marriage must have produced as many broken homes and personal tragedies as the morals of Hollywood. Both Damian the ascetic and Heloise the deserted wife have a claim on our sympathy as historians; and both found their supporters in their own day. Between the unbending demand for the enforcement of celibacy and the view of the 'Anonymous of York' that it was entirely proper for the clergy to be married there were many possible positions. The Anonymous (writing at the turn of the eleventh and twelfth centuries) was propounding opinions already obsolescent; and clerical marriage found few defenders in the mid and late twelfth century. But if the field narrowed, the subtleties of the problem were more fully appreciated. The twelfth century was an age of growing sophistication in lay circles as well as clerical. Nowhere was this more true than in the world of love and of marriage; in that century (whatever the lot of womankind as a whole) the romantic ideal was born, under whose spell we still live. It is the variety and the subtlety of the view-points which give my subject its interest, and also its intractability. Clerical marriage is an exceedingly delicate topic, though it has not always been delicately treated.[2]

It appears that Pope Leo IX was more troubled by simony than marriage. He made some effort to reform the morals of the Roman clergy, and may have done something more; but the two contemporary accounts of his great councils north of the Alps do not

[2] This is certainly true of H. C. Lea's great *History of Sacerdotal Celibacy in the Christian Church* (3rd ed., 2 vols., London, 1907), which, with all its faults, remains the only general account of the subject on a broad scale. There is an immense literature on the origins and the law of celibacy. Vacandard's account (*Études de critique et d'histoire religieuse,* I (Paris, 1905), pp. 69–120) is still valuable; for the law, see also A. Esmein, *Le mariage en droit canonique,* I[2] (Paris, 1929), pp. 313–41; J. Dauvillier, *Le mariage dans le droit classique de l'Église* (Paris, 1933), pp. 162 ff.; *Dictionnaire de droit canonique,* III (Paris, 1942), pp. 132 ff. For a general account of the reformers' campaign for celibacy, see A. Fliche, *La réforme grégorienne,* I (Louvain-Paris, 1924), pp. 30 ff., 190 ff., 335 ff., etc.

suggest that clerical marriage was even discussed: the target was simony.[3] One of these accounts was written by the great Cardinal Humbert of Silva Candida, whose principal literary effort was the *Libri tres adversus simoniacos*. But if simony had first place, clerical marriage was not far behind. Subdeacons and above had been forbidden to marry since the fifth century; and married men who entered orders had been forbidden to sleep with their wives since the fourth.[4] For centuries the attempt to keep the clergy in higher

[3] Anselm's *Historia dedicationis ecclesiae Sancti Remigii* and Cardinal Humbert's *Vita Leonis IX* (ed. I. M. Watterich, *Pontificum Romanorum . . . Vitae*, I (Leipzig, 1862), pp. 113 ff., 127 ff. – especially pp. 155–7). Humbert's authorship of the *Vita* has recently been established by two scholars working independently, Dr H. Tritz in *Studi Gregoriani*, IV (Rome, 1952), pp. 194–286, and Dr Richard Mayne in an unpublished Cambridge Ph.D. thesis. Leo IX dealt with the problem of celibacy in two surviving letters (Jaffé-Löwenfeld, *Regesta Pontificum Romanorum* – henceforth *JL*. – nos. 4279, 4308); and he prescribed celibacy for the clergy of Rome in 1049 (C. J. Hefele-H. Leclercq, *Histoire des Conciles*, IV, ii (Paris, 1911), pp. 1007–8 and notes). There is some later evidence that clerical marriage was dealt with at Rheims in 1049 and elsewhere in Leo's pontificate (ibid. pp. 1023–4 n., 1031); and Bonizo of Sutri attaches the decrees of 1059 and later (below, n. 12) to the Roman synod of 1050. Some or all of this evidence may be authentic (see now J. J. Ryan, *St Peter Damiani and his Canonical Sources*, Toronto, 1956, pp. 94–5, 101–2); but it is in marked contrast to the strictly contemporary evidence, and Bonizo is inclined to read back later developments (such as the personal influence of Hildebrand) into the pontificate of Leo IX. For the canon of 1050 we have only Bonizo's word, and the unsupported testimony of Bonizo is scarcely evidence.

[4] For the legal authorities, cf. n. 2 above: the bulk of them are laid out in Gratian, *Decretum*, D. 27, cc. 1, 8; D. 28, 31, 32, *passim*; D. 81, cc. 15–34; D. 82, cc. 2, 5; D. 84, cc. 3–5; cf. also C. 15, q. 8, *passim*; C. 27, q. 1, c. 40; for sons of priests, D. 56, *passim*; for hereditary benefices, C. 8, q. 1, c. 7 (cf. cc. 3–6). These include many of the decrees of papal councils from 1059 onwards, as well as the earlier material; decrees not in Gratian were issued at the papal councils of 1096 (cc. 7, 12, Mansi, *Concilia*, XX, coll. 935–6), 1099 (c. 13, ibid. col. 963), 1107 (c. 4, ibid. coll. 1223–4), 1119 (Toulouse, c. 8, ibid. XXI, col. 227), 1123 (c. 3, ibid. col. 282), 1131 (cc. 4, 15, ibid. coll. 458, 461; cf. Gratian, D. 28, c. 2), 1148 (cc. 3, 7, Mansi, coll. 714, 715). The decrees of 1018 are in Mansi, op. cit. XIX, col. 353 (cf. Hefele-Leclercq, op. cit. IV, ii, p. 919). I have nothing to say in this article of the more abstruse matrimonial impediments to ordination, e.g. 'bigamy'. It is impossible to discuss here to what extent this material was known throughout Europe. It is certain that the main lines of the law of celibacy were widely known in England throughout

orders away from the weaker sex had been a favourite activity with all kinds of reformers; and as recently as 1018 one of the last of the Tusculan Popes had insulted his ancestors by reviving the ancient decrees. The reformers regarded simony, the sin of Simon Magus, as an attempt to sell the Holy Ghost, a conception so blasphemous as to be evidently the fruit of error, and hence a heresy. Soon they erected by its side the heresy of Nicholas the Deacon of Antioch, who was by a confusion supposed to be the author of the heresy of the Nicolaitans.[5] Cardinal Humbert is the first person known to have applied the title Nicolaitans to all married clergy. But their greatest enemy among the reformers was Peter Damian, who stated the case against them in four of his most eloquent epistles.[6] It is impossible to do justice in a sentence to the wealth of rhetoric, of argument, of biblical and patristic learning which this great ascetic poured out in the most cultivated Latin of the century. He took his stand on his own sacramental theology and on the law of the Church. He cited a chain of texts to show that clerical marriage was forbidden; and he built up a vision of the sacred nature of the Eucharist and of the office of the priest who celebrates the Eucharist. Just as Jesus was born of a chaste Virgin, so his re-birth in the blessed sacrament must be

the period (see below, pp. 78, 96); and the fresh developments were repeated in Norman councils of the mid eleventh and in English councils of the early twelfth century. From the middle of the twelfth century both Normandy and England were beginning to be plentifully supplied with expert lawyers to interpret the law. Furthermore, even before Gratian, the outline of the law could easily be reconstructed from the popular collections of Burchard of Worms and Ivo of Chartres.

[5] Nicholas of Antioch is mentioned in Acts vi. 5, and the Nicolaitans in Rev. ii. There is no reason to suppose that there was any connection between them. Rev. ii. 14, 15 hint that fornication was one of the sins of the Nicolaitans, and in course of time the title came to be attached to almost any sect liable to this kind of error (cf. Hastings' *Encyclopaedia of Religion and Ethics*, IX (Edinburgh, 1917), pp. 363–6).

[6] Humbert, *Adversus Nicetam,* ed. C. Will, *Acta et scripta* (Leipzig-Marburg, 1861), cc. 25 ff., pp. 147–50; Damian, *Ep.* v, 13, *Opuscula*, XVII, XVIII (Migne, *P*[*atrologia*] *L*[*atina*], CXLIV, coll. 358 ff.; CXLV, coll. 379–424), and cf. also *Epp.* v, 4, 14–15 (*PL,* CXLIV, coll. 344 ff., 367 ff.). For the development of sacramental theology, see R. W. Southern in *Studies in Medieval History presented to F. M. Powicke* (Oxford, 1948), pp. 36 ff. and references there given.

solemnized by a priest sworn to chastity. The attack on clerical marriage was closely associated with the new sacramental theology, with its growing emphasis on the objective nature of the Real Presence, and the growing sense that the priesthood and all who stood by the altar at mass were a race apart, 'separated for the work'. This sense made the reformers all the more aware that clerical marriage tended to assimilate the clergy to their lay surroundings. Marriage produced children and the desire for hereditary succession; and a benefice became more and more like a lay fee, passing from father to son. It may well have been this consideration which produced the law forbidding the ordination of the sons of priests, a law made definitive by Urban II at the end of the century. But the relation of marriage and inheritance cannot be expressed simply; and an attenuated form of hereditary benefice survived the onslaughts of the reformers.

When Peter Damian treated clerical marriage as heretical, that is, as a matter of faith, he erred. It could not be, and has not usually been regarded as more than a matter of discipline; such it was seen to be so soon as the Papacy won the allegiance of any part of the eastern Church, in which marriage for the lower clergy became not merely pardonable but compulsory in the later Middle Ages. But as a matter of discipline celibacy has been strictly maintained for all but a small minority of the Roman Catholic clergy from that day to this; and the law has been very little altered since the twelfth century. Indeed, to anyone who has toiled with the incoherent complexities of the law of marriage in the eleventh and twelfth centuries, there is a simplicity and consistency about the laws of celibacy which is wholly admirable.

Before 1059 it was already the law that no subdeacon or above might marry and that everyone entering these higher orders must take an oath of chastity; but a married man who was ordained did not put away his wife – he was still married, but must live with his wife as though she were his sister.[7] Underlying these provisions were two vital principles, which did not always live together in perfect harmony: the sanctity of marriage and the sanctity of orders. Some reformers might regard woman as man's worst enemy, and there was plenty of anti-feminism in all the

[7] Gratian, *Decretum*, D. 28, cc. 1, 5, 14; D. 32, c. 18; etc.

circles in which it customarily flourishes; but the rights of a properly married wife were carefully safeguarded. It was always maintained that ordination did not dissolve a marriage and that a husband could only be ordained with his wife's consent. In earlier centuries it had been common for a married man to enter orders late in life. But in the twelfth century it came to be thought that marriage was not a suitable foundation for a clerical career; that a married clerk was too likely to lapse and commit fornication with his wife; in general that the arrangement put too great a strain on both parties. Alexander III (1159–81) laid down, first that the vow of chastity necessary to the ordination of a married man must be taken by both parties, and then that while the wife lived no married man might be promoted to a bishopric unless his wife took the veil.[8]

So far the defence of marriage; but from another angle the fortress of matrimony had already been breached and the status of a married woman undermined. Hitherto the normal doctrine had been that if a clerk married, the marriage was valid; but if he persisted in leading the life of a married man, he forfeited his orders and his benefices. Thus the marriage of Abelard and Heloise was perfectly valid, although it was illegal and should have entailed for Abelard the loss of his benefices;[9] and as Heloise

[8] *JL.*, 14,104, also in the *Decretals* of Gregory IX – henceforward X – III, 32, 5–6.

[9] It used to be argued that if Abelard was not yet a subdeacon, the marriage was not only valid but legal. This can no longer be maintained, for two reasons: – 1. He was certainly a canon (*Historia calamitatum*, ed. J. T. Muckle, *Mediaeval Studies*, XII (1950), p. 188), and there is some evidence that he was a canon of Sens; there is no evidence that he was a canon of Paris, though it is quite likely that he was (ibid. n. 81 and the passage from Rémusat's life there quoted). Canons were forbidden to marry by the English council of 1076, and by a Norman council of 1080 (below, n. 31; T. P. McLaughlin, *Mediaeval Studies*, III (1941), p. 94) – decrees given general validity at Clermont in 1095 (ibid. pp. 95ff.), and subsequently repeated by further English and French councils. These decrees condemned canons who married to forfeit their benefices (indeed, they seem to have applied to all who committed fornication). That this rule was known in the diocese of Paris is certain: Ivo of Chartres had stated it in a letter to the Bishop of Paris only a few years before Abelard's marriage. 2. In any case, there is no reason to doubt that Abelard was in higher orders. He himself assures us that it was an abuse for a canon

pointed out when opposing the marriage, it ended Abelard's chances of clerical promotion. But in 1123 it was decreed not merely that all clerics in higher orders were debarred from marriage, but that any marriage they entered was to be broken.[10] Thus, one by one, the doors were closed; and if we meet a subdeacon, deacon, priest, or bishop after 1123 with a lady on his arm, we guess that she is probably not his wife. The decree of 1123 has come in for much criticism, and it undoubtedly contributed to the confusion in the order of matrimony so conspicuous in the mid twelfth century: it added greatly to the number of unofficial liaisons which might be felt by the partners to be marriages, but were not recognized by the law and could be broken at will. But it was the natural culmination of the attempt to make full celibacy the unambiguous law of the Church; and it had more effect than all the enactments and endeavours of the preceding half century.

In Gratian's *Decretum* (*c.* 1140) there is collected a great deal of ancient lumber on this subject; so much so that he at one moment arrives at the triumphant (and characteristic) conclusion that marriage is permitted for priests![11] But the dead wood is swiftly dispersed by the application of principles unusually sound for Gratian: some of the authorities which seem to permit marriage are disposed of on the historical ground that at one time celibacy was not enforced, and others because the discipline of the eastern Church differs from the western. The full law of celibacy is established, and only one serious obscurity remains. A famous decree of Gregory VII of 1074 (itself a repetition of decrees of

not to be (*Ep.* 8, cit. E. Gilson, *Héloïse et Abélard*, English trans. (London, 1953), p. 172). The word 'clericus' on which M. Gilson bases his view that Abelard was not at this time in orders at all was used in a variety of ways: in the passage in question it is contrasted, not with 'presbiter', but with 'laicus' – it is being used in the broadest (and commonest) sense, 'a member of the clerical order'. We do not know what his orders were, but he may well have been a priest, as he certainly was within a few years of becoming a monk (ibid. p. 67). M. Gilson has argued (ibid. chs. 1–2) that legal impediments and the threat of deprivation were not of major consequence to either party in their discussion whether to marry; and this we may (in the main) accept.

[10] I Lateran, c. 21 (Mansi, op. cit. XXI, col. 286).

[11] D. 28, *dictum post* c. 13.

1059 and 1063)[12] had ordained that the faithful were not to attend the masses of clergy known to have intercourse with women. The original meaning of the decree is not certain. It was written when there was much controversy about the validity of sacraments administered by heretics, and Urban II had to explain that Gregory's decree did not mean that the masses of married clergy were invalid. Urban's exposition is far from clear, but it ought to have meant – and was taken to mean – that the faithful laity were to be enrolled as allies against the delinquent clergy. If the clergy were contumacious, their congregations were to strike.

In the second half of the twelfth century and the early thirteenth the laws of celibacy were little altered. Alexander III narrowed the entry of married clergy to higher orders; he and his successor dealt with individual cases as humanely as was compatible with complete rigidity on the basic principles. Thirty decretals of the twelfth-century Popes (prior to Innocent III) found their way into the *Decretals* of Gregory IX; and without making a comprehensive search I have found about thirty-nine more dealing with celibacy cases.[13] A high proportion of surviving decretals on any subject refer to England, but in this instance the proportion is remarkable: of the sixty-nine decretals counted, forty-four certainly deal with English cases,[14] twenty with continental, and

[12] Mansi, op. cit. XIX, coll. 897–8, 978, 1023–5 (cf. Hefele-Leclercq, op. cit. IV, ii, pp. 1167–8, 1230, V, i, pp. 90–1). The authenticity of the decree of 1063 is not quite certain. Urban's solution is in Gratian, *Decretum*, D. 32, *dictum post* c. 6.

[13] The decretals on this subject in X are in I, 17; I, 21; III, 2–3; IV, 6; cf. also III, 32, 5–6; V, 31, 4. I have no space here for full references to those not in X.

[14] Of the decretals listed in n. 13, the following were addressed to England: X, I, 17, 2–11; III, 2, 4–6; III, 3, 1–2; IV, 6, 3 (there is a critical edition of X, I, 17, 2 in *Papal Decretals relating to the Diocese of Lincoln*, ed. W. Holtzmann and E. W. Kemp, Lincoln Record Society (1954), no. 5; X, I, 17, 3 is a part of an important decretal addressed to the Bishop of Worcester, which is printed in full in *Gilberti Foliot Epistolae*, ed. J. A. Giles, II (London, 1846), no. 368 – it later formed the basis of the first canon of the council of Westminster of 1175, for which see below, n. 63; X, III, 2, 4 and III, 3, 1 formed part of a single decretal, *JL*. 13,813). The proportion of English cases in X, I, 17 is especially striking – this title deals with the sons of priests and problems of inheritance.

the remaining five cannot be located. One of these five is a remarkable letter of Alexander III of more than doubtful authenticity, granting a personal privilege to some unnamed clerk in higher orders to marry and retain his benefices.[15] The forger might evade the law by such means as this, and its rigour could on occasion be relaxed by papal dispensation. But when Innocent III breathed new life into the campaign for celibacy in 1215 the battle had already been waged for 150 years with remarkable vigour and consistency.

My interest in this campaign and its results in England are with clerical marriage as a social institution which, however illicit, was recognized as such. I am not interested in what would be regarded in any age as immorality. For this reason I shall make little use of the evidence of penitentials, moral reformers, and satirists. The perennial aberrations of mankind are of little concern to the historian, and every medieval poet had read the sixth satire of Juvenal. Clerical marriage has suffered by being studied too little concretely, and I aim to make it as concrete as I can. This involves a certain amount of self-denial. In particular, I must confine my attention mainly to the upper clergy, and leave the lower to students of episcopal registers and Gerald of Wales.[16]

The division into upper and lower clergy is fundamental, though the distinction can be exaggerated and the line too clearly drawn. Bishops, archdeacons, canons, and all the regular clergy lie above it; the rank and file of the parish clergy lie below. But a member of the upper clergy – a clerk possessioner in the

[15] *Collectio Brugensis*, XXII, 3 (ed. E. Friedberg, *Die Canones-sammlungen zwischen Gratian und Bernhard von Pavia*, Leipzig, 1897, p. 152). In the same collection (XXXVII, 1) is a decretal about a forger who was a priest's son, and claimed to have a papal letter declaring this no impediment from orders.

[16] For the English lower clergy in later centuries, there is a useful catena of references collected by H. G. Richardson in *Trans*[*actions of the*] R[*oyal*] *Hist*-[*orical*] *Soc*[*iety*], 3rd ser., VI (1912), pp. 120–3; cf. also J. R. H. Moorman, *Church Life in England in the Thirteenth Century* (Cambridge, 1945), pp. 63–7. For the twelfth century the *locus classicus* is Gerald of Wales, *Opera*, II (ed. J. S. Brewer), pp. 168 ff., IV, pp. 313 ff. (and cf. the references in J. Conway Davies, *Episcopal acts relating to Welsh dioceses*, II, Historical Society of the Church in Wales (1948), pp. 459 f., 465 ff.); but Gerald's charges are exceedingly confused and the value of his evidence very difficult to assess.

Lollard phrase – might reside on his cure and lead the life of the lower clergy; and there is no way to decide where to place the highly educated parish priests who wrote *The Owl and the Nightingale* or (possibly) the *Cloud of Unknowing*. For our purpose, however, the distinction is necessary.

How far the lower clergy were affected by the Gregorian reform is hard to say. Kings and churchmen had legislated with vigour against clerical incontinence in the early eleventh century.[17] In the second half of the twelfth (when the married bishop was scarcely to be met and even the married archdeacon was becoming rare) Pope Alexander III was forced on numerous occasions to denounce the frequency not merely of married clergy but of hereditary succession in the English Church. Papal decretals had a particularly good chance of survival in this country and the English bishops were particularly active in submitting their problems to Rome; but even so the proportion of English cases among the decretals of this period suggests that the problem here was particularly acute.[18] Cases of marriage and inheritance recur throughout the Middle Ages. But by the second half of the thirteenth century married clergy seem to be an exceptional problem; and the bulk of the evidence is for clerical immorality of a kind normal in a world very prolific in untrained clergy.[19] I imagine, then, that if married clergy were common in eleventh-century England, the Gregorian reform had, over two centuries, a considerable effect. There is no doubt that some clergy were

[17] The legal and other evidence about the attitude to celibacy in England in the early eleventh century is fully discussed by R. R. Darlington in *E*[*nglish*] *H*[*istorical*] *R*[*eview*], LI (1936), pp. 404–7, 411.

[18] For the proportion of English decretals see W. Holtzmann, *Papal Decretals relating to the Diocese of Lincoln*, p. xvii. The reason for the high proportion in general has been much discussed: it is due in part at least to the work done by English canonists in collecting decretals – perhaps mainly, as is argued by Dr C. Duggan in *Twelfth-Century Decretal Collections* (London, 1963). There is certainly no reason to suppose that the proportion of surviving decretals which are directed to England reflects at all closely the proportion originally sent.

[19] Cf. the studies referred to in n. 16: the evidence has not yet been sifted by regions or in closely circumscribed chronological periods – and only thus can any conclusions be drawn from the scandals recorded in bishops' registers or the papal dispensations granted for the ordination of the sons of priests.

married in the eleventh century – but we can be confident that the number was large only if we rely on gossip and hearsay. It may be true that 'there is no smoke without fire', but a mountain of smoke can be raised by the feeblest of fires. Among the lower clergy the effect of the reformers' work is very difficult to gauge.

It is estimated by Professor Knowles and Dr Hadcock that there were a little more than 1,000 monks in England in 1066; by 1200 the number of regular clergy had probably increased more than ten-fold.[20] The figure cannot be proved exactly, but it cannot be far wrong; and this is the most concrete indication of the success of the campaign for celibacy. The English population itself may have increased, but not on this scale. Peter Damian and Hildebrand had founded a movement designed to sweep all religious communities and all clergy who could live in a community into institutes based on a recognized rule of life, founded on vows of chastity and obedience and lived in common. Their efforts led to the formation of numerous houses of Augustinian canons all over Europe.[21] In England we know of sixty-six houses of canons at the time of the Conquest – living a life based on a rule, on misrule, or on no rule at all. By 1200 nearly half (including three cathedral chapters)[22] had been swept away, virtually all being translated or absorbed into a regular establishment, thirteen specifically becoming houses of canons regular.

The greatest change in the regular population, however, came from another quarter: well over half the English regulars of the late twelfth century were Cistercians. And their enormous numbers (estimated at over 5,000 in 1200, including lay-brothers) raise a problem of great complexity. There can be little question that the number of upper clergy in England had multiplied many times between 1050 and 1200. The increase of regulars had not been made entirely at the expense of the seculars; indeed, it is probable that the upper secular clergy were more numerous in 1200 than in 1050, and certain that there were royal clerks and cathedral

[20] M. D. Knowles and R. N. Hadcock, *Medieval Religious Houses* (London, 1953), pp. 359–65, esp. p. 364.

[21] Cf. J. C. Dickinson, *The Origins of the Austin Canons and their introduction into England* (London, 1950), esp. ch. 1.

[22] Durham, Norwich, and Rochester (1083, *c.* 1094, 1080).

prebendaries in far greater profusion. Where, then, did the increase come from? Was the clerical profession more popular, or was it easier to rise from the ranks of the lower clergy? The answer is that both forces must have been at work. When we estimate the effect of the Gregorian reform on the quality and the morals of the lower clergy, we must remember that it is probable that the cream of the profession was being skimmed – more than ever before or since, save possibly in Counter-Reformation Spain – for the benefit of the royal service, the cathedral chapters, and, above all, the monastic houses. But in the main, the increases probably came from the upper classes: the appeal of the clerical profession was very powerful in a century under the spell of St Peter Damian and St Bernard, when standards of education and learning were undergoing revolutionary advances, and when it was fashionable to be a monk or a learned clerk.

Within the ranks of the secular clergy the century following the Conquest saw changes as momentous as those in the monastic orders. The novelty of the institutes founded by Damian and his followers does not mean that formal rules for canons were unknown before the papal reform. The rule of St Augustine itself (however much altered or interpolated since it left the master's hand) was of great antiquity; and many houses of canons were nominally subject in the eleventh century to rules compiled or devised by the reformers of the eighth and ninth centuries.[23] All the English cathedrals and some proportion no doubt of the lesser minsters were subject to a communal rule with strict enforcement of celibacy in 1066. But not all the communities adhered to these rules, and some (even of the cathedrals) were so small and poor as scarcely to be able to maintain their status as communities at all. The bulk of the cathedral chapters of post-Conquest England were in every sense entirely new foundations.[24]

Just as every subaltern is supposed to have a field-marshal's baton in his knapsack, so every member of the upper clergy was a potential bishop. Only a few attained to the office; but if a section

[23] Cf. K. Edwards, *The English Secular Cathedrals in the Middle Ages* (2nd. ed., Manchester, 1967), pp. 8 ff.

[24] St Paul's is the only English cathedral which provides any real evidence of continuity through the Conquest.

of the clergy were debarred from promotion, we should feel doubtful if they were properly called 'upper clergy' at all. Between the translation of St Dunstan to Canterbury in 960 and the accession of Cnut in 1016 a majority, and probably nearly all the English bishops, were drawn from the monasteries;[25] the upper secular clergy, if such a body may properly be said to have existed, are buried in total obscurity. Under Cnut and the Confessor a rapidly growing number of bishops were drawn from the royal service, from the clerks who provided the staff of the King's chapel, of his 'chancery' and 'chamber'. The royal clerks throw a remarkable light on the condition of the English secular clergy in the early eleventh century. We know at least thirty-four by name, and of these some seventeen won bishoprics. Of the thirty-four, there is reason to suppose that fifteen or eighteen were not of English origin; of these, the majority came from France and Lorraine, and three were Normans. Even allowing for the Confessor's partiality for the associates of his exile, it does not look as if the English Church was organized to support on its own resources a distinguished secular clergy. Nor was it economically organized for the purpose. A century later Thomas Becket largely maintained the 'port' of royal chancellor out of the numerous benefices which he held in plurality, with a nucleus of prebends and cathedral dignities. The prebendal system was not in existence under the Confessor; and although there were some cases of scandalous pluralism, it was probably commoner for royal clerks to be supported by grants of land, like the grants from which Leofric was later able largely to endow the bishopric of Exeter.[26] The English secular clergy of the twelfth

[25] M. D. Knowles, *The Monastic Order in England* (Cambridge, 1940), pp. 697–701. There is no known case of a non-monastic bishop in this period; but the origins of a certain number are not known.

[26] Albert of Lorraine and Regenbald were certainly holding parish churches in plurality, though whether as quasi-lay proprietors or as rectors or both is not clear (for Albert, see J. H. Round, *Commune of London* (Westminster, 1899), pp. 36 ff.; *C*[*ambridge*] *H*[*istorical*] *J*[*ournal*] x (1951), pp. 122, 124–5; for Regenbald, Round, *Feudal England* (London, 1895), pp. 421 ff.; F. E. Harmer, *Anglo-Saxon Writs* (Manchester, 1952), pp. 59–60; etc.). The greatest single landholder was Stigand, whose fabulous possessions have been indexed by O. von Feilitzen, *The Pre-Conquest Personal Names of Domesday*

century was in most respects the creation of the Norman Conquest.

Archbishop Stigand was as good an abuse as a usurper with reforming pretensions like William I could wish to find at Canterbury. He had preyed on the Confessor with even greater success than the Kemps and the Booths later preyed on Henry VI. He held two bishoprics and allegedly some abbeys besides; his translation to Canterbury was uncanonical for almost as many reasons as the law could devise. He was the very image of Simon Magus. But one crime was never laid to his door; there is no early evidence that he was either married or incontinent.[27] Indeed, it is remarkable how little evidence of this particular abuse can be found before the Conquest. One of Cnut's chaplains had a son who became Abbot of Winchcombe; Stigand's brother Aethelmaer had a wife; so apparently had the Bishop of Lichfield; and Albert of Lorraine founded a dynasty in the chapter of St Paul's.[28] But both Albert's son and his prebend may well have come to him after the Conquest.

If we add to this picture of the English clergy evidence drawn from the periphery, the vision is less innocent. At St David's and Llandaff in the late eleventh century we find dynastic bishoprics,

Book (Uppsala, 1937), pp. 374–5. For Edwards' grant(s) to Leofric, see *The Exeter Book of Old English Poetry*, ed. R. W. Chambers, M. Förster, and R. Flower (London 1933), pp. 5, 15. Guibert de Nogent takes it as a matter of course that a man should make his pile as chaplain to the Confessor (*PL*, CLVI, col. 909). In addition, the perquisites of office may have been as profitable as royal gifts. (For all this, see now F. Barlow, *The English Church 1000-1066*, London, 1963.)

[27] That Stigand was married is asserted in a long footnote in E. L. Cutts, *Parish Priests and their People* . . . (London, 1898), pp. 262–3, which lists cases of married bishops, etc. There are some errors and almost no references given for this catalogue, which must be treated with the utmost caution; I have found no support for the statement about Stigand.

[28] For Godmann, Cnut's chaplain, see T. J. Oleson, *The Witenagemot in the reign of Edward the Confessor* (Oxford, 1955), p. 125; for Aethelmaer, *Domesday Book*, II, fol. 195; for Leofwine, Bishop of Lichfield, Lanfranc, *Ep.* 4 (cf. J. Tait in *Essays in History presented to R. L. Poole*, ed. H. W. C. Davis (Oxford, 1927), pp. 155 ff.); for Albert of Lorraine, above, n. 26. A list of benefactors of New Minster, Winchester, of the early eleventh century contains the name of a priest's wife, but her husband's standing in the Church is quite uncertain (*Liber Vitae*, ed. W. de G. Birch (London-Winchester, 1892), p. 58).

archdeaconries, and every kind of family influence in cathedral chapters and in the surviving remnants of the great Welsh monasteries.[29] At Durham, in the early eleventh and again in the early twelfth century, we find a bishop who could marry his daughter into the local nobility; in the late eleventh century, the Dean and Treasurer of Durham at least were married men. But before the century was out the Durham chapter had been ousted by monks; and in 1114 the Treasurer's son, Eilaf, was attacked in the last stronghold of the family, the church of Hexham, of which they were hereditary priests, by the arrival of Augustinian canons. But Eilaf retained a life interest in the church, and lived to see his son Ailred a monk at Rievaulx.[30] How far these conditions were peculiar to the north and west of Britain, we cannot tell.

In 1076 Archbishop Lanfranc passed his first decree against married clergy. It was a kindly answer to a difficult situation. For the future, no clergy are to marry, no priests or deacons to be ordained without a pledge that they are not married. The parish clergy who are married are permitted to keep their wives; only to canons are wives entirely forbidden.[31] This has usually been taken to reflect the English scene, and it may be so. But in some respects Lanfranc and his colleagues were none too sensitive to the special needs of their new subjects, and it is equally likely that

[29] For married clergy in the Welsh Church, see the remarkable tables of succession to the churches in Archenfield (Herefordshire, on the Welsh border) in the *Liber Landavensis* (ed. J. G. Evans (Oxford, 1893), pp. 275 ff.); for a general account of the evidence, see J. Conway Davies, op. cit. II, pp. 457–60, 464–8, 491–537; see esp. p. 535 (of the bishopric of Llandaff): 'For more than a century after the Norman Conquest the bishopric was reserved for the family; for more than a hundred and fifty years after the Norman Conquest the archdeaconry was reserved for the family. The chapter of Llandaff seemed almost a closed corporation reserved for the Llancarfan family.' There is exaggeration in this, and some of the evidence for family relationships is tenuous; but what can be established is striking enough.

[30] J. Raine, *The Priory of Hexham* (Surtees Society, 1864), pp. l–lxvii; F. M. Powicke, Walter Daniel's *Life of Ailred* (Nelson's Medieval Texts, 1950), pp. xxiv–xxxvi; Symeon of Durham, ed. T. Arnold (Rolls Series), I, pp. 122–3, 215 ff.; II, p. 316.

[31] D. Wilkins, *Concilia Magnae Britanniae*, I, p. 367. For Lanfranc's treatment of celibacy, cf. his *Epp.* 21, 62.

the decree was as much the fruit of Norman as of English experience; it was undoubtedly based on the Norman legislation of the preceding decade. The one distinguished English bishop of native origin active in 1076, Wulfstan of Worcester, made no use of the escape clause in his treatment of the married clergy of his diocese.[32]

The Norman clergy were by repute among the most uxorious in Europe.[33] Even here the extent of clerical marriage and hereditary succession cannot be at all exactly estimated. We cannot trace in detail the succession to any office lower than bishop, and the office of bishop was too important to become hereditary in eleventh-century Normandy. There is an isolated case of a man who granted his hereditary archdeaconry to the Abbey of St Évroul in the middle of the century;[34] and there is a great deal of evidence to show that the upper clergy formed a more normal part of the Norman aristocracy than Gregory VII and his associates would have wished. Robert, son of Richard I Duke of Normandy, was count of Évreux, and in that capacity had a wife and at least three sons. He was also Archbishop of Rouen.[35] In three ways he represented characteristic features of

[32] *The Vita Wulfstani of William of Malmesbury*, ed. R. R. Darlington (Camden 3rd ser., XL, 1928), pp. xxxiv, 53–4. An enactment similar to that of 1076 had been made in the Norman council of Lisieux (*c.* 1064, cc. 2–3, ed. L. Delisle, *Journal des Savants* (1901), p. 517), condemning priests married since the council of Rouen (1055–63; *PL*, CXLVII, col. 278). A more stringent canon was passed at Rouen in 1072 (Mansi, op. cit. XX, coll. 33 ff.).

[33] Gaufridus Grossus, *Vita Bernardi Tironiensis*, c. 6, §51 (*PL*, CLXXII, col. 1397), written after 1116, but referring to the period *c.* 1100, gives a circumstantial account of clerical marriage as a normal element in the social scene in Normandy, and relates how Bernard of Tiron, preaching continence in Normandy, was nearly lynched by the wives of the clergy; Orderic tells the same tale of John of Avranches, Archbishop of Rouen, when he promulgated the decree of 1072 (ed. Le Prévost-Delisle, II, p. 171). We shall presently see how high a proportion of the controversial literature in favour of marriage was written in Normandy (below, p. 88 and n. 43).

[34] 'Archidiaconatum quoque, quem in feudo ab antecessoribus suis de archiepiscopo Rotomagensi tenebat . . . dedit', *Orderic*, II, p. 132. The phraseology is very strange, but there is no obvious way of emending the text.

[35] Ibid. II, p. 365; cf. the *Acta* [*archiepiscoporum Rotomagensium*], *PL*, CXLVII, col. 277.

the Norman Church. He was of the ducal family, and the genealogy of the Norman dukes in the eleventh and early twelfth centuries includes seven Norman bishops, three of them archbishops of Rouen.[36] He was Count as well as Bishop, and so reminds us of Ivo, Bishop of Séez and lord of the notorious house of Bellême for over thirty years in the middle of the century, and Odo of Bayeux, the Conqueror's half-brother and Earl of Kent.[37] Archbishop Robert was married, and so takes his place with about a dozen other distinguished Norman clerics of whom we are informed.[38] This number is not excessively large; and the evidence is very fragmentary – in some respects the Normans showed their

[36] (1) Robert, Archbishop of Rouen (989–1036 or 7), son of Duke Richard I (*Orderic,* IV, p. 294, etc.; *Acta,* loc. cit.). (2) Mauger, Archbishop of Rouen, son of Duke Richard II (William of Jumièges, *Gesta Normannorum ducum*, ed. J. Marx (Rouen-Paris, 1914), p. 119; *Acta,* loc. cit.; etc.). (3) Hugh, Bishop of Lisieux (*c.* 1050–77), grandson of Duke Richard I (cf. *Orderic*, II, pp. 39, 71 and D. C. Douglas, *E.H.R.*, LXI (1946), pp. 154 f., 140). (4) and (5) Hugh Bishop of Bayeux (died *c.* 1049) (William of Jumièges, p. 102; *Orderic*, III, pp. 416, etc.) and John of Avranches, Bishop of Avranches (1061–68/9) and Archbishop of Rouen (1068/9–79) (William of Jumièges, p. 137; *Orderic*, II, p. 374, etc.), sons of Rodulf, count of Ivry, half-brother of Duke Richard I. (6) Odo, Bishop of Bayeux (1049/50–97), half-brother of the Conqueror (see n. 37). (7) Richard of Kent, Bishop of Bayeux (1135–42), grandson of Henry I (*Orderic,* V, pp. 31, 45).

[37] For Ivo, see G. H. White, *Trans. R. Hist. Soc.,* 4th ser. XXII (1940), pp. 81 f., 88; for Odo, D. C. Douglas, *The Domesday Monachorum of Christ Church Canterbury* (London, 1944), pp. 33 ff., etc., and the study by V. Bourrienne, 'Odon de Conteville évêque de Bayeux . . .', *Revue catholique de Normandie*, VII–IX (1897–1900). (See now also D. Bates's Exeter Ph.D. thesis on Odo.)

[38] Hugh and Roger, Bishops of Coutances (L. C. Loyd, *Yorks. Arch[aeological] J[ournal]*, XXXI (1932–4), pp. 99 ff.; *Orderic*, IV, p. 415); Radbod, Bishop of Séez (see n. 40); Sampson Treasurer of Bayeux (see n. 39); Norman, Dean of Séez (see n. 40); Anger of Bayeux (see p. 91); Fulk, Dean of Évreux (*Orderic*, II, pp. 20, 397); Robert, Archdeacon of Évreux and Adelis his wife had a son Gilbert, who occurs in 1099–1100 (J.-J. Vernier, *Chartes . . . de Jumièges,* I (Rouen-Paris, 1916), no. 40); Gilbert d'Évreux, Precentor of Rouen and chaplain of Henry I, had at least four sons, including William Prior of Ste-Barbe-en-Auge (chronicle of Ste-Barbe, ed. R.-N. Sauvage in *Mémoires de l'Académie . . . de Caen* (1906), pp. 19 ff.); the sons of an Archdeacon and of the Dean of Coutances witness a charter of *c.* 1140 (*Cartulaire des îles normandes,* Société Jersiaise (Jersey, 1924), no. 175). The last three are the only instances in which it is not certain that the family was raised in the eleventh century. For other cases, see next note.

characteristics most clearly only after crossing the Channel. But we have evidence of two striking phenomena: first, of family groups within the chapter of Bayeux (the only cathedral of whose personnel we are at all well informed),[39] and secondly of the existence of certain powerful and purely ecclesiastical families – the family of Radbod, Bishop of Séez, father of an Archbishop of Rouen; of Sampson, Treasurer and possibly Dean of Bayeux, later Bishop of Worcester, brother of one Archbishop of York, father of another, father also of a Bishop of

[39] A witness list of 1092 contains a large number of canons of Bayeux, including Ralph de St Patrick and John his son, Anschetil de St Vigor and Ralph his nephew (V. Bourrienne, *Antiquus Cartularius ecclesiae Baiocensis*, I (Rouen-Paris, 1902), no. 22); also Ranulf, son of Thurstin and Osbert, son of Thurstin (just possibly Ranulf Flambard and his brother: cf. *C.H.J.*, x (1951), p. 130 and n. 18); Odo, son of Oger, who was father of Matthew, Archdeacon of Worcester (Bourrienne, op. cit. I, no. 22; II, no. 362) – and Odo's father may have been Oger, Precentor of Bayeux (Bibliothèque Nationale, MS. Latin 5423, p. 144). The list contains six other men with patronymics, but there is no evidence that their fathers were canons or clerics. Apart from the list, Serlo, canon of Bayeux, poet and controversialist, was son of a priest (see n. 43); and it is possible, though not certain, that Anger of Bayeux held a position in the chapter there (cf. below, p. 91). But the most distinguished family group was that of the brothers Thomas and Sampson, successive Treasurers of Bayeux. The children of a priest (William of Malmesbury, *G*[*esta*] *P*[*ontificum*], ed. N. E. S. A. Hamilton, p. 66) called Osbert, and Muriel his wife (*Liber Vitae ecclesiae Dunelmensis*, ed. J. Raine, Surtees Society (1841), pp. 139–40), both the brothers won English bishoprics. Thomas I became Archbishop of York (1070–1100; cf. *Hist*[*orians of the*] *Ch*[*urch of*] *York*, ed. J. Raine, II, p. 99); Sampson, like his brother, was chaplain to the king and Treasurer of Bayeux (*Orderic*, II, p. 249, III, p. 266; H. W. C. Davis, *Regesta Regum Anglo-Normannorum*, I, (Oxford, 1913), no. 147; cf. Bourrienne, op. cit. I, no. 23), and also possibly Dean (William of Malmesbury, *GP*, p. 289) before he became Bishop of Worcester (1096–1112). Sampson had at least two sons, Thomas II, Archbishop of York (1109–14; Eadmer, *Hist*[*oria*] *Nov*[*orum*], ed. M. Rule, p. 208; Malmesbury, *GP*, pp. 289–90) and Richard de Douvres, canon and Bishop of Bayeux (*c.* 1107–33; Bourrienne, op. cit. I, no. 23; *Hist. Ch. York*, II, p. 124). Humphrey (two of the name), Hugh, and Roger Bovet were canons of Bayeux in the mid and late twelfth century: Hugh and Roger held the prebend of Cartigny (Bourrienne, op. cit. I, nos. 96, 124 ff., 283–4, etc.). Hugh Bovet also claimed a canonry at Salisbury by hereditary right, but since he was only seven when his father died, he had some difficulty making good the claim (*JL.* 14,098). Some of these families may have been reared before the fathers were ever in orders.

Bayeux; and of Norman, Dean of Séez, father of a bishop, grandfather of two more, great-grandfather of a fourth.[40]

Before we can compare these conditions with the affairs of the Normans in England, we must remove two of the difficulties and misunderstandings raised by problems of this kind. To us, as to Gregory VII, it makes little difference whether Sampson was subdeacon or bishop when he begat his children.[41] But in contemporary eyes it made a world of difference: the special stigma which attached to the son of a priest (and by that much the more of a bishop), was rarely transferred to any lower order.[42] I know of no case of a bishop having children after his promotion in England or Normandy in the eleventh or twelfth century, save Robert of Normandy as Count of Évreux – and perhaps, though I cannot prove it, Ranulph Flambard of Durham. Thus, when I talk of a bishop as father of a family, the family is presumed to have been conceived before the bishop's consecration.

[40] Radbod, Bishop of Sèez in the 1020s and 1030s, was father of William Bonne-Ame, Archbishop of Rouen 1079–1110 (*Orderic*, II, pp. 64, 213, etc.); for Sampson of Worcester, see above; for Norman, Dean of Séez, F. Barlow, *Letters of Arnulf of Lisieux* (Camden 3rd ser., LXI (1939), pp. xi–xii and notes).

[41] Sampson was a subdeacon when he became bishop in 1096 (Eadmer, *Hist. Nov.*, p. 74), and was presumably such throughout his career as a canon and dignitary at Bayeux. The first certain evidence of Norman canons being forbidden to marry is in 1080 (cf. n. 9 above); but in any case a canon in lower orders was an abuse.

[42] The prohibition against the ordination – outside a monastery – of a priest's son was extended to all illegitimate children in the council of Poitiers of 1078 (Mansi, op. cit. xx, coll. 498–9). But this local decree never became the law of the Church. 'Son of a priest' was a recognized term of abuse, against which it seems to have been regarded as sufficient defence to show that the father was not in *priest's* orders. Cf. Herbert of Bosham's brilliant repartee to Henry II in *Materials for the History of Thomas Becket*, ed. J. C. Robertson, III, p. 101. Becket must have been retailing current gossip when he so described Reginald fitzJocelin (M. D. Knowles, *Episcopal Colleagues of Archbishop Thomas Becket* (Cambridge, 1951), p. 19 – where for twenty-three read thirty-three). Jocelin, his father, was either an Archdeacon when Reginald was conceived, and so most probably a deacon (all the English archdeacons of this period whose orders are known were deacons) or already Bishop of Salisbury – the former is more likely! But it is possible that we take these stories too pedantically, and that 'priest' in this context was popularly taken to mean a clerk of any kind, like OE. 'preost'.

The papal reform and the investiture contest produced a number of pamphlets, and in reply to the abuse poured by reformers on married clergy and the stringent demands of the canons several treatises were written on their behalf. At least four were written in Normandy – two anonymous defences of marriage written in the 1060s and 1070s; a defence of the right to ordination of the sons of priests by a canon of Bayeux; and a pair of treatises, one on each of these issues, by the brilliant writer commonly known as the Anonymous of York.[43] The Anonymous may have visited England, though his connection with York is pure hypothesis; his background and his milieu lay certainly in Normandy. In his writings the traditional attitudes and customs of the Norman Church were defended with all the panoply of the new logic. Old-fashioned views dressed up in novel dogmatic forms produced opinions of an extreme and startling nature. But the Anonymous's defence of clerical marriage is among the least eccentric of his writings, because he was defending a position which other contemporaries did not hesitate to defend. It was widely held that sons of priests should not suffer for their parents' supposed delinquency.[44] But the Anonymous presently became entangled in his doctrine of predestination, where neither we nor his contemporaries can follow him. Similarly the text 'melius est enim nubere, quam uri' was the conventional foundation

[43] For these writings (mostly printed in *Libelli de Lite*, III) see H. Böhmer, *Kirche und Staat in England und in der Normandie* (Leipzig, 1899), pp. 168 ff.; A. Fliche, *La réforme grégorienne*, III, pp. 13–38. For Serlo of Bayeux (himself the son of a priest) see H. Böhmer, *Neues Archiv*, XXII (1897), pp. 722–38. The most recent study of the Anonymous, his origin and his thought, is by G. H. Williams, *The Norman Anonymous of 1100 A.D.* (Harvard Theological Studies, XVIII, 1951); cf. R. W. Southern, *The Making of the Middle Ages* (London, 1953), p. 93 n. Williams does not seem to realize how eccentric and how heretical the Anonymous's thought was, and so makes him out to be a more responsible and influential person than he can possibly have been (he even suggests that he was an archbishop). His defence of clerical marriage is in *Libelli de Lite*, III, pp. 645 ff. (Ed. K. Pellens, *Die Texte des Normannischen Anonymus*, Wiesbaden, 1966, pp. 204 ff. Cf. R. Nineham in *J. Eccles. Hist.*, XIV, pp. 31 ff.)

[44] The Anonymous's tract on priests' sons is in ibid. pp. 649 ff. Ed. Pellens, pp. 116 ff., 209 ff.; see also the approximately contemporary works of Serlo of Bayeux (pp. 579 ff.) and Theobald of Étampes (pp. 603 ff. and below, n. 48).

for the defence of marriage: to refuse the clergy the right to marry was to invite those who had no vocation to celibacy to far worse crimes. 'The apostle laid it down that "a bishop should be the husband of one wife". He would hardly have made this ruling', commented the Anonymous, 'if it were adultery, as some assert, for a bishop to have at one time both a wife and a church – two wives, so to speak. . . . For Holy Church is not the priest's wife, not *his* bride, but Christ's.'[45] Along these lines the institution was defended; and if the defence was not always coherent and sometimes led plainly to heresy, the defenders can hardly be blamed. Like the men who supported lay power against the papal onslaught, they were defending deeply felt but often incoherent attitudes against a coherent ideological system many centuries old.[46] If clerical marriage was undoubtedly illegal at the turn of the eleventh century, both a married clerk and his wife could feel that they had some noted thinkers on their side, and the support of a considerable body of public opinion. But their days were numbered. The defenders of clerical marriage were so active in Normandy partly for the very reason that the reformers were active there too.

Between the Conquest and 1123 a number of canons were passed in England against the married clergy. Lanfranc's comparatively mild decree was followed by more stringent attempts to enforce the law in Anselm's two councils of 1102 and 1108.[47] To set beside the Norman Anonymous we have little overt polemical literature, save the fierce defence of priests' sons by the Oxford lecturer Theobald of Étampes; but Theobald's writing pre-

[45] Op. cit. p. 646. In the text I have omitted his characteristic 'Quod quia de scripturis sanctis non habet auctoritatem, eadem facilitate contempnitur, qua dicitur.'

[46] For the defence of lay power, see W. Ullmann, *The Growth of Papal Government in the Middle Ages* (London, 1955), pp. 344–58, 382–412.

[47] The decree of 1076 (Wilkins, *Concilia*, I, p. 367) appears to have been preceded by a decree from the council of 1070 (c. 15, ibid. p. 365); it was followed by canons 5–8 of the council of 1102 (ibid. p. 382; for the attempt to enforce these canons, cf. the letters in Anselm, *Opera Omnia*, ed. W. S. Schmitt, IV (Edinburgh, 1949), pp. 165–70; V (1951), p. 287), and by the council of 1108, the whole of whose canons were devoted to the subject (Wilkins, op. cit. I, p. 388). For later councils, see nn. 61–3.

supposes that the clerical father had been at fault.[48] Nevertheless, the concrete evidence for the behaviour of the higher clergy shows clearly that a substantial section followed the practices noticed among the Norman clergy; and the English evidence reveals with greater clarity than the Norman the connection between clerical marriage, the inheritance of benefices, and the social structure of the Church.

For the English Church as a whole, the evidence is almost as fragmentary as the Norman. Occasional cases of incontinence in high places may be found in any century, and it is difficult to pin-point the moment when clerical marriage became really exceptional. A large majority of the upper clergy known to have had children between 1050 and 1200 had had their families, at latest, by about 1130; by the middle of the century there is a noticeable falling off. What was happening can be gauged from three of the most celebrated cases of the second half of the century. Two letters written by John of Salisbury in 1156 describe the case of the scandalous Walkelin, Archdeacon of Suffolk. They were addressed to Pope Adrian IV:

> 'He has ordered that a bastard whom his concubine bore while he was on his way back from you, should be called by your most sacred name of Adrian. He, the father of this child, has now left the lady pregnant, but has made a most provident disposition for the future, to wit that, if the child happens to be a boy he shall be called Benevento, because his father has gone on a pilgrimage to that place, while if it is a girl, she is to be called Adriana.[49]

This is an isolated scandal; though, if we may believe John of Salisbury's letters, Walkelin was not the only incontinent archdeacon in the diocese of Norwich. At about the same time Osbert of Bayeux, Archdeacon of Richmond, was deposed from his

[48] *Libelli de Lite*, III, pp. 603–7; for Theobald, cf. R. Foreville and J. Leclercq in *Analecta Monastica*, IV (=*Studia Anselmiana*, XLI), pp. 8–118.

[49] *Letters of John of Salisbury*, ed. W. J. Millor, H. E. Butler, and C. N. L. Brooke, I (Nelson's Medieval Texts, 1955), nos. 14–15; cf. nos. 78–9 for the Archdeacon of Norfolk.

archdeaconry for the murder of St William of York.[50] Osbert became a layman, and founded a knightly family. It is possible that as Archdeacon he was already married, since he sprang from one of the most celebrated clerical families of the early twelfth century. He was nephew to Thurstan, Archbishop of York from 1114 to 1140, a prelate of considerable distinction. Thurstan's brother was Bishop of Évreux, and his father, Anger or Anskar, was a distinguished married clerk from the Bessin who settled with his wife Popelina in London, and became (with both his sons) a canon of St Paul's.[51] Anskar was married; Thurstan and Audoen evidently not; and Osbert, if married, was also a miscreant. The habit of marriage died more slowly in the great curial family of Roger, Bishop of Salisbury. Roger's wife or concubine, Matilda of Ramsbury, was still active at the time of her husband's death in 1139. Their son became for a time King Stephen's Chancellor. Of Roger's nephews, two were bishops; and Nigel of Ely himself had a son, Richard fitzNeal or Richard of Ely, Royal Treasurer and Bishop of London from 1189 to 1199. Richard's successor as Treasurer was his kinsman William of Ely, the last of the family known to have achieved distinction, and the last clerical member of the family known to have been a father. William died in 1222.[52]

[50] For Osbert see C. T. Clay, *Yorks. Arch J.*, XXXVI (1944–7), pp. 277–9; Dom Adrian Morey, *C.H.J.*, X (1952), pp. 352–3; *Letters of John of Salisbury*, I, pp. 261–2.

[51] *C.H.J.*, X (1951), p. 124.

[52] For Roger himself, Nigel, Bishop of Ely, Richard fitzNeal, and Alexander Bishop of Lincoln, see *D[ictionary of] N[ational] B[iography]*; for Richard, see also *Dialogus de Scaccario*, ed. C. Johnson (Nelson's Medieval Texts, 1950), pp. xiv ff. and *passim*; H. G. Richardson, *E.H.R.* XLIII (1928), pp. 161 ff.; for William of Ely, Richardson, *Trans. R. Hist. Soc.*, 4th ser., XV (1932), pp. 45–90, esp. pp. 47, 60, 90. Matilda of Ramsbury is mentioned by name in *Orderic*, V, pp. 120–1; for her son Roger le Poer, see ibid, and *Gesta Stephani*, ed. K. R. Potter (Nelson's Medieval Texts, 1955), p. 52. On the strength of his name 'le Poer', a connection has been conjectured between Roger and Herbert and Richard Poore, successive Bishops of Salisbury at the end of the century; and it has been established that the Poores were sons to Richard of Ilchester, a leading exchequer clerk and Bishop of Winchester 1174–88 (cf. Stubbs, introduction to Howden's *Chronica*, IV, p. xci n.; *D.N.B.* *s.v.* Poor, Richard of Ilchester, etc.). There is plausibility in these suggestions,

About nine years earlier, in 1213 or 1214, occurred the death of Richard Junior, canon of St Paul's, last of the most prolific of all the clerical families of twelfth-century England.[53] Its founder, Richard de Belmeis I, had been Bishop of London from 1108 to 1127. As bishop he had control, though not undisputed control, of appointments to the thirty prebends of his chapter. Two of his sons and four of his nephews at least were promoted by him; and the glory of the family was maintained by his nephew Richard de Belmeis II, who was bishop from 1152 to 1162. By a strange irony, Richard II's successor was also related to him, though not closely; but the family connection of Gilbert Foliot was untainted by any suspicion of clerical marriage. 'The Lord deprived bishops of sons, but the devil gave them nephews.'[54] The decline of clerical marriage did not mean the end of nepotism or even of inheritance. Both found pastures new in a world of celibate clergy. When we witness the pathetic struggles of Peter of Blois and Gerald of Wales in their grey hairs to prevent their nephews securing their choicest benefices,[55] we can see that already, by the end of the twelfth

but no solid evidence on which to support them. Matilda of Ramsbury may well have been connected with Azo of Ramsbury, Archdeacon of Wiltshire (*Register of St Osmund*, ed. W. H. R. Jones (Rolls Series), I, pp. 215, 351) and probably Dean of Salisbury from before 1139 to *c.* 1145, *Notes and Queries for Somerset and Dorset*, XXIII (1942), pp. 319 f.) and his brother Roger, canon of Salisbury and Archdeacon of Wiltshire after Azo (*Register of St Osmund*, I, p. 351, cf. p. 349, etc.; *Historia et cartularium mon. Gloucestriae*, ed. W. H. Hart (Rolls Series), II, p. 106).

[53] For what follows, see C. N. L. Brooke, *C.H.J.*, X (1951), pp. 111–32, especially pp. 124 ff.; for the Belmeis family, see Stubbs's introduction to Ralph de Diceto, I, pp. xxi ff., xxvi ff., and Brooke, art. cit., pp. 125–7.

[54] This celebrated dictum is assigned to Alexander III by Gerald of Wales, *Opera*, II (ed. J. S. Brewer), p. 304.

[55] Two letters of Peter of Blois relating to his nephews are preserved in a manuscript at Erfurt (Amplonian MS. F.71, fos. 190r–v, 196r–v. I owe these references to Mr R. W. Southern who kindly lent me photostats of the MS.). For Gerald of Wales's troubles with his nephew Gerald, see *Opera*, III, p. 325, and especially the *Speculum Duorum* (of which there is an account by W. S. Davies in *Archaeologia Cambrensis*, LXXXIII (1928), pp. 111–34. An edition by Dr M. Richter is promised.)

The exchange of benefices in later centuries (of which this is only one aspect) is discussed by A. Hamilton Thompson in *The English Clergy and their Organisation in the later Middle Ages* (Oxford, 1947), pp. 107–9, but both the

century, the technique of succession and exchange was firmly established, by which the younger members of a clerical family obtained possession of the family heirlooms throughout the later Middle Ages.

Peter and Gerald had both written love lyrics in their youth, like every good scholar of the day; but in the long run they were strict upholders of celibacy.[56] The clerical element in their families was by no means based on clerical marriage; and in this it is in marked contrast with the episcopate of Richard de Belmeis I. Only two of the Belmeis promoted by him were his own children; but in return for his share of the spoils, he permitted a number of benefices to pass to the sons of canons. We know that at least a quarter of the canons were married in the period 1090–1127; that at least eight dignities and prebends passed from father to son. This information comes almost entirely from the St Paul's prebendal catalogue, which must have been carefully kept at this period; and its authors showed no scruple about entering in the successions to various prebends: 'Albert of Lorraine, Hugh his son', 'Quintilian Archdeacon, Cyprian his son', 'Roger Archdeacon, son of Robert Archdeacon' and so forth. Most of these men are little more than names, but there is no reason to suppose that many were disreputable; in the case of the family of Thurstan of York, quite the contrary. The chapter had its black sheep, among whom the family of Ranulph Flambard, Bishop of Durham and Canon of St Paul's, was conspicuous. But there is nothing to suggest that the canons of St Paul's were exceptionally domestic among English chapters at this time. Nor can we tell whether the convention had its roots in England or in Normandy, since both races were represented among the married canons. Unfortunately this early prebendal list is the only oasis of light in the general obscurity.[57]

phenomenon in general and its use to further family interests in particular await a full critical study.

[56] For Gerald and Peter's lyrics, see F. J. E. Raby, *Secular Latin Poetry in the Middle Ages* (Oxford, 1934), II, pp. 110–11, 323–4.

[57] Cf. Brooke, art. cit.; and for Flambard, pp. 124, 129 ff. It is possible, though not entirely certain, that he was Dean (but see D. E. Greenway in J. Le Neve, *Fasti Ecclesiae Anglicanae, 1066–1300*, I (London, 1968), pp. 97–8); there is no doubt that he was a canon of St Paul's.

By the time of Richard's death in 1127, the halcyon days when nepotism and heredity could flourish side by side were drawing to a close. Of hereditary succession there are seven or eight cases known at St Paul's before 1127, two between 1127 and *c.* 1150, and only one – and that a Belmeis – thereafter. No doubt local conditions, in the shape of ascetic bishops and an obscure but evidently powerful ascetic movement within the chapter,[58] contributed to this comparatively speedy uprooting of an established custom. But the date fits so well with the other evidence about when celibacy became fashionable throughout the upper clergy that we may take it that in this respect St Paul's accurately reflected the state of things throughout England, and perhaps in many corners of Europe besides.

Our view of the English scene has shown that in many ways the assimilation of social arrangements lay and ecclesiastical is much as the more fragmentary Norman evidence might lead us to expect. We have few parallels for Archbishop Robert the Count of Évreux, though many clerics were engaged in very secular pursuits – one canon of St Paul's may have been sheriff of eight counties, and Thomas Becket led an army in the campaign of Toulouse.[59] But the great clerical families (always with some lay members, but often owing their power wholly to their grip on the Church) and the hereditary benefices flourished in the English Church between the Conquest and the Anarchy. There were many celibates; but clerical marriage was sufficiently common to be safe and even respectable. In the middle of the century – among the higher clergy – it died; more swiftly where ascetic ideals won a firm foothold, more slowly in families with a long tradition of the clerical paterfamilias.

My last word must be some brief appraisal of why the institution died when it did. In part it was simply because of the passage of time and the impact of the reformers' attack. A social revolution

[58] Cf. M. Gibbs, *Early Charters of the Cathedral Church of St Paul, London* (Camden 3rd, ser. LVIII (1939)), p. xxxiii.

[59] For Hugh of Buckland, cf. Brooke, art. cit. p. 124, n. 70; for Becket's part in the campaign of 1159, see especially FitzStephen in *Materials for the History of Thomas Becket,* III, pp. 33–4, and the *Continuatio Beccensis* and Robert of Torigni in Torigni's *Chronique*, ed. L. Delisle, II, p. 174 and I, p. 325.

takes time to accomplish, and two generations had to be born under the stigma of illegitimacy before the attack could have its effect. The attack came to a crescendo in the 1120s, with Celestine II's decree making invalid all marriages contracted by clerks in higher orders. This decree was solemnly repeated in three English councils in the same decade.[60] Chroniclers like Henry of Huntingdon (himself a hereditary archdeacon) might sneer at these decrees and tell stories about the legate and the Archbishop who promulgated them,[61] but there is no doubt that their impact was felt. They were repeated in later councils in various forms, and the first and most elaborate decree of the great council of Westminster of 1175 was directed against married clergy and hereditary benefices.[62] But by then the offence was rank only among the lower clergy.

The formal campaign is the first and most obvious cause, but I doubt if it was – directly – the most important. Celibacy had been the law of the Church since the fourth century, and it is far

[60] 1125 (Wilkins, op. cit. I, p. 408), 1127 (ibid. p. 410), 1129 (ibid. p. 411; Henry of Huntingdon, *Historia Anglorum*, ed. T. Arnold, pp. 250–1; *Anglo-Saxon Chronicle*, E, *s.a.* 1129 followed by several later writers); cf. also 1138 (Wilkins, op. cit. I, p. 415), and below, at n. 62.

[61] Henry of Huntingdon, pp. 245–6 on John of Crema; pp. 250–1 (and cf. *Anglo-Saxon Chronicle*, E, *s.a.* 1129) on the way in which Archbishop William's simplicity was duped by Henry I, who accepted fines from the married clergy and allowed them to keep their wives. The substance of the second story is very likely correct; the tale of John of Crema's incontinence is less plausible – a memory of a different kind of his important mission is given by Gilbert Foliot, writing in 1166 (*Epistolae*, ed. J. A. Giles, I, no. 194, pp. 282–3 (ed. A. Morey and C. N. L. Brooke (Cambridge, 1967), no. 170 pp. 240–1)). Henry of Huntingdon was certainly the son of a cleric; the grounds for thinking that he succeeded his father as archdeacon are given by T. Arnold in his introduction to Henry's *Historia*, pp. xxxi–xxxiii and notes.

[62] Wilkins, op. cit. I, p. 477 (the best text is in *Gesta Henrici Secundi* . . . , ed. Stubbs, I, p. 85); cf. also 1195, c. 17 (Wilkins, op. cit. I, p. 502) and 1200, c. 10 (p. 507), based on the Third Lateran Council of 1179, c. 11. The canon of 1175 was based on a decretal of Alexander III addressed to the Bishop of Worcester, 'Inter cetera sollicitudinis', *JL.* 12,254 (printed in full in *Gilberti Foliot Epistolae*, ed. J. A. Giles, II, no. 368, from the *Collectio Belverensis*). Both decretal and canon make a frequent appearance in the early decretal collections.

from clear why the mere reiteration of the law, however powerfully supported, should have been so startlingly successful. Decrees enjoining celibacy, indeed (as Prof. Darlington has shown), were almost as common in England before the Conquest as after.[63] Rather we must look at the situation of western Europe as a whole in the early twelfth century. The revival of learning and all that went with it – the movement we call the twelfth-century renaissance – owed much to the stimulus of the papal reformers; but even more conspicuously, it was the Papacy's most potent ally. To take an obvious example, the revival in the study and technique of law enabled the Papacy for the first time to operate through a network of courts enforcing a highly wrought and sophisticated legal system. The world in which Gratian floated his astonishing *Concordia discordantium canonum* about 1140 was ripe to receive it. The generation which witnessed its appearance had been brought up to accept the standards of their schools, where they learnt to know and respect the law of the Church, and so the law of celibacy. In St Paul's in the second and third decades of the century, the married clergy still flourished, though in decline. In contemporary Paris, Heloise and Abelard both reckoned already that their marriage would be the end of Abelard's career.

So far I have spoken from the point of view of the Church or of the clerical husband; finally, and more speculatively, we must consider the lady's point of view. There was a poetical genre of some popularity in the twelfth century which took the form of a debate as to whether a clerk or a knight was the better lover; since the authors were mostly clerks, the victory usually went to the clerk. But in one poem in which a clerk woos a lady, his hopes are most rudely dashed. 'Respuo moechari; volo nubere', says the lady, with a rare attack of brevity.[64] 'Adultery I repudiate: I want to get married' – we can never know how many potential wives of clerics answered their suitors in this manner after the decree of 1123. It must certainly have made it increasingly difficult

[63] See above, n. 17.

[64] The poem is by Matthew of Vendôme, and is edited by W. Wattenbach, *Sitzungsberichte der k. bayer. Akademie der Wiss. zu München, Philos.-philol. und hist. Classe,* II (1872), p. 599, cited Raby, op. cit. II, p. 34.

Plate I. The Bishop blessing.
From *The Benedictional of St Æthelwold*
(see pp. 167–8)

PLATE II. Rome, San Clemente

for the upper clergy to find mates in their own class. It is a misfortune that we know so little of the class known in happier days as the 'priestesses'.[65] We know a little of Matilda of Ramsbury. the name only of the illegitimate Percy who consented to live with Hugh du Puiset when he was Treasurer of York.[66] But for more personal evidence we have to turn to the continent and to Heloise, and Heloise – though she points to many of the problems in the case – was so exceptional a person as to be the worst possible basis for any generalization.[67]

One of the most startling changes in European society in the twelfth century was the rise of the Romantic ideal, the appearance north of the Pyrenees, in European dress, of the Arab and

[65] This title was commonly used in the sixth century (cf. E. Vacandard, *Études de critique et d'histoire religieuse,* I (Paris, 1905), p. 110).

[66] For other names, see above, notes 38, 39, Brooke, art. cit., pp. 123–4 and notes; for Matilda, above, n. 52. For Alice de Percy, see William of Newburgh, ed. R. Howlett, *Chronicles of the Reigns of Stephen, etc.,* II, pp. 440–1, *Complete Peerage,* revised ed. X, p. 442 n.; for their son Henry du Puiset, *Historiae Dunelmensis scriptores tres*, ed. J. Raine (Surtees Society, 1839), p. 18, and *The Priory of Finchale* (Surtees Society, 1837), pp. x, 46. William of Newburgh implies that Hugh had liaisons with more than one lady, and lists three sons; but it is probable that Bouchard du Puiset was Hugh's nephew, not his son (cf. *Gesta Henrici Secundi,* II, p. 85; Roger of Howden, *Chronica,* ed. Stubbs, III, p. 16, etc. Howden, the author of both these works, was a well-informed Northerner who, unlike William of Newburgh, preferred sound information to gossip as evidence). Alice de Percy subsequently – but still during Hugh's lifetime – married Richard de Morville (*Complete Peerage*, loc. cit.). This shows that she did not regard her liaison with Hugh du Puiset as a binding marriage. (On Hugh, see now G. V. Scammell, *Hugh du Puiset, bishop of Durham* (Cambridge, 1956).)

[67] For the Heloise of history, see the brilliant book of E. Gilson, op. cit. and the brief but profound appraisal by Dom David Knowles in *Studies* (1941), pp. 43–58, esp. pp. 48 ff. (reprinted in *The Historian and Character and Other Essays* (Cambridge, 1963), pp. 16–30, see above, p. 55). Out of the many ways in which Heloise illuminates our problem, I select two. Whoever her father may have been, she was brought up in a cathedral close, and thus gives us a rare glimpse not only of a clerical wife, but also of a child of that lost society. More important, her genius elicited from Abelard himself (in his letters to her), and more particularly from Peter the Venerable (in the letter he wrote to her after Abelard's death), two of the very few really lofty statements of the doctrine of Christian marriage written at this time.

Spanish conventions of romantic love.[68] In the wake of courtly love came a more refined appreciation of the relations of men and women, higher regard for the strength and the sanctity of the weaker sex; and in collaboration with the efforts of the Church and the civilizing influences of the age, a strengthening of the bonds of marriage. It may seem a paradox to associate the higher view of marriage with courtly love; since the orthodox opinion of the more extreme adherents of the 'religion of love' was summed up in the famous judgement attributed to the Countess of Champagne, Queen Eleanor's daughter, that love and marriage are incompatible.[69] But powerful as was the notion of love as adultery in the more artificial courtly circles, its importance has probably been exaggerated. In every age and every stratum of courtly literature there are hints that the union of love and marriage is both possible and desirable; it is surprising in how many romances it is a married couple who live happily ever after. The truth is that in a world in which Christian sentiment and courtly love both flourished – even if a full conceptual synthesis had to wait for Dante or beyond – every possible view of the relations of courtly love and married love, of the love of man and the love of God, was possible and likely to be held. The priest's concubine might be decked out in jewels from the altar, she might have a measure of security with a good husband; but from the mid twelfth century on, her position was neither dignified nor romantic. As the Church's doctrine of marriage became clearer and saner, the difference between marriage and concubinage became lucid,[70] and marriage based solely on

[68] It seems to me highly probable that Hispano-Arab influences played a decisive part in the origin of the European tradition of courtly love; but I am aware that it is most imprudent for a historian to express an opinion on this much-vexed question. (See p. 34.)

[69] The judgement is given in Andreas Capellanus, *De Amore*, ed. E. Trojel (Copenhagen, 1892), pp. 152–5 (English trans. J. J. Parry (New York, 1941), pp. 106–7). It has been suggested that the English romances are more moral in their attitude to love and marriage – by and large – than the French (cf. M. A. Gist, *Love and War in the Middle English Romances* (Philadelphia, 1947), pp. 1 ff., esp. p. 8).

[70] The way in which the canonists solved the problem of what constituted a valid marriage is shown in detail by J. Dauvillier, *Le mariage dans le droit classique de l'Église* (Paris, 1933).

comfort and appetite found other competitors: a new and more lofty attitude to marriage found classical expression in Peter the Venerable's letter to Heloise. It is easy to exaggerate the swiftness and the extent of the change; but it is easy, too, to understand why the ladies of the later twelfth and thirteenth centuries were inclined to say 'volo nubere'.

5

Approaches to Medieval Forgery[1]

A lecture delivered in the Institute of Historical Research, University of London, on 7 December 1967, and, in a modified form, in the University of Liverpool on 24 January 1968 and first published in the Journal of the Society of Archivists, *III, no. 8 (1968), pp. 377–86 (with two plates: see n. 19). Its purpose is to clarify the general context of eleventh- and twelfth-century forgery, not to solve particular problems, and full documentation is not possible or appropriate. Some of the issues here discussed formed the theme of A. Morey and C. N. L. Brooke,* Gilbert Foliot and his Letters *(Cambridge 1965), chapter viii (with further references in appendix III); and there is a general discussion, on rather different lines, by H. Fuhrmann and others in* Historische Zeitschrift, *CXCVII (1963), pp. 529–601.*

THERE is a famous passage in Lord Acton's paper on 'German schools of history' in which he claimed that '. . . a crust of designing fiction covers the truth in every region of European history. The most curious of the twenty-two thousand letters in the correspondence of Napoleon, that of 28th March 1808, on his

[1] This paper is concerned with documents, and only touches e.g. relics incidentally. Strictly perhaps the word forgery should only be used of imitations of genuine documents made with fraudulent intent; but one purpose of this survey, which is inevitably both general and highly selective in its treatment, is to plot the ambiguous territory between documents which are in a full sense authentic instruments of the authority which produced them and

Spanish policy, . . . proves to be a forgery, and the forger is Napoleon. Whole volumes of spurious letters of Joseph II, Marie Antoinette, and Ganganelli are still circulated. Prince Eugene should be well known to us through his autobiography, the collection of six hundred of his letters, and the *Life* by Kausler. But the letters are forged, the *Life* is founded upon them, and the autobiography is by the Prince de Ligne. The letter from the Pruth, which deceived the ablest of the historians of Peter the Great, is as fabulous as his political testament. So too are . . . the life of [Columbus] by his son, one of the trials of Savonarola, Daru's acts of the Venetian inquisitors, the most famous of the early Italian chronicles, the most famous of the early privileges and charters of almost every European country'.[2] And so the catalogue goes on. In practice, however, for most historians, dodging the forger is an occasional exciting hazard, not a normal part of his daily routine, though there are some exceptions: the archaeologist who deals with the artefacts of certain parts of the world, and the numismatist who deals in ancient or medieval coins from whatever source, have constantly to be on the lookout.

One of the few areas where the crust of designing fiction over the literary sources is so thick that the historian must always consider the possibility of forgery is the period stretching from Pseudo-Isidore in the mid ninth century to Geoffrey of Monmouth and the Westminster forgers in the mid twelfth; forgery then was an entirely respectable activity. I do not mean that it was no crime: this is a point on which there has been some misunderstanding, and it is best cleared up at the outset. Amid the Christmas festivities of 1125, when the Westminster forgers were in the prime of life, all the moneyers of England were gathered by the Bishop of Salisbury and mutilated, because a number of them had en-

those which are wholly bogus, and also the ambiguities surrounding the intention of the men who produced inauthentic documents or altered genuine ones. A particularly striking example of both these difficulties is the Anglo-Saxon diploma: see Dr Chaplais's articles cited below, n. 32. Hence no precise definition of forgery is attempted in the text.

[2] *Historical Essays and Studies* (London, 1907), pp. 363–4 (this paper was first published in 1886). I was first introduced to this passage, more than twenty years ago, by an unpublished paper by Prof. P. Grierson, in which the allusive references were very ingeniously disentangled.

gaged in forging coins.[3] This was rough justice on secular men who blasphemed, as it were, against Caesar's image. Forgers of seals and documents were clerks, and so exempt from physical penalties; but there is no reason to think that most men consciously drew a distinction between one kind of forgery and another – save perhaps to observe that a royal or papal seal was an object of greater value and majesty than a mere penny. 'We know that the Church is the vessel of the fisherman who has no peer', wrote John of Salisbury, in the name of the Archbishop of Canterbury, about a generation later: 'we do not doubt that the Roman pontiff is the vicar of the chief among the Apostles: as the helmsman with his tiller guides the ship, so he by his seal's control guides the whole Church, corrects it and directs it. Thus the falsification of that seal is a peril to the universal Church, since by the marks of a single impress the mouths of all the pontiffs may be opened or closed, and all forms of guilt may pass unpunished, and innocence be condemned.'[4] And later in the century a Pope, who could not be unaware of what happened to his own seal, was constrained to observe of a clerk who had forged that of Philip Augustus that he should be unfrocked, degraded, branded, and exiled – but not mutilated, because he was a clerk.[5] Another of John of Salisbury's letters contains a *cri de cœur* to the Pope for a ruling on the punishment suitable for forgery, because cases were too common for the Archbishop to be able to ask for a judgement on every occasion. The subject of this letter was the son of a former Archdeacon of Llandaff, whose crimes were apparently numerous. 'To say nothing of carnal vice, we have heard from a multitude of persons that he is guilty of arson, robbery and all manner of crimes. With much zeal and effort, we have often re-established peace between him and his adversaries, but every time peace has come back from the encounter torn and sadly changed . . .'[6] His culminating depravity was revealed when he was charged with *lèse-majesté* for forging a papal bull – which the

[3] *Anglo-Saxon Chronicle,* E, *sub ann.* 1125.

[4] *Letters of John of Salisbury,* I, ed. W. J. Millor, H. E. Butler and C. N. L. Brooke (Nelson's Medieval Texts, 1955), p.109.

[5] Morey and Brooke, p. 130.

[6] *Letters of John of Salisbury,* I, pp. 97–8.

Archbishop confirmed was highly suspect for its peculiar style and erasures. There is a cloud of witness that forgery was regarded as a very heinous crime in the twelfth century.

None the less, it was also entirely respectable; and so common as to form an exceptional problem for historians of the centuries leading up to the twelfth, whose slender stock of documentary survivals was so considerably improved by the forgers. How and when it started, I know not; but its first great peak clearly came when the author of Pseudo-Isidore forged a large book full of papal letters in the interests, it seems, of an obscure episcopal quarrel now forgotten; and when a clerk of the Bishop of Le Mans forged another large book in an attempt to rewrite the feudal land law in the interest of the Bishop.[7] No one seriously surpassed these men in volume; but forgery was apparently at its most widespread, and a most characteristic part of the scene, in the first sixty years or so of the twelfth century. Then it rapidly declined into its normal place among human crimes.

These facts were already in some sense apparent to the scholars who laid the foundation of the critical study of medieval documents in the seventeenth century.[8] The eminent Bollandist, Father Papebroch, issued in 1675 a general warning against early charters, especially those produced by Benedictine monks, with a particular reference to the monks of St-Denis. His charges were not unfounded, but they were somewhat too sweeping; and the contemporary Benedictines looked round for a pamphleteer to defend them. The pamphlet that emerged was the *De Re Diplomatica*, a substantial folio, perhaps the most notable of all the great works of scholarship of Jean Mabillon, for in it he laid the scientific foundations for both palaeography and diplomatic. Only occasionally does it reveal its controversial origin. In the famous list of rules, which includes the fine principle that a document should be judged not by one but by every element and

[7] See W. Goffart, *The Le Mans Forgeries* (Cambridge, Mass., 1966), esp. chap. v, secs. 4, 5 (on this important study, see the interesting critique by J. van der Straeten in *Analecta Bollandiana*, LXXXV (1967), pp. 473–516). For current views on Pseudo-Isidore, see Goffart, pp. 66 ff.

[8] The story of the *De Re Diplomatica* is told (with full references) by D. Knowles in *The Historian and Character and other Essays* (Cambridge, 1963), pp. 221 ff.; the quotation at the end of this paragraph is on p. 223.

criterion possible – a principle as true now as in 1681 – there is a slight crack of the whip when Mabillon suggests that if forgery is a crime, then false accusations of forgery deserve their forfeit too.[9] But on the whole it was notably charitable as well as immensely learned, and Father Papebroch, perhaps the second most erudite scholar in Europe, after a long pause, wrote his celebrated letter of recantation. 'Count me as your friend, I beg of you. I am not a learned man, but I desire to be taught.'

Mabillon gave the study of documents a comprehensive frame of sensible rules, and established certain criteria of judgement; and the tradition of scholarship which he passed on to his disciples set the pattern for the study of medieval forgery for several generations. The problem was to distinguish the genuine from the false, and to avoid hypercritical judgement. Amid all the growing subtlety of nineteenth-century diplomatic, especially the new ideas fostered by the tradition of Sickel and Bresslau in Austria and Germany, this remained the central interest – the establishment of the genuine documents or the genuine element in interpolated documents. My own first steps in diplomatic were taken in the appendix on the forgeries of St Augustine's Canterbury attached to Wilhelm Levison's Ford Lectures.[10] For this reason, perhaps, I have always been more interested in the forger than in the forgery; and in a general way it can be said that the most notable advances in recent years in this field have lain in the investigation of forgery through the forger's eyes. We have long known that many documents cannot be placed in simple categories – genuine or spurious – that a great number fall into intermediate pigeon holes: badly copied, tendentiously copied, deliberately altered, improved, brought up to date – and so forth. Scholars have developed an elaborate casuistry to describe the numerous shades of grey into which documents fall. But until quite recently very

[9] *De Re Diplomatica* (Paris, 1681), pp. 241–2 (nos. iv, viii).

[10] *England and the Continent in the Eighth Century* (Oxford, 1946), Appendix I. The chief monuments to the work of Sickel are the *Institut für Österreichische Geschichtsforschung* and the volumes of *Diplomata* in the *Monumenta Germaniae Historica*; and of Bresslau the famous *Handbuch der Urkundenlehre* (3rd edn., 2 vols., 1958–60). A vital constituent in my own approach to all problems of diplomatic has been Professor Galbraith's emphasis, in all his writings on the subject, on the *human* context in which documents are framed.

little attention was paid to the forger, or the tendentious copyist, as a human animal. Now the wheel has turned, and we have had a number of studies in recent years from the forger's point of view, studies which ask, not 'Is this document genuine or forged?', but 'What has this document to tell us of the world in which it was born?' – and are prepared for that world to be a forger's world.

Papebroch, we have seen, submitted to Mabillon; but some of their disciples continued to dispute, and in the process one of the most remarkable contemporary documents in medieval forgery was bandied about and itself branded with infamy.[11] And so it was left to Levison to dig it out of oblivion. It is a copy of a letter from the Archbishop of Rouen to Pope Adrian IV which is preserved in the archives of Canterbury Cathedral. The Archbishop describes how he had been present in a papal council in 1131 when the Pope had asked the Abbots of Jumièges and St-Ouen at Rouen if they could establish their claims to exemption from episcopal control by authentic privileges. The Abbot of St-Ouen hesitated; then the Bishop of Châlons intervened and observed that when he had been Abbot of St-Medard at Soissons, 'one of his monks named Guerno in his last confession admitted that he had been a forger, and among other fictitious documents which he had written for various churches, he declared, with tears of repentance, that he had defended the church of St-Ouen and the church of St Augustine at Canterbury with spurious papal bulls; and that he had received some precious ornaments as the price of his wickedness and had taken them to the church of St-Medard'. And Levison proceeded, by subtle criticism of surviving bulls and early charters, to show Guerno's hand at work in the documents of St Augustine's, of St-Ouen, and St-Medard, and also of Peterborough Abbey; and observed that St-Medard was famous even in Guerno's own day for bogus relics.[12] In an ill-conceived article published in 1950–1, I myself attempted to add to Guerno's stock the famous Canterbury forgeries, on which the claim of the Archbishop to primacy of all England was first given its historical ground. For all but a fraction of the Cathedral's *spuria* this was

[11] For what follows, see Levison, pp. 206 ff.

[12] Levison, pp. 210–11; the letter is quoted on pp. 207–8.

demolished (urbanely, but conclusively) by Professor Southern some years later; but a better success attached to a brief note at the end of my article which suggested that Guerno had a worthy successor in the mid twelfth century who worked for Westminster, Ramsey, Bury, and St Peter's Ghent.[13] It had long been known that Westminster had what James Tait called a 'factory of forgeries',[14] which had somehow contributed to the work of other houses, such as Coventry and Ramsey; my own point was that one might well reckon it likely that it was a forger and not just forgeries which these other houses borrowed from Westminster. I based this view on comparison of witness lists of impossible charters attributed to William I. But I was quite unprepared for the extent of evidence of this which has been unveiled in recent years by Dr Chaplais and Mr Bishop.

Just after the end of the Second World War my father and I visited Aberystwyth to look at the muniments of Hereford Cathedral, then deposited in the National Library of Wales for safe keeping. They include a group of charters from Gloucester Abbey, among them a charter which had aroused suspicion, but never been nailed a forgery, attributed to William the Conqueror. This writ seemed to us to be in an eleventh-century hand, and the seal, although repaired – so that certainty was impossible – to be properly attached. There was some reason to doubt the grounds on which it had been suspect, and I came away with the firm impression that it was genuine.

In 1957 Dr Chaplais and Mr Bishop published their *Facsimiles of English Royal Writs to A.D. 1100, presented to V. H. Galbraith.* Hitherto it had been accepted doctrine that Edward the Confessor had used three, and that William I and William II had each used two, seal matrices. Bishop and Chaplais laid out a list of originals of these three kings to which seals are still attached, dividing them into writs otherwise supposed genuine and writs otherwise supposed forged; and to the genuine one seal of each king, and to the forged the other, is always attached. Evidence of handwriting

[13] *Downside Review*, LXVIII (1950), pp. 462 ff.; LXIX (1951), pp. 210 ff. – esp. p. 230; R. W. Southern, *English Historical Review*, LXXIII (1958), pp. 193–226.

[14] J. Tait, in *Essays in History presented to R. L. Poole*, ed. H. W. C. Davis (Oxford, 1927), p. 159 n.

confirmed in a number of cases that spurious originals for different religious houses came from the same stable.[15] The enormous bulk of the surviving work of this atelier is for Westminster Abbey, and no one doubts that its headquarters lay there. If Guerno's disciple who forged the Canterbury privileges gave the Archbishop of Canterbury his primacy, Westminster Abbey owes its unique privilege of being the site of the coronation of English kings and queens first and foremost to the Westminster forgers. The Gloucester writ can now be shown, both by hand and by seal, to come from this workshop.

In 1962 Dr Chaplais carried his investigation a stage further, to the point of identifying the Westminster forgers.[16] So greatly did they increase the store of documents of their age that we can never hope to be exactly sure how many were involved, still less how much was known by how many folk about their work at the time. But Dr Chaplais has isolated three men who were clearly at the heart of it. First of all, he has identified the hand of one of the scribes of the charters of Abbot Herbert of Westminster (who died in or about 1136) as the scribe of the three great charters of Edward the Confessor for Westminster; and another hand, which wrote for Herbert's successor, Gervase, King Stephen's illegitimate son, wrote writs attributed to the Confessor and the Conqueror for Westminster and other houses, and a variety of other documents; most oddly of all, he seems to have provided Abbot Gervase with a spurious charter from his own father, King Stephen. The writ of the Conqueror for Gloucester to which I referred is in his hand. Chaplais has also shown, by a display of verbal and stylistic parallels, that the more ambitious diplomas for Westminster reveal the hand, or at least the mind, of the Prior of Westminster, Osbert de Clare.

I must confess that when first I read the article, I found it hard to believe that Osbert really composed forgeries; but the evidence

[15] *Facsimiles* . . ., ed. T. A. M. Bishop and P. Chaplais (Oxford, 1957), pp. xix ff. Further evidence as to handwriting is given by P. Chaplais in *A Medieval Miscellany for D. M. Stenton*, ed. P. M. Barnes and C. F. Slade (Pipe Roll Soc., lxxvi, 1962), pp. 91 ff. For the Gloucester Abbey charter (now at Hereford) see *Facsimiles*, p. xxi, no. xi, and p. xxii n.

[16] *Medieval Miscellany*, pp. 89–110.

is cogent, and in course of time I came to see that it was not only inescapable on textual grounds, but also not so improbable on human grounds as I had supposed.[17] Osbert was a dedicated man: his whole life was devoted to fostering the interests of his abbey, its patron saint, St Peter, and its most notable relic, the body of Edward the Confessor. He quarrelled with successive abbots because they were not sufficiently dedicated; he narrowly missed the abbacy, so far as we can tell, because he was too single-minded a man for an office so near the King and the Court. He was sent twice into exile for setting obedience to St Peter and St Edward before obedience to the Abbot and the King; he rewrote the earlier life of Edward the Confessor and supplied other communities with lives of their patron saints.

Although evidently allies, Osbert de Clare and the Abbot's clerks were men of different backgrounds and different skills. It is clear from Dr Chaplais's reconstruction that the clerks were professional scribes; and it is clear that they were professional forgers in a sense different from that which we could apply to Guerno or to Osbert de Clare. Fifty years later forgery was becoming less common; and yet still causing sufficient concern for Pope Innocent III, soon after his accession in 1198, to issue a bull giving a list of the techniques by which forgery could be perpetrated.[18] I have always been struck by the contrast between his list and earlier comments on the same problem. The letter of John of Salisbury speaks of errors of style, of erasures, and of spurious seals; and this is a characteristic statement for the early or mid twelfth century. Innocent was concerned above all with his seal: all but one of the list describe various dodges relating to the seal and the last alone refers to other methods of forgery. One technique described is to take a genuine bull, cut off the seal, and reattach it to a spurious document. This involves cutting the strings and re-tying them in such a way as to hide the join; or else heating

[17] Cf. Morey and Brooke, loc. cit., esp. pp. 139 ff.

[18] *Reg. Innoc. III,* ed. O. Hageneder and A. Haidacher, 1 (Graz-Köln, 1964), 520 ff. (lib. i, no. 349), cf. pp. 333 ff. (lib. i, no. 235); cf. R. L. Poole, *Lectures on the History of the Papal Chancery* . . . (Cambridge, 1915), pp. 152 ff.; C. R. and M. G. Cheney, *Letters of Pope Innocent III concerning England and Wales* (Oxford, 1967), pp. xxii f.

the top of the lead bulla or seal, inserting the strings coming from the new, bogus parchment, and then closing the top of the seal again with pincers. There are two bulls in the Public Record Office, almost exactly contemporary in date with Innocent's rules, purporting to grant indulgences in the interests of the nuns of the small priory of Wix in Essex, which exactly illustrate this method.[19] The seals are genuine; the parchments undoubtedly false. In one case it is just possible to detect, in the other quite impossible to detect, the marks of the pincers. These are the work of highly qualified professionals.

We know these two documents to be forgeries because of their handwriting. This is not a hand from the papal chancery, but it is one of the two hands which wrote many of the early charters of Wix priory, of which the P.R.O. still contains a substantial proportion. In some cases, these documents clearly hide legal chicanery: at least, the nuns were involved in tiresome and worrying lawsuits and some of the documents were probably altered to improve their case. Some again may replace charters defaced by damp, which the nuns in a mood of panic felt to be useless or inadequate. But in the main these two professional forgers seem simply to have rewritten the muniments, no doubt to increase their fee. Students of forgery always look for an immediate and powerful motive, no doubt rightly. But a comparatively modest difficulty can lead to a very extensive forgery, on the analogy of what Dickens said of the English law. 'The one great principle of the English law is, to make business for itself. There is no other principle distinctly, certainly, and consistently maintained through all its narrow turnings. Viewed by this light it becomes a coherent scheme, and not the monstrous maze the laity are apt to think it.'[20]

Such a story presupposes a situation something like this. The nuns of Wix were troubled by legal difficulties, and we may pre-

[19] S.C. 7/9, nos. 2, 5, ed. W. Holtzmann, *Papsturkunden in England*, I, II (Berlin, 1931), nos. 314, 329; cf. Brooke in *Medieval Miscellany for D. M. Stenton*, pp. 45 ff., esp. pp. 47–8, 57. I am much indebted to Dr P. M. Barnes, Mr L. C. Hector, and Mr H. C. Johnson, formerly Keeper of the Public Records, for help with these bulls. (S.C. 7/9, no. 2, and an enlargement of its seal, comprised plates I, II, of the original article.)

[20] *Bleak House*, chap. XXXIX.

sume that being nuns they turned to their male legal advisers; or perhaps they knew enough of the world to know themselves that there were folk about who were expert in improving one's muniments. The two forgers were evidently given a free hand to sort and explore and tidy up. I am convinced the nuns knew that they were improvers, not just investigators; but I am equally convinced that they were given a free hand and that the nuns had no idea of the extent of their labours until they were presented with the bill.

Their productions make dull reading when compared with those of Osbert de Clare; and many would never have been suspect had they survived only in copies. This may start disquieting reflections in our minds. Mr Bishop has shown that of the 750 or so surviving original writs of Henry I, Stephen, and Henry II, a high proportion, perhaps as many as 300, are not the work of professional royal chancery scribes.[21] How many of these, we may ask, are the genuine products of casual scribes or of the beneficiaries, properly authorized? We may probably reckon a large majority authentic, and this seems to be Mr Bishop's view; and there are copious indications that forgery was in decline. But the Wix charters reveal just how difficult it is to be sure of the authenticity of twelfth-century documents. At one time it was fashionable to set up the authority of the authentic charter as objective and decisive and always to be preferred to the subjective, biased, imperfect view of the chronicler. Nowadays historians know nothing of infallible testimony; whatever our period, be it the third millennium B.C. or the twentieth century A.D., we handle evidence, and try to deduce from all the evidence we can muster what it has to tell.

Guerno, the Westminster forgers, and the Wix forgers reveal between them in what I believe to be a characteristic way both a shift and a decline: a shift from the monastic scriptorium to the professional atelier, and the decline of forgery as a respectable art.

The shift is part of the general trend away from the monastic scriptorium which is characteristic of the later stages of the

[21] *Scriptores Regis* (Oxford, 1961), esp. pp. 1, 3–4, 9, 14; on p. 11 he notes that about 450 are the work of royal scribes; on the origin of most of the rest he speaks with considerable caution.

twelfth-century renaissance. In the eleventh and twelfth centuries the monasteries were still sufficiently inspiring as leaders of fashion to attract a wide variety of talent, and craftsmen who were monks were still not rare. Outstanding examples of the early twelfth century were Roger of Helmarshausen, author of precious reliquaries of outstanding craftsmanship, and the anonymous monk who passed under the name Theophilus and wrote the Treatise on *The Various Arts*; it is indeed likely that Theophilus and Roger were one and the same man.[22] It is probable that the order best provided with craftsmen, anyway of the more practical arts, was the Cistercian, and that the presence of trained masons among the Cistercian lay brothers explains the extraordinary uniformity of plan and style, and the high standard of masonry, of twelfth-century Cistercian architecture.[23] After the twelfth century the Cistercians no longer attracted the same range of recruits; the leadership in talent passed elsewhere; and the decline of monastic craftsmen is doubtless at least one of the explanations of the disappearance, at the end of the twelfth century, of the

[22] Theophilus, *De diuersis Artibus*, ed. and trans. C. R. Dodwell (Nelson's Medieval Texts, 1961), pp. xl ff.

[23] The scanty direct evidence as to Cistercian master masons is laid out in M. Aubert, *L'architecture cistercienne en France* (2nd edn., Paris, 1947), I, pp. 97 ff. There is clear evidence that the Cistercians themselves played a conspicuous part in their own building enterprises in early days, and the uniformity of style and plan which they show over exceptionally wide areas makes it clear that there must have been skilled craftsmen within the order able to help direct the efforts of local builders; and this is confirmed by the uniformly high quality of Cistercian masonry. This is in marked contrast, for instance, to much Norman masonry in England of the two generations before the arrival of the Cistercians, whose poor quality presumably reflects in large measure an acute shortage of skilled masons due to the exceptional building effort of the Norman conquerors. The Cistercians were also involved in an exceptional building effort, but this led to no deterioration of standards; and this strongly suggests that they recruited skilled masons among their lay brothers, as they recruited other craftsmen of advanced skills – it is surely to such men, rather than to the eminent choir monks whom the documents name, that the Cistercians owed their style, and the recruitment of lay brothers in early days helps to explain over a wider front the comparatively advanced nature of Cistercian technological achievement. On the Cistercian style see F. Bucher in *Comparative Studies in Society and History*, III (1960–1), pp. 89–105, and works there cited.

Cistercian style as something separate from the other local styles of Europe.

Great traditions do not die overnight, and (to switch to a different field) some of the characteristics of late Anglo-Saxon drawing can still be seen in the thirteenth century in the artistry of Matthew Paris. But Matthew was an exception to prove the rule: in his chauvinist prejudices he was a man of the nineteenth century, which loved him; as monk, artist, historian, hagiographer, and forger he was a man of the twelfth century.[24] This particular combination was indeed a symbol of one aspect of the twelfth-century renaissance; and among many precursors of Matthew Paris let me choose a more attractive figure, from the early twelfth century: also a monk and calligrapher, historian and hagiographer – or biographer rather, for Eadmer's *Life of St Anselm* has been revealed to us in recent years by Professor Southern as the first and most effective intimate biography of its age.[25] His particular gift was to reveal personality in reported speech. From the fifth century B.C. to the eighteenth A.D. it was common form for historians to put speeches in their characters' mouths, to give variety and colour, to impart the character's thoughts (supposed or real), or the author's comments; and no one supposed that this was either to be taken literally or to be regarded as lying. There are indeed a number of cases in which the reported speech means more than this, and Eadmer's is clearly one. He had a sense, inspired no doubt by Anselm's particular gifts, that speech was the essence of his hero and the way to relate his views and personality; and we can see in the lesser characters, and especially in the *Historia Novorum*, a deliberate attempt to state their point of view in succinct but characteristic phrases: he seems to have taken particular delight in reproducing the staccato blasphemies of William Rufus. When Anselm rebuked the King for his treatment of the monasteries, Rufus made his famous retort: 'What business is that of yours? Are not the abbeys mine? You do as you like with your manors and shall not I do as I like with my abbeys?' Anselm replied, 'They are yours to defend and guard as their patron; but not

[24] See R. Vaughan, *Matthew Paris* (Cambridge, 1959).

[25] R. W. Southern, *St Anselm and his Biographer* (Cambridge, 1963), esp. chap. IX; *Vita Anselmi*, ed. Southern (Nelson's Medieval Texts, 1962).

yours to assault or lay waste . . .'.[26] The doctrine and counter-doctrine of the Eigenkirche have never been more succinctly stated, not even by Ulrich Stütz himself. In this case one can see clearly enough that Eadmer is at work on a faithful portrayal of a scene; we have not sufficient ground to assume that these were the exact words used. In the account of the enquiries leading up to the marriage of Matilda and Henry I, he is very much concerned to defend Anselm's part in the affair; this leads him to claim objectivity: 'My conscience is my witness, I have described the order of events just as I saw and heard them, for I was present, giving favour neither to one side nor the other; and I have set out the maiden's actual words as spoken, not to assert whether they were true or false'.[27] Again, we may doubt whether Matilda's long speech is to be taken for *ipsissima verba*; but we may accept that Eadmer's statement was entirely reasonable in a world not used to precise reporting, in that he had made far more effort than was normal to be precise.

There is another interest in this passage: it is a curious way for a loyal subject to refer to a reigning queen. Clearly Eadmer was much more concerned with the monastic circle of his readers than with opinion in the royal Court. The early Archbishops of Canterbury were buried in St Augustine's Abbey; Eadmer was brought up with the bones of the later Archbishops, Dunstan and Ælfheah, and so his history of recent events starts with the age of Dunstan, and mostly consists of his own living saint, Anselm.[28] Dunstan, Ælfheah, and Anselm constitute for Eadmer the real world. Rufus, Henry I, and Matilda belong to the twilight of secular affairs. In this context we can understand the passage in which Eadmer introduced into his narrative the famous Canterbury forgeries. Under the year 1120 he wrote: 'In these days there arose a fervour of research into the authorities and ancient privileges of the primacy which the church of Canterbury claims over

[26] *Historia Novorum*, ed. M. Rule (Rolls Series, 1884), pp. 49–50; trans. C. Bosanquet (London, 1964), pp. 50–1. On the Eigenkirche in England, see esp. F. Barlow, *The English Church, 1000–1066* (London, 1963), pp. 186 ff.

[27] Eadmer, ed. Rule, pp. 121 ff., esp. pp. 125–6; trans. Bosanquet, pp. 126 ff., esp. p. 131.

[28] On the relics of Canterbury Cathedral see Southern, pp. 260 ff.; below pp. 170–4.

the church of York.' The reason was the imminent failure of Canterbury's case, which had fallen into the hands of ignorant foreign bishops. Recent precedents were not enough; ancient authority was needed. 'And so many took pains in this investigation, as we have said, avowed the justice of God's Church, and with great care inspected the secret corners of ancient chests and holy gospel books hitherto serving solely as adornments to God's house. And lo! how the wish of the just man who loveth was not deprived of its reward: some privileges were found, firm in all points and supported by papal authority, by God's revelation.'[29] Hugh the Chanter of York refers to these 'bulls of privilege concerning the dignity and primacy of the church of Canterbury, which the monks had lately "found or thought up" ' – 'inuenerant uel cogitauerant' – and gives a lively account of the rough handling they received in the papal Curia; and more recently Professor Southern has observed that 'without a great deal of special pleading' one cannot acquit Eadmer 'from the charge of knowing that the privileges were forgeries and knowing that his account of their origin was false'.[30]

Historical truth is a fine thing; but if you live in a world in which Dunstan, Ælfheah, and Anselm preside every moment of the day and night over a tightly knit community, it may well seem a pious duty to extend the normal limits of historical description so that Truth in another sense shall not be denied in and to God's Church, Christ's own Church, Canterbury Cathedral. Many books could be written on the crimes inspired by loyalty; like all virtues it can lead us to heaven, but also direct to hell.

Such feelings were roused with equal fervour in defence of monastic properties or the properties of cathedral chapters; and in defence of monasteries which claimed exemption from episcopal control. Primacy and exemption demanded forgery: in the form in which they were claimed in the eleventh and twelfth centuries they were entirely new ideas, though their protagonists, for the most part, could not realize this. It was incomprehensible

[29] Eadmer, ed. Rule, pp. 260–1.

[30] Hugh the Chanter, ed. and trans. C. Johnson (Nelson's Medieval Texts, 1961), p. 105 (cf. pp. 114–15); Southern in *English Historical Review*, LXXIII (1958), pp. 225–6.

to them that earlier generations had not taken greater pains to preserve privileges they must have had. Similarly with land. In England the high watermark of forgery was the period between the new chaos of the Norman Conquest and the establishment of order, or growing legal precision, in the reign of Henry II.[31] By then forgery was more difficult, perhaps more dangerous; and in any case the forger had done his work. But it was a cosmopolitan world, and these are but the local expressions of movements which embraced much of western Christendom. Indeed, there had been forgery in England before the Conquest, and it may even be the accidents of survival which lead us to suppose the twelfth century to be its golden age. Yet there is clearly a sense in which the spread of literacy and of written instruments of land tenure made the eleventh and twelfth centuries, in a special sense, the period of the shift from oral to written testimony. The opportunities, the temptations, and the urgent calls of duty in such a period were quite exceptional. Osbert de Clare may well have known how diplomas were made in the eleventh century: it was apparently quite normal for the King to issue a writ telling a bishop to compose a diploma in his own or his community's interest.[32] This diploma would be embellished with signatures, but always made by the scribe not by the signatories; it had no seal. The Confessor must have intended the monks of his favourite monastery to have everything they wished; if his diplomas were defective or missing, this could only be attributed to criminal negligence. When Osbert died, he knew that he would tread a steep

[31] Morey and Brooke, pp. 128 ff.; it may be, as Dr N. P. Brooks has suggested to me, that this survey underestimates the quantity of English forgery before 1066.

[32] See F. E. Harmer, *Anglo-Saxon Writs* (Manchester, 1952), pp. 38–41 and nos. 7, 26, 55, 68; cf. Chaplais in *A Medieval Miscellany for D. M. Stenton,* p. 88. The peculiar difficulty of deciding what is 'authentic' and 'original' in pre-Conquest charters has long been recognized, but it has recently been placed on a new footing by Dr Chaplais's important articles 'The Origin and Authenticity of the Royal Anglo-Saxon Diploma' and 'Some Early Anglo-Saxon Diplomas on Single Sheets: Originals or Copies?', *Journal of the Soc. of Archivists,* III, no. 2 (1965), pp. 48–61; III, no. 7 (1968), pp. 315–36. Furthermore, the study of pre-Conquest charters has also been given a new foundation by Prof. P. Sawyer's *Anglo-Saxon Charters: an annotated List and Bibliography* (Royal Historical Soc., 1968).

and narrow path, and if he was fortunate come to the gate of heaven; and there he would be met by St Peter and St Edward, and we need not doubt that he was haunted by the questions they would ask. Yet I confess that it takes an effort of imagination to see into the mind of a man who prepares for his encounter with St Edward by planning the forgery of three or more charters in Edward's name each the size of a modest tablecloth.

Forgery in this age, then, illustrates a piquant episode in the history of loyalty; a key stage in the history of law; and reflects the inventive powers of the generations which created the twelfth-century renaissance. It was not confined to charters. The Book of Llandaff, whatever lay behind it, represented a bold attempt to bring the Welsh Church into the twelfth century and counter the effects and the chaos of the Norman Conquest of Glamorgan.[33] It consists of forged charters and saints' lives sometimes equally bogus; and it hints at the third type of forgery of the age. The greatest of the saints of Llandaff was St Teilo, and in the *Life of St Teilo* it is reported that an unseemly dispute over the relics led the saint, shortly after his death, to provide three copies of his own body.[34] The jewelled reliquary raised on a great shrine behind the high altar was the centre of the design of many of the greatest churches of the twelfth century; and in a certain number the completed shrine was a monument to fiction as well as to art. St Benedict lay at Fleury-sur-Loire; but it was inconceivable to the monks of Monte Cassino that he meant to. The monks of Ely blasphemously claimed that St Alban had gone to Ely in the Danish troubles and never returned; this his own monks at St Albans strenuously denied.

It may well seem to anyone who has studied the forgeries of Durham of the 1180s and of Wix of the 1190s, or of Lewes of the 1220s, or other smaller groups, that forgery was far from rare even after 1160. The difference is that down to the 1150s everyone

[33] Brooke in *Studies in the Early British Church,* ed. N. K. Chadwick (Cambridge, 1958), pp. 218 ff.; cf. *Celt and Saxon,* ed. N. K. Chadwick (Cambridge, 1963), pp. 312 n., 322 n. for criticisms of this paper, especially that by C. W. Lewis in *Morgannwg,* IV (1960), pp. 50–65 (see now the London Ph.D. thesis by Dr Wendy Davies).

[34] *The Text of the Book of Llan Dâv,* ed. J. G. Evans and J. Rhys (Oxford, 1893), pp. 116–17.

engaged in it. I exaggerate, of course; but not very much. Almost all the English monastic communities which claimed exemption from episcopal control forged to support their claims, and most can be shown to have forged in the early or mid twelfth century. In the past scholars have stressed – I have stressed myself – the legal changes of the century as explanation of the decline which set in thereafter; these, and the completion of the task, are undoubtedly important elements in the story.[35] But I am now inclined to place greater emphasis on the trend with which I opened: the shift from amateur to professional. So long as the work was done wholly within the monastic and other religious communities, the moral issue was one merely of conflicting loyalties: forgery was a crime when other types of folk engaged in it. But when the time came that if one wished to forge the procedure was to call in an outside professional, the case was somewhat different. I do not believe the risk of exposure much affected the issue. It would have been easier for Osbert de Clare to admit to forgery – and offer himself to martyrdom – than for the Wix forgers who were common criminals. No doubt euphemisms were in vogue, and it is disappointing that we do not know what they were. Guerno on his deathbed was a forger (*falsarius*); but to the monks of St Augustine's Canterbury or Peterborough he appeared, no doubt, as an expert archivist, or 'improver' of muniments. Osbert de Clare, Geoffrey of Monmouth, and Matthew Paris were historians. If the Wix forgers rewrote a large number of documents simply to increase their fee, Guerno and his like evidently rewrote large numbers too without altering their purport, to make them more impressive.

An older generation of scholars looked at forgeries mainly for the sake of the genuine element behind them; we now realize that this can only be considered if one studies first the men who wrote, rewrote, adapted, altered, or forged the documents as we now have them. I have recently been trying to reconstruct lists of

[35] Cf. Morey and Brooke, pp. 132 ff. On the Durham and Lewes forgeries, see G. V. Scammell, *Hugh du Puiset bishop of Durham* (Cambridge, 1956), Appendix IV; H. Mayr-Harting, *Acta of the Bishops of Chichester* (Cant. and York Soc., 1964), pp. 62–70. On forgery in the late Middle Ages, see L. C. Hector, *Palaeography and Medieval Forgery* (London and York, 1959).

tenth- and eleventh-century English abbots. Monastic communities had long and tenacious memories, and many left good annals behind which give us precise years of accession and death. But much of the material consists of the enormous lists of signatories to Old English diplomas. It is doubtful if any of these were drawn up in the assemblies which they describe, and no surviving pre-Conquest diploma has autograph signa. Every list depends therefore on its scribe's knowledge and accuracy, and it is perfectly possible that forgers sometimes worked off notes as reliable as authentic scribes; indeed, in this world the distinction between the genuine and the forged sometimes becomes as hazy as it was to Osbert de Clare and Eadmer.

Equally striking is the other reflection to which our picture of the mid-twelfth-century situation must compel us. The extraordinary thing is that many of these forgeries were produced in court at one time or another, and taken seriously. Some were clearly never intended to be used in this way. The monks of Gloucester got the Bishop of Worcester to send a covering letter to the Archbishop of Canterbury, in or about 1148, with a copy of a quite imaginary charter of the reigning king; this charter never existed, and details in the drafting of the copy which was made for the Archbishop reveal that it was intended merely to be a model for a genuine confirmation from the Archbishop. The pretended royal charter, and the Archbishop's well known admiration for and trust in the Abbot of Gloucester, Gilbert Foliot, made the conspiracy comparatively certain of success.[36]

Yet forgery was so widespread at this time that it must have been common knowledge that this sort of thing was happening, at least in certain circles. There is, I think, some evidence for this in the way in which it was parodied. In or about 1138 Geoffrey of Monmouth issued his *History of the Kings of Britain*; whatever else it was, it was a clever parody of genuine historical writing by a man who knew more than we do of the inward story of the Welsh forgeries of his age.[37] William of Malmesbury had written in the 1120s: 'Arthur is he of whom the Breton ditties still burble; but he was plainly worthy not to be dreamed of in bogus tales,

[36] See *Celt and Saxon*, pp. 272 ff., 279 ff.

[37] *Studies in the Early British Church*, pp. 205 ff.

but made the subject of true histories [*ueraces historiae*, an echo of a famous passage in Bede], as one who long upheld his falling land, and drove on to war the unbroken spirits of his fellow-countrymen'.[38] Geoffrey retorted by inventing a 'true history' of King Arthur, which is the centre-piece of his book; and by apostrophizing William in his epilogue. 'The kings . . . of the Saxons I leave to William of Malmesbury and Henry of Huntingdon: but I forbid them to say anything about the kings of the Britons, since they have not that book written in Breton which Walter archdeacon of Oxford brought out of Brittany; which is a true account of their history; and which I have thus in these princes' honour taken pains to translate into Latin.'[39]

Thus was born a convention which reappears in vernacular dress in countless romances of the late twelfth and thirteenth centuries. In its simplest form it is the convention that the romancer makes his story respectable by stating its source, or sometimes by simply disclaiming responsibility; thus Chrétien of Troyes lays the blame for his *Lancelot*, the most immoral of his works, on the Countess of Champagne. The only surprising thing is that some literary critics have believed him: surprising, because in the majority of cases the source is plainly fictitious; and it is evident that the convention, as it developed, depended on a fictitious contrast between the historical truth of the romance and an obviously imaginary or misleading origin. Thus a clear path leads from Geoffrey's Breton source, or his statement that the Laws of Malmutius had been written in the British tongue, translated into Latin by Gildas and into English by King Alfred and are still in force, to the claim of the author of the prose *Queste del Saint Graal* to have copied from a French translation of a Latin original made by Walter Map; or of Wolfram von Eschenbach in his *Parzival* to have corrected Chrétien out of a book by Kyot of Provence, who had it from the Arabic.[40] The conte was the work of a Cistercian

[38] *Gesta Regum*, ed. W. Stubbs (Rolls Series, 1887–9), I, 11.

[39] *Historia Regum Britanniae*, Epilogue (ed. A. Griscom, New York, 1929, p. 536).

[40] *Historia Regum Britanniae*, ii. 17, iii. 5, ed. Griscom, pp. 275, 282; for Map and Wolfram, see introd. to forthcoming revised edn. of Map's *De nugis curialium*, ed. and trans. M. R. James (Oxford Medieval Texts).

or his disciple; Wolfram was a semi-illiterate knight. We may doubt whether these characters knew at all precisely what it was to have lived in the world of Osbert de Clare. But they were heirs of the world of creative fancy in which Eadmer, monk and bishop-elect, and Geoffrey, secular canon and bishop, had lived and moved and had their being.

At the end of the day, as historians, we owe Geoffrey of Monmouth and Osbert de Clare some respect. They lacked the first, most vital quality of our calling: they played with truth. But they also played with techniques of research, not perhaps with the brilliance of William of Malmesbury or the author of the Book of Llandaff, but with a notable gusto. Geoffrey worked mainly in Oxford, Osbert in London, or rather in Westminster. Of Geoffrey it may be said that he founded the Oxford history school; and of Osbert (I hope) that he earned a passing thought in the Institute of Historical Research of the University of London.[41]

[41] See Origin of this essay.

6

Thomas Becket[1]

A revised version of a lecture given in Liverpool in December 1956.

ON the afternoon of Tuesday, 29 December 1170 (just over 800 years ago) four knights with their retinues visited the Archbishop of Canterbury at his palace near Canterbury Cathedral. About an hour later, when the Archbishop had gone to the Cathedral to hear vespers, the knights broke in after him, and assassinated him in

[1] The most recent interpretation of Becket is in David Knowles, *Thomas Becket* (London, 1970); see also his character studies in Knowles, *The Historian and Character and Other Essays* (Cambridge, 1963), chapter 6, and the centenary number (no. 65, 1970) of the *Canterbury Cathedral Chronicle*, which has a series of interesting papers by various authors. Knowles, *Thomas Becket,* pp. 172 ff., has a brief account of the lives etc., and a short bibliography; see also E. Walberg, *La tradition hagiographique de S. Thomas Becket* (Paris, 1929); on the letter collections, A. Morey and C. N. L. Brooke, *The Letters and Charters of Gilbert Foliot* (Cambridge, 1967); the indispensable corpus of sources remains the *Materials for the History of Thomas Becket*, ed. J. C. Robertson and J. B. Sheppard, 7 vols. (Rolls Series, London, 1875–85). For the circles in which Becket moved, see A. Saltman, *Theobald archbishop of Canterbury* (London, 1956); Knowles, *The Episcopal Colleagues of Archbishop Thomas Becket* (Cambridge, 1951); A. Morey, *Bartholomew of Exeter* (Cambridge, 1937); A. Morey and C. N. L. Brooke, *Gilbert Foliot and his Letters* (Cambridge, 1965); for the historical context, Z. N. Brooke, *The English Church and the Papacy from the Conquest to the reign of John* (Cambridge, 1931); C. R. Cheney, *From Becket to Langton* (Manchester, 1956); C. Duggan, *Twelfth Century Decretal Collections* (London, 1963).

the public view. The news spread rapidly – around the city, then to the corners of England, and all over Europe, to the Court of France, and to the papal Court in Rome. The conscience of Christendom was profoundly shocked. Outside the circle of his personal enemies, Thomas Becket was hailed at once as a martyr for the faith. The rumour spread that miracles had occurred at his tomb; soon the reports of miracles became numerous, then they came in floods; in 1173 he was formally canonized by the Pope. Even those who had opposed him most bitterly when he was alive submitted to him when he was dead; and the greatest of them, King Henry II, did public penance in the streets of Canterbury, walked barefoot, stripped to the waist, and submitted to a flogging by bishops and monks.

To what extent Henry had really been responsible we shall never know; and that is only one of the mysterious elements about this strange affair. But although it has its mysteries, the main sequence of events has little else in common with a modern detective story. The knights were no obscure assassins, but men of position in the royal Court and in the parts of England where they lived. Nor was their work done in secret. The made their act as public and sacrilegious as possible: to kill a priest was sacrilegious, to kill an archbishop even more so; though they may have wished to do their work elsewhere, they made the sacrilege doubly bad by killing him on consecrated ground. And it is the public nature of the murder, the drama with which the main actors intentionally surrounded it, which makes it so exciting and so strange.

Why was Thomas Becket murdered? The answer lies deep in the social organization of England and Europe in the twelfth century, and more immediately, in the personality of Thomas Becket himself.

Custom and social tradition are often very stable, very tenacious things; and the fact that English society has changed so rapidly in recent centuries is one reason why its history is particularly fascinating and illuminating today. In a sense this is especially true of medieval history. We cannot study the world in which Becket lived without realizing how profoundly different it was from our own. As the psychologists tell us, human nature does change; we need to make an effort of imagination and sympathy to understand the characters of these men.

Becket's life lies in the central part of the ages of faith, when most people in western Europe, in western Christendom, acknowledged, though in many different senses, the spiritual headship of the Pope. From the mid twelfth century, there were numerous heretics in western Europe, but almost none in England. Education in the schools in the twelfth century was broadly based; but the intellectual horizon was, by our standards, narrow, because so many of the subjects we study in schools and universities were hardly known, or, if known, hardly subjected to any kind of scientific discipline. Those few who went on to higher study were almost all clerics – that is, bent on a career as clergymen even if not yet in orders – and were mainly recruits for the more responsible positions in the Church. For practical as well as theoretical reasons Theology and Canon Law, the Church's law, were their main topics at the higher level. The great mass of the people was totally illiterate; the kings and a few great noblemen could read and write, but rarely do more than that; the parish clergy, similarly, were most of them just literate; education in our sense was confined to the privileged clergy – monks, canons, archdeacons, bishops, and higher civil servants, since all professions in which real literacy was needed had to be recruited from the higher, educated clergy. It was a very hierarchical society, with highly organized classes among clergy as well as laity. But it was not a rigid society: there was no caste system, and men of comparatively humble origin could on occasion reach the highest clerical positions, if they were lucky enough to find a patron to support them and send them to school.

The material of clerical education consisted of all the literature then known, the classics, the Bible, the fathers of the Church, the authorities of the Church's law. The lay aristocracy were brought up to the arts of war and justice, which were their chief functions in a feudal society. They were taught how to handle horse, sword, and lance; they practised their art in the tournament field and in battle; their sports were hunting and hawking. The literature they knew was an oral literature, sung to them by minstrels in their castle halls; tales of military prowess and heroism, of Roland

and Oliver and the other knights of the court of Charlemagne, and – the new fashion of Becket's own day – the knights of King Arthur's court and the Round Table. The ideals and aspirations of the two classes were widely different, however closely the classes might be connected by ties of blood, and the fact of living together in the same country, often under the same roof.

Thomas Becket was the son of a burgess of knightly stock, a man bred to the arts of war, but not wealthy enough to set up on his own as a country squire. He lived in London, and his son, who had the benefit of schooling in London and Paris, was set to work as clerk to a city merchant. A stroke of fortune removed him from that work to a position ideally suited for a young man of brilliance and ambition. He became one of the clerks of Theobald, Archbishop of Canterbury, and rapidly came to be recognized as one of the most promising of the talented circle which the ageing Archbishop had gathered round him. In October 1154, his chief rival in Theobald's court, Roger of Pont l'Évêque, became Archbishop of York, and within a few months Becket had been promoted to positions which assured him wealth, influence, and fame. Theobald made him Archdeacon of Canterbury, the foremost position in his own administrative service; and when the young Henry II succeeded to the throne at the end of the year, the Archbishop suggested Becket to him as a suitable royal Chancellor. At that time the Chancellor was one of the leading royal ministers, and under Becket he rapidly became the first officer of state. Theobald knew Becket's ability, his readiness to please, his charm, and remarkable gifts; but he can hardly have realized how completely Becket would throw himself into the job. To combine the archdeaconry with the chancellorship was an odd mixture, which Becket solved in a way not uncommon at the time, by merely ignoring his duties as Archdeacon. Theobald had hoped, maybe, to keep an eye on the young King through his Chancellor; and there is evidence that he himself hoped Becket would succeed him as Archbishop. But in these years, between 1154 and 1162, when Becket was Chancellor, the Archbishop only saw him when he came to Court. Becket had an imaginative vision of what the position of Chancellor involved, and lived up to it. He was soon the King's indispensable adviser and boon companion; his right-hand man in all his schemes; in private life and education a churchman, a statesman in everything else. Nor need we doubt that he enjoyed it. He had hunted and hawked as a young man; and later in life, when in disguise, he was once detected by the way he appraised the performance of a hawk. He enjoyed the active life; the splendour and panache of the royal Court. He was still comparatively young when he became Chancellor (thirty-six to the King's twenty-one).

Henry was not an easy master. He was a passionate, mercurial, temperamental man; but he was also extremely impulsive, and Becket quickly won his affection. He certainly seems to have been extravagant, but also successful: to have deployed to the full his capacity for administration, his imagination both in planning royal enterprises and in sympathetic understanding of the best way to serve the King. If he had died Chancellor, we should remember Becket as a great and rather worldy royal servant; we might even have had some idea of his brilliance if contemporaries had bothered to tell us about it. Even so, his name would have been known only to historians and specialists.

It seems almost as if circumstances had conspired to cut short Becket's career as a minister. The old Archbishop had clearly at one time or another had his eye on Becket as his successor; the King, having found in him so admirable a servant, was determined to have him in the most crucial office of all, the archbishopric of Canterbury. When the time came to elect a new Archbishop, as far as we know only two dissentient voices were raised: the voice of Gilbert Foliot, Bishop of Hereford, later of London, an ex-monk and one of the outstanding men in the British Church, who regarded Becket as scarcely a churchman at all, and who, without openly coveting the position of Archbishop himself, doubtless thought he should be offered it; and the voice of Becket himself.

Becket became Archbishop in the middle of one of the great periods of conflict in the Middle Ages, that between Church and State. It was a conflict in which he was soon to be actively involved. Everyone in western Christendom, apart from the heretics and the Jews, acknowledged the spiritual headship of the Pope; but in practice this might mean any of a variety of different things. Everyone who had any coherent idea on the problem of Church and State, on the problem of the relation between the lay and spiritual society, between clergy and laity, reckoned that God had set in the world two kinds of authority: temporal and spiritual – as we should say, the authority of the policeman and the authority of the priest.

In practice, it was neither suitable nor possible that the same man should exercise both kinds of authority; each was a full-time job and each demanded very different qualities. Thus the authority was delegated to two different hierarchies, the ecclesiastical hierarchy, with the bishops at its head, and the Pope as the ultimate authority in all spiritual matters, and the secular hierarchy, with kings and emperors at its head. Everyone expected that most of the time the two authorities would work harmoniously together, each getting on with his own task, aiding each other when necessary. But the problem which this fundamental view failed to answer was the problem of the no man's land, the boundaries, between the two territories. Above all, if conflict arose between the authorities of Church and State, who was to decide it?

This was perhaps the greatest political issue of the Middle Ages, and certainly one of the most fundamental divisive factors in any medieval kingdom. A number of different views were held. By the time of Becket's death, two views were the most common. The view which the Papacy had maintained for many hundreds of years, and was by now very widely held by educated churchmen, was based on the functions which the two authorities had to perform. The lay powers ministered to man's earthly ends, to his mortal life: the ecclesiastical to his spiritual ends, to his immortal life. Clearly, they argued, the latter is a higher function, and in cases where the authorities conflict, and in all cases where moral and religious questions are involved, the Church must decide. On medieval premises this was difficult to contradict, and it was always the most coherent and consistent of the doctrines propounded. But there were none the less powerful grounds for holding a different view.

The Papacy had been reformed in the mid eleventh century, and from then on came to be an increasingly powerful factor in European politics. But in the centuries which preceded the papal reform, it had been common for the powerful monarchs of

Europe to direct the affairs of the Church in their kingdoms. The papal reform itself had been inaugurated by the intervention of the German Emperor, Henry III. The memory of what men like Henry III – or, indeed, like Charlemagne, who ruled most of western Europe at the beginning of the ninth century – had done, was a powerful force in moulding the opinion of the lay aristocracy and of those clergy not imbued with papal doctrine.

The conservative traditions and tenacious customs of medieval peoples and kingdoms preserved a strong sense of the place the monarch should hold in the affairs of Church as well as State; and the ceremonies of anointing and crowning a king were held by all to confer a special character on the monarch, and by some to make the King some kind of priest, with spiritual as well as temporal authority. Against this view the Papacy set its face; and in all matters of doctrine the Papacy gained ground in the twelfth century, as its claims became more widely recognized, especially among the educated clergy. But the strength of conservative opinion, often unanalysed, still made for great respect for the person and office of a King, and a strong prejudice against any attempt by the Church to dictate to a King how he should behave.

In practice it was the position of the bishops themselves that caused most of the difficulty and roused most of the conflicts. A bishop was a leading figure in the Church's hierarchy, a lord spiritual; he had also a crucial place in the secular hierarchy, as a landholder and a royal counsellor. On more than one occasion in the eleventh century the Archbishop of Canterbury had permitted a bishop to be arrested by the King on the ground that he had committed his offence as a baron not as a bishop. At the height of the quarrel Thomas Becket addressed Henry II as lord and King and spiritual son.

The bishop's spiritual office was not only lofty; it was felt by reformers to be the key to good order in the Church. But the King reckoned himself almost equally dependent on the loyalty and effectiveness of the bishops. They were not only barons, they were traditionally the element among the baronage most inclined to peace and loyalty. When the King was on campaign, furthermore, a bishop, like any other baron, had the duty of providing him with a contingent of knights; and in this sphere in particular an insubordinate bishop was prejudicial to good order and military discipline. If we wish to understand why Henry II was so incensed when his bishops claimed, as spiritual lords, to be independent of his jurisdiction, to be solely his fathers in God, we have only to imagine the feelings of a divisional commander in a modern army, who discovers that one of his brigades is commanded by an Admiral.

In practice, the difficulties raised by the dual position of the bishop were solved by compromise; but we shall not understand the Becket controversy if we do not realize that however exclusive the claims of the Church might be, in practice the English kings had claimed and on most occasions vindicated the right to sit in judgement on their bishops when purely secular issues were at stake. However theoretically powerful, the pure theory of the papal view of the relations of lay and spiritual power could not in practice be enforced without compromise; and the compromises acknowledged the practical power of the conservative lay tradition in which Henry II put his trust. And it was not only in the eyes of the Pope and clergy that the issues seemed sacred. For laymen felt equally strongly that kingship was sacred, obedience a religious duty (at least when they were not themselves engaged in rebellion), and that a spiritual aura surrounded the feudal bond which tied bishops to their king. Add to this an old and growing sense of social cleavage between clergy and layfolk, and one can see why the conflict, when it came, was deep and bitter.

All these difficulties were only too well known to all the principal actors in the tragedy whose course we are about to follow; and they had inherited a knowledge of the techniques devised by the preceding generations to prevent them from leading to open strife. The conflict that ensued on Becket's appointment was the result of Becket's own character and the circumstances in which he became Archbishop.

The archbishopric of Canterbury was the most crucial office in the kingdom; its holder was the King's first councillor, and exerted an authority in the Church which could be decisive in any conflict which arose. A pliant and obedient Archbishop was one of Henry's dearest ambitions; and who could be more suitable for this office than his confidant, his leading minister, his close friend

Plate III. The thirteenth-century screen, with squints pierced in the fourteenth or fifteenth century, at Stanton Harcourt, Oxfordshire (see p. 165)

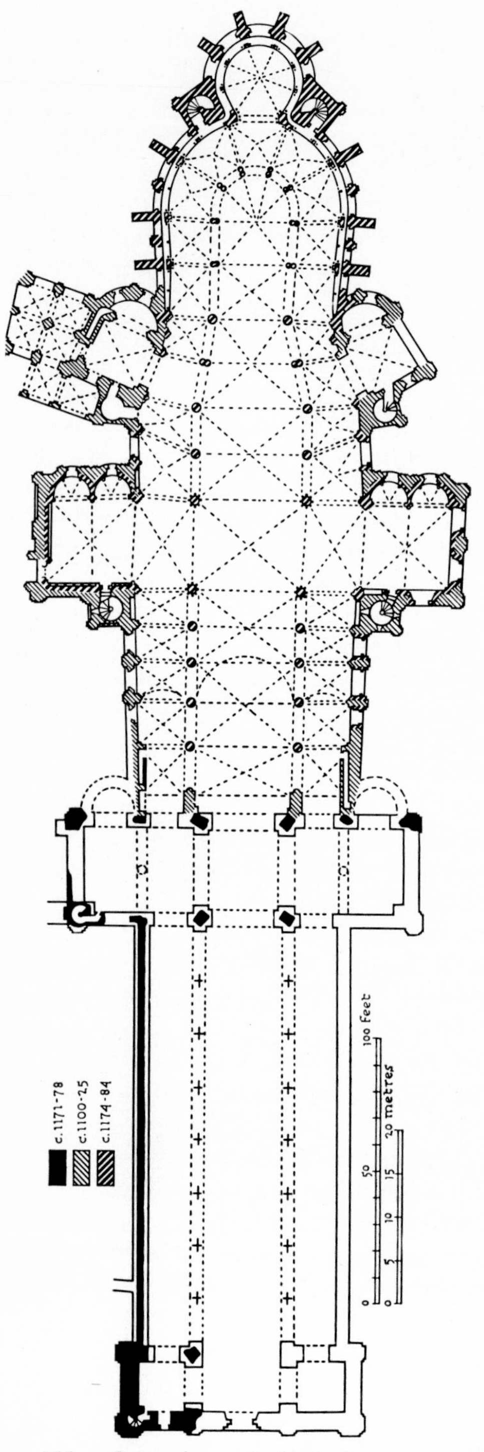

Plate IV. Canterbury Cathedral, *c.* 1071–1200
(see pp. 172–5, esp. 173n.)

Thomas Becket? How completely Henry had misunderstood Becket is a measure of the difference between a layman and a cleric in that age. It was a cleavage of understanding as deep as any national cleavage today. But in fairness to Henry one must admit that Becket was evidently a man whose deepest thoughts were a mystery to his contemporaries whether laymen or clerics; and the change that came over him seems to have surprised everyone. Becket was a man of charm who pleased and impressed superiors and inferiors alike; but it was always difficult to penetrate behind his mask. Men in the Middle Ages had a strong sense of office, of the nature of an office, of an ideal of how it should be performed; and although they failed to live up to it every bit as frequently as we do today, it provided for many conscientious men a framework in which to live their lives, and this often hides their personalities from us. Becket was doing nothing unusual in attempting to live up to such an ideal as royal Chancellor and as Archbishop; what was unusual was the imaginative intensity with which he conceived his tasks, and so the radical nature of the change when he became Archbishop. In a moment of time, he seemed to become a different man – from civil servant to spiritual leader. It was a dramatic change; but we must not think of him as a mere actor. It was conviction and tradition which made him see the part he had to play and made him live that part.

Nor is this the whole story. As Chancellor, Becket had enjoyed the patronage of both Archbishop and King. At times, it seems, Henry might have been inclined to suspect that Becket was in some measure Theobald's spy in his household. Such was the nature of patronage in the Middle Ages that the suspicion could not be entirely false: the Archbishop had certainly expected help from Becket, who was his archdeacon as well as the King's Chancellor. The situation may well have induced Becket to exaggerate his devoted service to the King to convince Henry of his wholehearted loyalty. When Becket himself became Archbishop and acted so differently from the King's expectation, we can understand the bitterness of Henry's disillusionment; behind Henry's taunt of treachery for Becket's behaviour in 1164 lay, very likely, a deeper charge, that he had deceived him and played him false when Chancellor. However this may be, the debt he owed to both his patrons made his situation extremely difficult both as Chancellor and as Archbishop. Circumstances, furthermore, compelled him to make some effort to convince the world that he was going to try and be a real Archbishop, not too unworthy a successor to great Archbishops like Lanfranc or St Anselm, or his old master Theobald; above all, he needed to disillusion the King. But it is fairly clear that it was not only circumstances, powerful as they were, which compelled Becket to act as he did; but a human trait in his character with which we cannot help sympathizing. It is likely that he felt the necessity not only to convince the King, the bishops, and his old friends that he could be a spiritual father, but also himself; a deep unsureness of himself which made him unwilling to confide his inner troubles to his friends and so increased the mystery which surrounded his actions, forced him to put his own capacity dramatically to the test.

At Canterbury he immediately became an archbishop in deed as well as word; and also, because his chapter was a chapter of monks, a kind of abbot. He began to lead the life of a monk, practised severe austerities, and wore a hair-shirt. Some of this was kept a secret at the time; but the general drift of the change soon became widely known. In due course it reached the ears of the King; and more disturbing still, Henry learnt that Thomas was not playing the part he had planned for him.

Henry II's notions of how the compromise between Church and State should work out in practice were based, like so many of his ideas of government, on what his grandfather, King Henry I, had done. By placing a royal minister in the see of St Augustine, he hoped to set on foot the restoration of his grandfather's position *vis-à-vis* the Church, to see fully established once again what he called his grandfather's customs. Some of these customs were clean contrary to the Church's law; but they had been customary, and it is impossible not to sympathize with Henry's desire to have them so again – many indeed, including some of the most uncanonical, he had already, to some extent, enforced. He soon found that Becket was disinclined to let him contravene the letter of the Church's law; and the discovery began the slow and painful process of the King's disillusionment. When Henry eventually understood what Becket was at, his enmity became implacable; he believed Becket to be a traitor, and treachery was the one sin no feudal lord could ever forgive.

The quarrel began with a host of minor irritants – disputes on trivial legal cases which would normally have been solved by compromise, but which were exacerbated by the personal difficulties between King and Archbishop, and by Becket's growing intransigence. As he found his way more clearly, and gathered round him a small group of friends and disciples who accepted his principles and admired his change of life, his position became more coherent, his principles more outspoken. But Becket himself remained a very lonely figure; he had cut himself off from his old associates, lay and clerical, in the royal service; and even his friends were not entirely convinced by the change: they felt that the Archbishop still had a good deal of the old Adam in him, and must be prevented from doing himself or them a mischief. His most discerning friend, John of Salisbury, a man entirely prepared to go into exile for the principles which he and the Archbishop shared, clearly at this date felt a deep suspicion about Becket's state of mind. He has had much credit from modern historians for preaching moderation to Becket in the early years of exile, and recommending to him spiritual reading rather than the texts of canon law on which Becket based his more extreme claims. But it appears that John did not wholly trust his old friend, and thought he was working himself up into a frenzy; and John could not believe that Becket could stand alone against the King indefinitely. It seems to have taken about four years for Thomas to convince John of Salisbury that his conversion from Chancellor to Archbishop was genuine. Small wonder that modern historians have disputed about it.

This is the central problem in any interpretation of Becket's character. What was the nature of his conversion in 1162 and the years following, and to what extent was it genuine? To this no fully satisfactory answer can be given, partly because it evidently puzzled contemporaries as much as it does us. Two things are reasonably certain. The first is that it was his vision of what was due to the new office which enabled Becket to make the external change so rapidly. The second is, that if a true conversion took place, it cannot have taken place so rapidly as appeared. A real conversion from one way of life to another cannot happen suddenly; conversion is a process, not an event.

The problem itself remains, and many different answers have been given to it. To some, Becket has appeared an arch-hypocrite, the villain of a conflict which need never have happened; to others his conversion has seemed wholly genuine, even if somewhat more prolonged than appeared from the outside; others again have commended his character while condemning his principles.

Thomas enjoyed his position as Chancellor; even as Archbishop he did not immediately lose his love of display or his interest in falcons; while he was Chancellor there must have been a great deal that was exciting, a strong sense of achievement in his work. But he may not have found the life entirely satisfying. He must have known that his old master, Archbishop Theobald, was dissatisfied, that others were criticizing him for his worldliness; and it would be surprising if he had never pondered how he would behave in the not very unlikely event of his being asked to succeed Theobald. He may have had a vision at least of some other way of life to which, as a churchman, he had once, and might again, aspire. The seeds of his conversion may have been sown in a deep dissatisfaction bred some years before he became Archbishop. This provided him with the possibility of the rapid external conversion when he was promoted; but there is plenty of evidence that when he first became Archbishop he was still deeply unsure of himself, still lacking the broader foundation on which such a conversion must ultimately rest.

The King believed that he had set a pliant royal servant in the see of Canterbury. As time passed, it became increasingly clear that this was not so. A series of awkward incidents revealed that Becket was not prepared to be subservient and would not accept compromises on points of friction. If clergy engaged in crime, could they be treated as criminals in the royal courts? This was only one of many issues; but it was a crucial one, since it touched the status and spiritual independence of the clergy on a sensitive point. To the King it seemed essential for the preservation of order that some kind of customary arrangement between the church courts and lay courts should continue in operation so that 'criminous clerks' could receive secular punishments as well as the purely spiritual forfeits—degrading and excommunication – of the Church courts. To Becket the Church's freedom was at stake; and within two and a half years of his consecration he was to show that his own freedom, perhaps his life, hung on the issue.

The quarrel between King and Archbishop came to a head in two famous councils in 1164. First, at Clarendon in January, Henry tried to get the English bishops to swear to a catalogue of the customs of his grandfather which he wished to see observed. A party among the bishops were for resisting the King, and expected Becket to support them. Up to a point he did so; but he felt insecure with the bishops, most of whom had not come fully to accept him. Insecure in his own position and in himself, and frankly afraid of what the King might do to him, he found his loneliness too much for him, and without consulting anyone, he gave in.

Immediately he became a figure of scorn to his colleagues and to himself; the Pope absolved him for his failure, but Becket none the less tried to escape from the country in order to consult the Pope more fully, perhaps to resign the see into the Pope's hands. His threat of flight, and of putting himself under the Pope's protection, finally determined Henry to make an end of him; so the trap was carefully laid. Becket was to be summoned to a council at Northampton in October and tried on purely secular charges – including that of peculation as Chancellor – for which imprisonment for life would be a light punishment as these things were then understood. If that failed, he was to be induced to resign. Becket knew that if he submitted to judgement he would have no mercy; and circumstances, once again, compelled him to take an extreme line, from which he never receded. He took the view that as a spiritual lord, as a bishop, as the King's father in God, he could not be tried at all on a criminal charge in a secular court, even for secular offences. He was better prepared for Northampton than for Clarendon, and behaved with greater firmness and greater dignity. The pressure and the strain were gruelling. But in the end, he screwed up his courage to make a parade of independence and ensure, in the only way possible, his immunity in practice from the King's anger. With his own hands he carried the Archbishop's cross into the King's presence as a symbol of defiance. One of his clerks asked his sternest critic among the bishops, Gilbert Foliot of London, if he was going to stand by and let the Archbishop carry his own cross. It seems that Foliot tried to take it from him – but Becket was a strong man physically, and Foliot no match for him – and Foliot then observed, 'He always was a fool and always will be.' That night Becket slipped away from Northampton disguised, and after a few days' adventure, reached the safety of the dominions of the king of France.

Becket sought the protection of King Louis VII of France for three reasons. First because the Pope himself, Alexander III (1159–81), was at Sens, in the royal domain; and he wished to consult Alexander, to lay his case in his hands, to resign his charge or fight on as the Pope decided; second, because Louis, in his later years, was a man of piety and good will who could be trusted to protect an Archbishop to whom he had offered hospitality; and thirdly, because Louis and Henry II were usually at war with one another, and Louis was therefore inclined to welcome Becket as a thorn in Henry's flesh. Even so, there were great risks: protection of Becket could prove dangerous to Louis, and the time might come that the two Kings would agree not to harbour each other's disloyal subjects; moreover, the Pope was seriously embarrassed by Becket's special appeal for his help.

In 1159, Alexander III's predecessor, the English Pope Adrian IV, had died; and two men were elected simultaneously to succeed him. More than half his pontificate was to pass before Alexander could reckon his position secure. At first the Emperor strongly favoured Alexander's rival, and Alexander was forced to flee from Italy; he was very dependent on the support of the French and English Kings. As the years went on, his fortunes improved and he was able to return to Italy; in the late 1160s the Emperor suffered reverses in Italy, and by 1170 the Pope felt free to proceed against Henry II. But in the early years he had to be cautious: he never wavered in his support for Becket, but refused to take decisive action such as excommunicating Henry. He played for time, to the frustration of Becket and his supporters.

From the end of 1164 until a month before his death Becket was in exile, either in Pontigny or in Sens, both on the territory of the French King. It was always doubtful whether Louis VII and the Pope would be powerful enough to protect him against the strong forces working for his destruction. In the comparative quiet of the French abbeys in which he stayed, Becket recovered his confidence in himself and his capacity to sustain his own cause; but he lost nothing of the intransigence of practice as well as of principle which made compromise with him extremely difficult, and often embarrassed the Pope in his efforts to make peace. From Henry's point of view the traitor, by flying, had confirmed his treachery; and many of the bishops, even those of them who accepted Becket's opposition to some of the principles of the Constitutions of Clarendon, thought that a measure of give and take would always be necessary in practice.

For six years Becket remained in exile, while effort after effort to arrange a reconciliation failed. The Pope slowly grew more resolute in Becket's support as the years passed, until finally, in 1170, when the various measures which he and the Archbishop had devised proved of no avail, the Pope lost patience. He authorized Becket to pronounce an interdict – the most powerful weapon in the Church's armoury, since it stopped all services save baptism and closed the churches – and behind this lay the threat that the King himself would be excommunicated. For the moment Becket held his hand. But meanwhile another trouble had arisen. Henry II wished to have his eldest surviving son, also called Henry (1155–83), crowned in his lifetime as the first step in a grand design to settle his lands on his family, and so that there should be no dispute about the succession when he died. Despairing of peace with Becket, who should have performed the ceremony, he arranged to have it performed by the Archbishop of York. This contravened the rights of the church of Canterbury, a very dangerous issue in a century when Canterbury and York were almost continuously in dispute about their rights and claims; and to avoid deepening the rift between Henry and Thomas, the Pope forbade the coronation. Becket hastened to deliver the Pope's letters; but although their contents were quite well known, the bishops pretended not to have received them. On 14 June the young King was crowned; and Becket held his hand no longer. Warned by this example of what happened if he hesitated to take extreme measures, and encouraged by his friends, Becket immediately prepared to launch the interdict, and at the same time sent violent complaints to Rome about the coronation. Henry's reaction to the threat of interdict was immediate; within a month he had patched up a reconciliation with Becket and made arrangements for him to return to England.

Meanwhile the Pope had heard of the coronation of the young King, and proceeded to strong measures; he sent letters excommunicating the bishops involved in the coronation, with a covering letter to Becket authorizing him to publish them. News travelled slowly to Rome; especially slowly, it seems, that summer. Whether Pope Alexander would have tempered his wrath if he had known of the reconciliation when he issued his anathemas we cannot tell; certainly he was not retracing his steps, and when he did hear of the reconciliation he viewed it with scepticism and misgiving. Nor was Becket in a mood to withhold the Pope's letters. He forwarded them, and then returned to England. He found the lay powers, acting under the young King's instructions, extremely suspicious; in effect Becket was kept a prisoner in Kent. It is clear that he had a foreboding of what was coming, and made no attempt to conceal the fact.

Becket speeded his own end by forwarding the Pope's letters; and he has been much criticized for doing so. But it is doubtful if the end would in any case have been long delayed; and he can certainly be acquitted of being in any sense suicidally inclined. He had learnt that there could be no true reconciliation while he lived. He can hardly be blamed for thinking he was entering a trap, and it is scarcely surprising that both he and Henry behaved like actors in a tragedy. But it is extremely doubtful if the final denouement was premeditated by the King. Reports of the Archbishop's activities were exaggerated, and the Archbishop of York seems to have stirred Henry to a fit of violent temper. 'A fellow who has eaten my bread,' he is reported to have said, 'has lifted up his hand against me! He . . . dishonours the whole royal race, tramples down the whole kingdom. A fellow who first broke into my court on a lame horse, with a cloak for a saddle, swaggers on my throne, while you, the companions of my fortune, look on!' Speeches reported by medieval chroniclers and biographers were commonly free compositions, not normally expected to bear a close relation to what had actually been uttered, and the story lost nothing in the telling. But whatever Henry really said, he precipitated the intervention of the four knights by his violent outburst. It stirred above all that sense of social cleavage which made the barons feel that Becket, though an Anglo-Norman by origin like themselves, was somehow an upstart and a foreigner, because although a clerk, he had done things that the King alone should do. T. S. Eliot in *Murder in the Cathedral* makes the knights give a highly rational account of their deed; their speeches are intended to make a dramatic contrast, certainly not to be historical. The original knights could have given no coherent account of what they were at, save that Becket was a traitor, and that they had treated him as such.

The Archbishop went to the Cathedral for vespers, and as he was entering the choir to go to his stall a hubbub broke out behind him in the cloister. The monks tried to stop the service and bar the gates; many of them fled. Some semblance of order was restored by the dignified behaviour of the Archbishop himself, who refused to fly, and waited by the altar of the Blessed Virgin in the north transept for the arrival of the knights, while a confused crowd of townsfolk and monks swept through the Cathedral. When the knights came there seems to have been some uncertainty in their minds how to proceed; they were troubled by the Archbishop's composure. One of them tried roughly to bundle him out of the church, as if afraid at the last of the sacrilege they had come to commit, but the Archbishop was a strong man, and could not easily be moved. The other knights seem to have known what they wished to do, but not how to begin. Presently one of them, Reginald FitzUrse, a vassal of Becket's, was stirred by the Archbishop's taunts to wave his sword and call the rest to action. The Archbishop just had time to commend himself, his cause, and the Church to God, St Mary, and the blessed martyr, St Denis, when FitzUrse was upon him. Three of the knights then set to work with their swords in earnest; the third blow brought him to his knees, and his last words, uttered in a low voice, were,

'For the name of Jesus and the protection of the church I am prepared to embrace death.' Then they scattered his brains on the pavement, and a cleric who had accompanied the knights shouted aloud: 'The traitor is dead; let us go.'[2]

[2] See E. A. Abbott, *St Thomas of Canterbury: his death and miracles* (London, 1898), I, esp. pp. 172, 159.

7

Heresy and Religious Sentiment: 1000–1250

A lecture delivered before the Anglo-American Conference of Historians on 15 July 1967. Since my purpose was to take stock and indicate lines of advance, it has seemed right to preserve the form of the lecture with minimal alteration and to provide only essential references: the articles and books of Professor Borst, Dr Russell, and Dr Fearns cited below provide references to most of the recent literature on heresy in this period.

When this was written, H. Grundmann's essential Bibliographie zur Ketzergeschichte des Mittelalters *(Rome, 1967), was not available to me; nor C. Thouzellier,* Catharisme et Valdéisme en Languedoc *(Paris, 1966; 2nd ed., Louvain-Paris, 1969). The latest discussion of the problem of eleventh-century heresy is by* R. I. Moore, *in* History, LV *(1970), pp. 21–36.*

NO one could say that medieval heresy was a neglected subject.[1] For several hundred years before 1000, references to heresy in western Europe are very scattered and sparse; much has occasionally been made of this or that stray reference, but on the whole the modern discussions are also sparse. Between 1000 and 1051 there are eight passages in chroniclers and the like, and a few

[1] In general, that is: in England the history of heresy in this period has been somewhat neglected until recently, at least in comparison with the attention it has received elsewhere (but see below, p. 145, n. 12; p. 145, n. 13). For what follows, see esp. p. 144, n. 9 below.

slighter references, which have formed the base for a very substantial literature, ringing the changes, refining, but rarely adding anything new in the way of evidence; a sort of Enigma variations. For fifty years after 1051 we have total silence. Even this has not silenced the pens of the modern scholars; there has been fervent discussion whether it is due to the disappearance of heresy underground or to the chroniclers' attention being claimed by rival excitements. Even here knowledge can be substantially advanced, as Professor Violante has shown by his investigation of the social background of popular religious movements in Milan and elsewhere.[2] But heresy as such only reappears after 1100; and its rise must be reckoned one of the most dramatic aspects of the twelfth century.

By the end of the century two major heretical movements had established themselves in many parts of western Europe. Both the puritan, quasi-Protestant movement of which Waldo and the Waldensians had come to be the centre, and the Cathars or Albigensians – who were dualists, that is to say regarded the flesh and the material world as wholly evil – had their main centres in southern France and northern Italy. In Italy the Waldensians still survive, and may be reckoned the oldest of Protestant communions; and if one describes them as heretics, this is certainly no term of opprobrium, but of convenience – for heretics they were in a world dominated by the authority of the western Catholic Church. Happily, in these ecumenical days, the term heretic must be reckoned in normal use merely a term of convenience.

Precisely how strong these heretical movements were we have no means of telling; and it is possible that the evidence of their strength in Provence and Lombardy blinds us to their comparative strength elsewhere – in northern France, the Low Countries, the Rhineland, northern Spain, and elsewhere. But the Cathars at least were highly organized in their main centres, and not elsewhere;[3] and in these regions they inspired the Catholic hierarchy with panic. It can hardly be said that the word panic in any measure

[2] C. Violante, *La società milanese nell'età precomunale* (Bari, 1953), esp. pp. 176 ff.

[3] For the Cathar bishoprics, see A. Borst, *Die Katharer* (Schriften der Monumenta Germaniae Historica, XII, Stuttgart, 1953), pp. 231 ff.

overrates the emotion which inspired the Holy Inquisition. However dignified its proceedings, however academic its principles, the Inquisition when it came, as a regular practice, to hand over recalcitrant heretics to the lay power essentially represented a marriage between the Church's spiritual condemnations of earlier times, and the popular horror of heretics which had condemned the rare heretics of the eleventh century to be burned – the traditional punishment for witchcraft.[4] It seems clear that the Popes of the late twelfth and early thirteenth centuries thought that they had a violent but temporary crisis to deal with; and in a sense they were right. In the long run the Waldensians became a small, persecuted group which barely survived and had little direct impact on the Reformation; the Cathars, who on any diagnosis by a moderately pessimistic Catholic might have seemed destined for total victory in certain areas in 1200, had by 1300 become an underground movement, and by 1400 had virtually disappeared. These two churches were not the only products of twelfth-century heresy; nor did the thirteenth and fourteenth centuries see heresy disappear – very far from it.[5] It is clear, meanwhile, that in the complex world of late medieval heresy, from which the Reformation was to come, the Waldensians were great pioneers, but not immediate precursors or founders of reform; and that the Cathars played a quite subordinate role.

Since the accession of Pope John XXIII much has been heard of *aggiornamento*, of the movement in the Roman Catholic Church – in the churches indeed – to abandon the siege-mentality of recent centuries, and come out to meet the world. It has been traditionally supposed that this mentality was the product of the Reformation and Counter-Reformation; but this is only partly true, and there is considerable justification for the thesis pressed

[4] On the legal development in punishing heretics, see H. Maisonneuve, *Etudes sur les origines de l'inquisition* (2nd edn., Paris, 1960); on burning heretics, cf. Brooke in *Eng. Hist. Rev.*, LXXVII (1962), pp. 137–8.

[5] Since this paper was written the whole subject has been illuminated by the appearance of Dr Gordon Leff's *Heresy in the Later Middle Ages*, I (Manchester, 1967). His starting point is *c.* 1250 and he excludes the Cathars, but he has much to say which is relevant to the present theme: e.g. on the early Franciscans, though in the context of his book they naturally appear as a source of new divisions rather than as a solvent of old.

so vehemently in Friedrich Heer's *Medieval World*,[6] that the closing of the gates took place in the late twelfth and thirteenth centuries. The Church indeed had been authoritarian and repressive before that; but the twelfth century was the first in which the western Church had been faced with the problem of mass apostasy. In the thirteenth century the Catholic Church scored one of its most sensational material triumphs – the defeat of the Cathars, a triumph which appeared at the worldly level to be the result of crusade and inquisition, and which appeared to justify the Inquisition in its prime. Whether persecution was truly the main cause of the Cathar decline is a problem to which every student will give his own answer; and our answers will depend in fair measure on our temperaments – on how much weight in human affairs we are prepared to allow cruelty and force to have had. There can be no question that force was very effectively used, and that the crusades mounted against the Cathars, especially those inspired by St Louis in the middle of the thirteenth century, led to the destruction of large numbers of Cathar *perfecti*. But there are other causes which evidently played their part, and there is at least one major difficulty in believing that persecution was the preponderant factor. The Cathar Church was equally strongly organized, so far as the evidence goes, in the south of what we call France and in the north of Italy: in each it had three bishoprics.[7] In France, especially under St Louis, persecution was highly organized, the Crusades effective, the Inquisition favoured. In Italy there was much variety of practice from city to city and from decade to decade. But it was contrary to the nature of Italian politics and Italian society that any policy of religious repression could be consistently maintained over a wide area. Pope Innocent III's outburst against the people of Assisi – a papal city – for electing a Cathar as *podestà* is a symbol of how things could work in Italy.[8] Yet the bishoprics sink from view both sides of the Alps in the mid thirteenth century; and so

[6] Translated J. Sondheimer, London (1962).

[7] Borst, pp. 231 ff. The multiplication of bishoprics may have been partly due to doctrinal differences which divided the Cathar Church in the late twelfth and early thirteenth centuries.

[8] K. Esser, 'St Franziskus und die Katharer seiner Zeit', *Archivum Franciscanum Historicum*, LI (1958), p. 239. It is not certain that the *podestà* was a believing Cathar.

far as the evidence permits us to reconstruct the story, the chronology of Cathar decline is the same in both countries. Of the Waldensians it is more difficult to speak with precision; but in general they seem to have felt the hand of the persecutor in France as heavily as the Cathars, and for that reason to have settled in remote regions of Italy, where they survived, diminished, but not extinguished. And some historians have been puzzled that the Waldensians survived but the Cathars not. It is clear that among the complex and obscure factors which explain this story, one is the rise in the thirteenth century of a movement of religious ideas and sentiment profoundly antagonistic to the ideas of the Cathars, somewhat less so to the Waldensians. Historical causes can never be weighed, and the kind of causes under discussion here could never be subjected to statistical analysis. To say that this movement was either more or less important than persecution in the fall of the Cathars is virtually meaningless, but one can say that it is more important to the understanding of how the Cathar movement was related to the history of western Europe at large in the eleventh, twelfth, and thirteenth centuries.

The most stubborn problems which have beset all who have tried to trace the chronological development of heresy between 1000 and 1200 are to find the original root and inspiration of heresy, and to explain the curious gap in the evidence between 1050 and 1100. From 1000 to shortly after 1050 there is a trickle of evidence; from 1050 to 1100 total silence; from 1100 to 1150 a stream, at times almost a river; from 1150 onwards a rising flood. On the basic issue of the source of these heresies, there is now fairly general agreement that behind the massive growth of the Cathars in the second half of the twelfth century there lies a period of active proselytizing by Bogomil missionaries from the Balkans and the Near East; and that this missionary work took place in a setting already favourable to its success. A western movement, reforming, dissenting, puritanical, met and absorbed the specific doctrines from the east. It is also agreed that before about 1140 there is very limited evidence among these heretical groups of specific dualism. On this ground some scholars have held that virtually all the heresies recorded before 1140 are of purely native growth, owing nothing to the Bogomils; and this view, strongly sustained by Professor Morghen – who has even argued against Bogomil influence after 1140 – has recently been revived in a modified form by Dr J. B. Russell, who provided a useful survey of the controversies in an article in *Mediaeval Studies* in 1963 and a conspectus of his own views on the period to 1140 in his interesting book *Dissent and Reform in the Early Middle Ages* in 1965.[9]

The other extreme is represented by Père Dondaine,[10] who has done more than any other living scholar to unearth new materials about the heresies of this period. Dondaine has held that the simultaneous appearance of related heretical systems in the opening years of the eleventh century and again in the twelfth cannot be satisfactorily explained unless we postulate a major external stimulus; and he has attempted to show that a majority of the heretical opinions adequately recorded in eleventh-century sources are Bogomil opinions or have Bogomil affinities; and that even if the lists are fragmentary and precise evidence of dualism absent, all the evidence is consistent with the view that we are shown by the sources a variety of aspects of a Bogomil iceberg.

Between these two extremes almost every conceivable position has been held, and I do not propose to wander far over this

[9] J. B. Russell, 'Interpretations of the origins of medieval heresy', *Mediaeval Studies,* XXV (1963), pp. 26–53; *Dissent and Reform* . . . (Berkeley and Los Angeles, 1965) (on which cf. *Jour. Theol. Studies*, new ser., XVIII, pp. 256–8). The studies to which I owe most are those by Borst (see above), Dondaine (see next note), Fearns (see below), Grundmann (see below), Ilarino da Milano ('Le eresie popolari del secolo XI nell'Europa occidentale', in *Studi Gregoriani*, ed. G. B. Borino, II (1947), pp. 43–89). Morghen's views are developed most fully in articles in *Archivio della* R. *Deputazione romana di Storia Patria*, LXVII (1944), pp. 97–151, repr. in his *Medioevo Cristiano* (Bari, 1951), and in *Accademia nazionale dei Lincei: XII Convegno 'Volta': Oriente ed Occidente nel Medio Evo* (Rome, 1957), pp. 84–104, 158–60. Also important are studies by J. Guiraud, *Histoire de l'inquisition au moyen âge* (2 vols., Paris, 1935–8); H. Maisonneuve (above, p. 141, n. 4); R. Manselli, esp. *Studi sulle eresie del secolo XII* (Rome, 1953); H. C. Puech, esp. 'Catharisme médiéval et bogomilisme', in *Accademia nazionale, ut supra,* pp. 56–84; Sir S. Runciman, *The Medieval Manichee* (Cambridge, 1947); C. Thouzellier, esp. 'Hérésie et croisade au xiie siècle', *Revue d'histoire ecclésiastique,* XLIX (1954), pp. 855–72. A selection of the basic texts is collected in J. V. Fearns, *Ketzer und Ketzerbekämpfung im Hochmittelalter* (Göttingen, 1968).

[10] See esp. A. Dondaine, 'L'origine de l'hérésie médiévale', *Rivista di storia della Chiesa in Italia,* VI (1952), pp. 47–78.

ground – but only to say that I myself reckon the most indispensable of modern authorities Professor Borst's exceedingly precise and careful study of the Cathars and their background, and Professor Grundmann's classic view of the wider field in *Religiöse Bewegungen im Mittelalter*.[11] It seems tolerably clear that neither extreme can be sustained. One cannot doubt that the ground was well prepared in the tenth and early eleventh centuries; that behind both the heretical movements and the larger movement for ecclesiastical reform which captured Rome itself in the person of Pope Leo IX lay a popular movement flowing in many channels. Dr Russell is indeed concerned to deny that anything very special happened about the year 1000: he believes that heretical outbreaks had occurred earlier and that it is only their frequency, and our evidence, which increases. This is to do less than justice to the concentration of evidence in the first half of the eleventh century. This evidence seems to presuppose a widely and strongly felt popular need not adequately met by the Church of the day. The disappearance of evidence after 1050 cannot be simply explained by the suggestion that late-eleventh-century chroniclers had matters more exciting to relate. There may be an element of chance, and total disappearance of heresies seems inconceivable. But a decline seems certain, and it is likely that the alliance of religious fervour and papal reform accounts for it. In the twelfth century one passes into a more complex and sophisticated world of thought and sentiment, and it is hardly surprising that the discontents should rise quickly to the surface again, nor that specific eastern influence should become in due course much clearer.

The clearest evidence of eastern influence before 1140 comes from the Petrobrusians, on account of the elaborate treatise of Peter the Venerable of Cluny against them, of which a new edition has been made by Dr J. V. Fearns.[12] He has also clarified their doctrine in an article.[13] In two particular ways they showed their

[11] Borst (p. 140, n. 3); H. Grundmann, *Religiöse Bewegungen* . . . (2nd edn., Hildesheim, 1961).

[12] J. V. Fearns, 'Peter the Venerable's "Epistola contra Petrobrusianos"' (unpublished Liverpool Ph.D. thesis, 1963) (now published in *Corpus Christianorum, Continuatio Mediaevalis* (1968)).

[13] J. V. Fearns, 'Peter von Bruis und die religiöse Bewegung des 12. Jahrhunderts', *Archiv für Kulturgeschichte*, XLVIII (1966), pp. 311–35.

western origin: they were not dualists, and although they condemned infant baptism, that was because they took baptism seriously, not because they condemned it altogether, as did the Bogomils and the later Cathars. But most of their other doctrines specified by Peter the Venerable show an affinity to the Bogomils closer than to any other contemporary heresies in the west; and it would be unduly sceptical to deny a link, though its nature is obscure and it does not follow that it was due to direct missionary work by the Bogomils, such as we know to have taken place a generation later. The Petrobrusian evidence also suggests that the heretical movements of the early eleventh century – though clearly dormant before 1100 – had not been entirely forgotten. More than this one cannot hope to know. But it is clear that Peter of Bruis (who gave his name to the Petrobrusians) and his like were preparing the ground for the later successes, both of the Bogomil missionaries who founded the Cathar Church properly so called, and of the development of Waldo and his followers, originally puritan but orthodox, into the heretical system of belief of the Waldensian Church.

At one time the major interest of historians was in the social origin and setting of these heresies. We have enough trouble on our hands here; and little will be said of the social aspect of the problem. Some earlier historians saw heresy as the outward sign of a class movement, here among merchants, there among peasants, and as a form of protest against the establishment. Two difficulties have made such views unfashionable: the first is that there is no adequate evidence to support them – they can be founded on faith alone; and the second is that such evidence as exists directly contradicts any class view narrowly conceived. That ideas spread along merchant routes, that the Cathars were known as the 'weavers' in areas where textile industries were strong, that Peter of Bruis was supported by a mob of peasants, the records do indeed reveal.[14] But they also show at many points that successful heresy involved a cross-section of society, including noblemen, leading city men, even the upper privileged clergy

[14] Cf. Grundmann, ch. III; Borst, p. 248. For 'textores', cf. *Letters and Charters of Gilbert Foliot,* ed. A. Morey and C. N. L. Brooke (Cambridge, 1967), nos. 157–8.

on occasion. There has been a reaction towards an interpretation in which theology and the world of ideas is more significant – a reasonable reaction, since it involves a shift from the realm of guesswork to that of evidence – but if it leads historians to ignore the social aspects of these movements, it will have gone much too far.

The purpose of this essay is to consider the way in which heresy has been related in recent studies to the religious movements of the age; to try to clarify this by taking some illustrations of the scope and nature of the world of religious sentiment in which it lived. It is hoped in the process to sharpen somewhat the focus of recent studies in three ways: to develop the theme that what is most fundamental is the development from a comparatively simple world of opinion in the eleventh century to one far wider, richer, more sophisticated in the late twelfth and early thirteenth centuries; to illustrate the ways in which vernacular literature and the history of art and architecture can enrich the Latin sources in the pursuit of this world of religious sentiment; and to show in brief how the reaction of St Francis of Assisi in particular to the problem of heresy in his own day reflects as in a mirror both the nature of the problem and the spiritual weapons (as opposed to the physical weapons of persecution) which conquered the Cathars.

Professor Grundmann has revealed the popular preacher as a characteristic feature of eleventh- and twelfth-century life:[15] a preacher will start as some kind of revivalist, but in intention Catholic, and will end, either with the founders of Tiron and Savigny and Prémontré, by founding a great monastic community and retreating, respectably, from the world, or, like Peter of Bruis and Henry of Lausanne, by becoming a heresiarch. When Henry of Lausanne came to Le Mans in 1116, the great Bishop Hildebert was on his way to Rome.[16] It never occurred to him that Henry was more than a fervent street-corner orator: he permitted him to give a course of Lenten sermons – no doubt he thought his flock much in need of them – and went on with his journey, leaving Le

[15] Grundmann, esp. ch. 1. There is of course a large literature on this: see esp. the additional chapter in Grundmann, 2nd edn.

[16] P. von Moos, *Hildebert von Lavardin* (Stuttgart, 1965), pp. 12–13.

Mans open to one of the most powerful heretical preachers of the century. It is indeed a striking and puzzling fact that orthodox popular preachers tended to become monks, abandon the world, and retreat behind the walls of monasteries; those who adhered to the apostolic life tended to become heretics, and in the long run to have almost a monopoly of effective popular preaching in some parts of Europe. It reveals the power of the monastic ideal in the twelfth century – and in particular, no doubt, the personal influence of St Bernard of Clairvaux on founders and would-be founders of new Orders. Within the Catholic framework, the apostolic life found remarkably little foothold or organization before the days of Francis and Dominic.

Too simple a dichotomy between heresy and orthodoxy tends to make the boundaries more clear cut than they can actually have appeared at the time; and, even more, tends to obscure the variety of opinion and sentiment of the twelfth century. The Petrobrusians were noted among other traits for their addiction to attacking churches and burning crosses: they objected, quite radically, to all the trappings of Catholic worship. To this Peter the Venerable, who presided in the great third Church at Cluny, the supreme expression of art and decoration and complex iconography in the service of the Church and of worship of the age, was bound to take exception. But Cluny's splendour notoriously excited the criticism of men more respectable than Peter of Bruis. No doubt the latter would have accepted gladly the terms of St Bernard's famous denunciation of Cluny if he knew them. To Bernard a church was a convenient, commodious, consecrated enclosure in which worship could take place.[17] Care might be lavished on its design; but the aim was not to attract the eye but quite specifically to avoid every distraction. However negative the aim, the Cistercian style and approach to church-design was in its way an extremely sophisticated expression of the contemporary concern to select proportions, to study ornament, to plan a building with a specific idea of its purpose and function in mind. Peter of Cluny

[17] On Peter and Bernard's controversy, see D. Knowles, *The Historian and Character and other Essays* (Cambridge, 1963), ch. IV, esp. pp. 63 ff.; on the Cistercian conception, F. Bucher in *Comparative Studies in Society and History,* III (1960–1), pp. 89–105; below, pp. 171–2.

would have agreed with his contemporary Suger, Abbot of St-Denis, that the sparkling jewels with which the reliquaries of St-Denis were crusted reflected God's glory and so brought the mind to God. Peter of Bruis would have agreed with St Bernard that every show of colour or ornament was a mere distraction, and would perhaps have agreed that whitewashed walls and plain glass were better suited to the purpose of a church than the coat of many colours of Cluny or St-Denis. But Peter of Bruis would have reckoned open air preferable to any oratory, and all the fuss about Cistercian church planning a ridiculous waste of time. Thus in this crucial matter there was as wide a variety of opinion as possible in the early twelfth century, and each of these three men could command an army of recruits.

It has often been assumed that this kind of variety of opinion was confined to outward things, like churches and ornaments, or to inessentials of belief; and that at the roots of things everyone was agreed, consciously or unconsciously, in their basic Christian Catholic faith. This kind of assumption tends to be sustained by obvious contrasts between the twelfth and the twentieth centuries. Today the Church, the churches, religious beliefs of every kind, have to struggle for their place in a free market, an Armageddon of conflicting opinions. Freedom of belief may not exist in a perfect form anywhere today, yet it is the clear aim and intention of all folk of liberal outlook in the modern world, whatever their own religious convictions. The new situation is the product (so far as one can understand a very complex and obscure process of causation) of the spread of tolerance, of humane and liberal sentiment, in recent centuries; and also of the revolution in intellectual climate which means that countless men and women today think that there is nothing ultimately obscure about the world, or (which can be a very different thing) nothing which makes the notion of a divine creator or saviour either necessary or plausible. This last situation, the confident rationalism or the scientifically based agnosticism which have come to be the dominant faiths among late-twentieth-century intellectuals, was indeed unthinkable in the twelfth century, at least in any recognizable form. This seems to be one of the major reasons why historians have tended to assume that religious doubt and religious tolerance were unknown in the twelfth century, and to make the religious climate of the age far more monochrome than it really was. All scholars have been aware of the great twelfth-century heresies, but original work in this field, unlike say work on the twelfth-century schools, or economic and social history, has been slow to penetrate the general thinking of historians.

The second obvious reason why historians have tended to play down or ignore the diversity of opinion that existed on matters of fundamental belief is that we are all traditionally trained to study, first and foremost, the Latin literature of the Church, which in its nature reveals uniformity rather than diversity, and when it shows us a heresy, shows us its learned side – the learned disputations of Cathars and Catholics, the writings of Wyclif and Huss. It comes as a considerable shock when one first makes serious contact with the *Parzival* of Wolfram von Eschenbach (of the very early thirteenth century), to discover that one of the most famous of medieval poems has as its central theme the problem of *zwîvel*, of doubt, and that at the heart of Parzival's doubt lay religious doubt. This is all the more striking because the grounds of doubt are not explored; Wolfram was essentially concerned with its consequences and with God's reaction to it. *Zwîvel* is a complex word, which involves much more than doubt in our sense; and articles and even books have been written on it.[18] The basic ingredients of the word in the early twelfth century appear to be intellectual doubt – not of God's existence, but of his willingness to *help* his people; and also the idea of distrust and fear; it is the opposite of understanding, of loyalty, and of trust. By Wolfram's time and in his own usage, the ideas of distrust and ignorance (not, in Parzival's case, disloyalty) have been joined by something most closely akin to our despair. Distrust in a very broad sense leading to blackness and despair are the fundamentals of Parzival's *zwîvel*; but ignorance is a vital element too – Wolfram uses *zwîvel* on occasion as the synonym for paganism, and faithlessness in the broad sense of the term. It is hard to believe that Wolfram was unacquainted with this range of thought and feeling, deeply religious man though he was; and one is left to assume that his

[18] see p. 10. On *zwîvel*, see the references listed in D. H. Green, *The Millstätter Exodus* (Cambridge, 1966), p. 354.

audience would be acquainted with it too. What is not taken for granted is the way back to faith and God's attitude to it. The poet urges on us that God finds merit in a man, even if he lose his faith, if he leads his life in strict accord with the code of his order. This is no formal legalism; Wolfram's account of knightly loyalty, *triuwe*, is a profound searching out of all that was best in chivalry, as he knew it; and in his analysis, as revealed in Parzival's adventures, a very wide range of human qualities is included. Of these one must suffice as an example. Parzival was married before he went on his unfortunate visit to the Grail castle, and his loyalty to his wife, his *triuwe* as a husband, is the first and most striking of his qualities. It is a love deeper and more abiding than the fever of courtly love (with which it is several times contrasted). Although it has to survive five years of separation, it is never strained even for a moment; love of his wife is Parzival's abiding motive even when his faith in God has been lost; and reunion with his wife and children is the supreme reward of his final success. Wolfram seems to be saying as follows: a feudal warrior has a special function in the world, a function clearly revealed in the life of his family and the life of warfare; his Christian duty lies first and foremost in this, to be faithful to his wife and family, faithful to his lord, faithful to the code of chivalry, and to show his *triuwe* in every human situation which arises. This matters more than theological orthodoxy; if he does this, God will be with him.

It is notoriously dangerous to argue from the ideas of a great poet to the opinions of ordinary men in the same age; but men of Wolfram's stature have this advantage, that they will often tell us things no one else bothers to tell us, and they will commonly reveal the width of the range within which opinions of their age could move. The notion of tolerance here struggles for expression; it finds expression in a much fuller form in Wolfram's second great epic, the *Willehalm*. But the argument of *Parzival* works on the assumption that his hearers are acquainted with religious doubt; and the argument of *Willehalm* assumes that men of good will have been known – whatever the Church may say – to change their religions. Parzival's doubt contains nothing of self-confident rationalism; it is part of a general doubt and blackness which envelops him, but doubt in a full sense it clearly is. If Wolfram can explore the realms of despair and doubt, he also reveals a sense of humaneness and tolerance often denied by historians a place among the characteristic qualities of his age. These were qualities which grew perhaps from a tiny seed; in a fair measure they may have been unique to him; in a fair measure they were clearly characteristic of the world in which he lived—as characteristic, maybe, as the authoritarian cruelty which allowed the Albigensian Crusade and inspired the Inquisition.

In a sense one can never hope to prove that any ideas of this kind were characteristic of any medieval period; the range of our evidence is invariably too narrow. But in the particular range of ideas and sentiments with which we are concerned, we have some striking examples of men who enshrined the basic contradictions of the eleventh, twelfth, and thirteenth centuries, in such a way as strongly to suggest that they drank in opposite opinions with the air they breathed, much as many folk today drink in Christian and agnostic assumptions, socialist and conservative, Democrat and Republican, with the air they breathe, and most of the time live happily unaware of the strange bedfellows in their brains.

Two basic contradictions are essential to this story. First the Christian view that the world is God's world and (however corrupt) remains his world, his creation, and so fundamentally good; against the Gnostic, Bogomil, and Cathar view, the dualist view to give it a single label, that the material world is wholly evil; that goodness can only exist in the world of the spirits, and in only a part of that, and so that salvation consists in an escape from the world, and especially from the world of flesh. The second contradiction is between two ways of combating the growth of error and false opinion in the world; the view that in the end only force will kill, and that every weapon of Church and State must be used to fight heresy, by crusade and inquisition; and the view that the growth of heresy reveals first and foremost some failure in the Church, a failure to communicate the faith to stir men to conversion; and that the right way to combat heresy is to make Christendom Christian, by preaching and example.

In the person of Peter Damian in the mid eleventh century one can see the two views of the world in one man's mind.[19] Damian was not a crypto-dualist; he was a Christian who thought the world so profoundly corrupted by sin that for much of the time in his writings the consequence seems to be that matter as he knows it is as foul and depraved as any Cathar could have thought. Peter Damian was a recluse who loved the hermit life, and yet was prepared to travel and to preach; he represented both the monastic and the apostolic urges of the age. His fierce disdain of human weakness, his intolerant asceticism, made him despise, in terms which would now be regarded as virtually heretical by almost all the sane branches of the Christian Church, the material world and the human body. The world of spirit is good; the world of the flesh (though created by God) hopelessly corrupt; the mingling of the sexes is the symbol of that corruption at its worst; marriage a doubtful legal cover for sin. Like Damian's equally austere though less fanatical younger contemporary, St Anselm, he thought that very few would be saved; only a monk had more than a sporting chance.[20] There are times in reading Damian when one feels that only a hair's breadth separates him from the dualists, and one can understand why his world proved such fertile ground for dualist missionaries from the east in the following century. It is interesting to observe that Waldo, the founder of the Waldensians, before he became a heretic, was made to abjure the view that all folk living in the world and not sworn to poverty were damned.[21] The dualists, the Cathars, went further than Damian in two essential respects; they said that the material world was wholly evil, even in its creation, and they repudiated the whole hierarchy of the Church of which Peter Damian was senior cardinal bishop. The Cathars indeed set up a hierarchy of their own.

But this was not the only difference between Damian and the Cathars. Cathar dualism made it impossible to regard Jesus as a

[19] Peter Damian's ascetic views have been fully analysed by R. Bultot, *Christianisme et valeurs humaines, A. La doctrine du mépris du monde*, IV (i) *Pierre Damien* (Louvain-Paris, 1963).

[20] Bultot, p. 132; cf. R. W. Southern, *St Anselm and his Biographer* (Cambridge, 1963), p. 101 (on Anselm): 'Few will be saved, and most of these will be monks'.

[21] A. Dondaine, 'Aux origines du Valdéisme: une profession de foi de Valdès', *Archivum Fratrum Praedicatorum*, XVI (1946), pp. 191–235, esp. 231–2.

real human being; and it is this which sets off Catharism, along with all the Gnostic and dualist sects of history, as heretical in a very special and extreme way. Damian was one of the first men to show an interest in reviving the cult of the human Jesus[22] – of which the chief evidence in his century were the revival of interest in his human mother, and the First Crusade to recover for Christendom the scenes of his earthly life. By this reviving interest, which went hand in hand with a new acceptance of human values, so alien to Peter Damian himself, western Christendom slowly came once more to see the world as God's world. And so when Wolfram enunciated with all his fierce pride in his own order and his own world, the goodness of Christian marriage in spiritual, domestic, and carnal senses, he was drawing out a layman's interpretation of the implications of a movement sponsored by many of the great theologians of the previous two generations; and when St Francis preached to the birds or put together a Christmas crib he was not engaged in traditional sentimentalities, but showing with the vivid art of one of the world's great teachers his belief in a doctrine precisely the opposite of the Cathars.

In Francis's day the cardinal bishopric of Ostia was held by Hugolino, who later, as Pope Gregory IX, was to canonize both his old friends and protégés, St Francis and St Dominic, and to set on a proper footing the formal organization of the Holy Inquisition.[23] The man who set the Inquisition in legal frame, who inspired the first official collection of papal decretals, and who inherited and enshrined in his own person the legal tradition of Alexander III and of Innocent III, might be supposed to have a purely legalist view of the problem of heresy and of proper relations within the Church's hierarchy. Certainly, Hugolino could look at these problems with a lawyer's eye; equally certainly he did not always do so. In the sacristy of the basilica of St Francis at Assisi may still be seen the bull of Pope Honorius III, Gregory's predecessor, which quotes in full, and confirms, the Rule of St Francis. It has sometimes been seen as a triumph for Hugolino

[22] Cf. R. W. Southern, *Making of the Middle Ages* (1953), pp. 235 ff.

[23] On Hugolino, see below, pp. 191 ff.; E. Brem, *Papst Gregor IX bis zum Beginn seines Pontifikats* (Heidelberg, 1911); R. B. Brooke, *Early Franciscan Government* (Cambridge, 1959), pp. 59 ff.; Maisonneuve, ch. v.

and legalism that the Rule, whose form had altered at every whim of the founder down to 1223, should have been set in a form so rigid and enshrined in a papal decretal. The opposite view seems nearer to the truth. For Francis held that the Rule of 1223 was in essence the original revelation of 1209, enshrined in words that had been dictated to him by Christ himself. In 1215 the Lateran Council had forbidden new religious Orders to be formed, and this had been interpreted as a prohibition on new Rules. It is alleged indeed that some version of Francis's Rule was paraded in 1215,[24] but whether this be true or not, it is reasonably certain that a prolonged attempt was made to force Francis to accept an existing Rule, as Dominic had done, as the basis for his Order; and that Hugolino lent a hand in trying to persuade the saint. The bull of 1223 represents an almost total victory for Francis, and in the end he must have had his Cardinal Protector Hugolino as an ally. At the centre of Francis's idea for his Order lay a conception of obedience which involved whole-hearted submission by the saint himself to Pope, cardinals, bishops, priests, friars, yes, and to the beasts of the field – so long as they submitted to the revelation he had had from God himself.[25] One can call it a mark of inconsistency, or one can call it a touch of greatness; but it seems clear, whichever way it is viewed, that Cardinal Hugolino had submitted to Francis's spell and consented to be his ally in promulgating a Rule based on a principle of obedience which was sanctified anarchy; just as, later on, Pope Gregory was to protest vehemently against the attempt to set Francis's wishes in a formal legal frame. The eleventh century cannot be understood unless it is seen that it found room both for a profoundly pessimistic view of the world and of man's destiny, and for a new vision of the humanity of Jesus; nor can the Church of the thirteenth century be understood unless it is realized that it saw the repressive autho-

[24] Cf. the discussion in Grundmann, pp. 146 ff.; Esser, *ubi supra,* p. 240 n. (and *Scripta Leonis,* ed. R. B. Brooke (Oxford, 1970), pp. 204–5 and n.)

[25] The promise of obedience and the demand for obedience are set firmly side by side in the saint's *Testament*; the beasts of the field are cited in his description of obedience in *Salutatio virtutum* (*Opuscula* (2nd edn., Quaracchi, 1941), pp. 21, 80–2). Cf. esp. P. Sabatier in *Franciscan Essays*, I (British Soc. of Franciscan Studies, 1912), pp. 1–17, esp. p. 17; D. Knowles, *From Pachomius to Ignatius* (Oxford, 1966), pp. 80 ff.; below, p. 204.

ritarian nature of the Roman Church set in a pattern which was not fundamentally to alter for several centuries, and also saw the authorities of the Church welcome with open arms – and open eyes – the sublime anarchy which inspired St Francis.

In their own ways and their own worlds Peter Damian and St Francis were concerned to harness and direct the movements in popular religion of their times; both felt most at home, according to the Italian tradition, in hermit retreats, but in many respects they lived in entirely different worlds. The popular religious movement of the late tenth and early eleventh centuries showed itself here and there in heresy; more widely and more frequently in activities which could be safely accepted under the umbrella of the Catholic Church. An example is the greatly increased popularity of pilgrimages – far and near; and of pilgrimages not only to the shrines and relics of the saints, but to any great ecclesiastical centre. One sees the aspirations of the eleventh century writ large in Norman England where the most ambitious of European peoples built on what they clearly regarded as (roughly speaking) a *tabula rasa*. They built a multitude of churches; but what is especially striking in relation to later architectural movements is that their cathedral and major abbey churches were enormous – as large as anything the Christian world has ever seen; their parish churches were commonly tiny. To say that the great increase in the size of churches which took place in the tenth and eleventh centuries in so many parts of Europe was due to rising population would be a superficial view of the case.

The Norman cathedral of East Anglia was nearly four times the length of its predecessor; now that the scale of pre-Conquest Winchester is known, the proportion there is found to be much closer;[26] yet the contrast between a string of chapels loosely tied together and a great basilica must have been striking. It is clear that Norman cathedrals were commonly far bigger than their predecessors, Norman parish churches much the same size. In England the importance of shrines and cult centres in the eleventh century tends to be dimmed by the (probably very temporary) Norman distaste for English relics. But otherwise it is a fair

[26] See M. Biddle in *Antiquaries' Jour.*, L (1970), forthcoming, for his final statement of the evidence; see also, below Ch. 8.

sample, on a grandiose scale, of the evidence of western Christendom at large. It may be that it is also superficial to relate size of great churches to the throngs of people who used them. The size of great churches was dictated by many factors. But the relation existed, and for France it is recorded with particular frankness and fidelity by Abbot Suger, who tells us not once but three times over that he embarked on the rebuilding of St-Denis because it was too small, and it was too small because of the vast throngs of pilgrims who came on the festivals of St-Denis and his colleagues to view the abbey reliquaries.[27]

Too little is known about popular religion in the eleventh century for precise and confident statements to be made about many aspects of it. But St-Denis reveals one clear centre. Within the screen, in choir and sanctuary, were the places set aside for the privileged, the monks, the few whom St Peter Damian and St Anselm reckoned to have a real chance of salvation. In the nave gathered from time to time a great throng of adherents; men and women hoping, as it were, to touch the hem of the garment of the true Christians within. The Church held out its arms to these folk in the eleventh century; it was not till the twelfth that the Cistercians built churches from which the laity were excluded; most of the great monastic churches of the eleventh century lay in centres of population or near main roads. In northern Europe great naves were built in part at least to shelter lay visitors from the climate and to make them feel in a measure part of Christendom. It is recorded by one contemporary[28] that when Pope Urban II preached the First Crusade he was quite conscious that one of its effects would be to provide Christian work for many of the most unruly elements in Christendom outside its confines; few greater blows have been struck for the peace of Europe than the preaching of the First Crusade. This was not quite immediately apparent, for the Pope unleashed a popular crusading doctrine very different from his own; a doctrine of holy war, which justified the slaughter of the heathen on the grounds that they were bound for hell in any

[27] *Abbot Suger on the abbey church of St-Denis,* ed. E. Panofsky (Princeton, 1946), pp. 42–3, 86–9, 134–5. See below, p. 167.

[28] Fulcher of Chartres: on this see *History of the Crusades*, ed. K. M. Setton, I (Philadelphia, 1955), p. 242.

case and so no harm could be done by speeding their passage.[29] The first non-Christians to fall under the eyes of the popular crusades were the Jews, and the Jewish massacres which accompanied the start of this and other crusades have lent a peculiar horror in modern eyes to the whole crusading movement. This horror, which I share to the full, may serve however to emphasize the distance between popular doctrines and the intentions of the Pope. In a similar way, the Church looked very different to the men who looked across the screens to the elect from the view of the elect themselves. But there was also common ground; and it is no coincidence that when the uncommunicative exteriors of great Romanesque churches burst into speech in the early twelfth century, it was a powerful presentation of Christ the King in apocalyptic setting at Moissac and of Christ the King supervising the Last Judgement and its consequences at Beaulieu and St-Denis which caught the eye of the adherents as they thronged round the west portals.

To use the division into the elect, or the perfect, and the adherents, is indeed to follow the jargon of the Cathars. The world of popular religion of the eleventh and early twelfth centuries very clearly provided fertile soil for the acceptance and spread of the doctrines of the Cathars. The eleventh-century world seems to have been a comparatively simple one; in some parts popular fervour could shade off into heresy indeed, but it was still possible for the Church to recover the respect of many of those who might otherwise have gone into heresy by harnessing the fervour and leading and guiding it. Not entirely, perhaps, but mainly. In the twelfth century the unity of western Christendom was destroyed. The twelfth-century heresies have never achieved the prestige of those of the sixteenth-century reformers, partly because only the Waldensians, now a comparatively small communion, can claim descent from them, and partly because we have not entirely grown out of a view of history in which the attitude of kings and princes is the determining factor. Nor can it be claimed that any twelfth-century heretical theologian whose works are known can bear comparison with the greatest of the sixteenth-century reformers.

[29] Cf. Brooke, *Europe in the Central Middle Ages* (1964), pp. 354 ff., esp. pp. 364–5.

There is no question here of taking sides in a dispute as to whether the Reformation really took place in the twelfth or the sixteenth century. The point is that so far as one can tell, the world of the eleventh century was a comparatively simple world, that of the twelfth much more varied. Humanism, asceticism, and dissent all flourished. In the course of the next two centuries the human Jesus and his human mother came to sit side by side – without displacing – the terrifying judge of St-Denis and the majestic king of Moissac and Vézelay. The Cistercians closed their churches to the laity, but St Bernard himself found in human affection the supreme earthly analogy for divine love, and in doing so paved the road which made possible a moderate revival of human values. Above all, the population of heaven increased. There can be few more decisive frontiers in doctrine than that which separates the Christian view that the world is God's world from the dualist's which (in various forms) makes the devil or an evil God the creator of the world. Yet in the realm of sentiment, it is hard not to think that the would-be Christians who, in half-despair, flocked to St Denis's church in the hope of a miracle – for nothing short of a miracle could save them – were nearer to the adherents who gathered to do service to the *perfecti*, the pure, the Katharoi, than to the lay world of Wolfram von Eschenbach. Wolfram was no doubt exceptional: in *Parzival* he countered the Cathar doctrine of the wickedness of matter and of human values to a degree which would have made even St Francis shudder. In *Willehalm* he took a story from the old world of the crusading epic and turned it on its head: instead of the heathen being cattle for the slaughter, they are God's handiwork.

The picture of religious sentiment revealed by these attitudes, and by all the surviving evidence from Latin and vernacular literature, from architecture and from art, is of a world of rapidly growing diversity. In every part of Europe we find evidence of diversity, though in different proportions in different places. This diversity did not disappear in the thirteenth century, but it shifted its ground and its balance; and some elements in it sharply declined. Among the most notable of these is the catastrophic decline of the Cathars. In a measure this was the fruit of persecution. As we have seen, it is hard to believe that this was the major cause, impossible to believe it the only cause. Still less can it be attributed to conversion. The career of St Dominic reveals how little fruit even the most expert of preachers could hope for in this direction. It is noticeable that St Francis never attempted to convert the Cathars by direct action. There is indeed remarkably little indication in his own writings or the early lives that there were any heretics in Europe at the time – little beyond a stern warning in the Rule about friars who fall into heresy, an occasional vague reference and one story about a single meeting with a heretic.[30] Yet Assisi looks down on the valley of Spoleto, where a Cathar bishop flourished throughout his lifetime; and on one occasion, it seems, a Cathar was made *podestà* of the city. In later life he traversed ground where they grew thickly, and of their existence the son of a merchant who traded over central and north Italy into the south of France can never have been ignorant. It seems that Francis had a deliberate policy of avoiding direct argument; and Dominic too, after the great change of direction to which he was inspired in his last years (partly perhaps by falling under Francis's spell),[31] turned his back on the heretics and made all Christendom his parish. In their different ways, these men were two of the most inspired teachers of the Middle Ages, and they seem clearly to have reckoned that the right way to combat heresy was to preach to the Church at large. If we compare Francis and Wolfram – almost exact contemporaries brought up in very different contexts – we can see how the ground was prepared for the spread of a doctrine more humane, less grim and forbidding, than that of the Cathars. It is an extraordinary paradox that the new world of sentiment and a harsh system of suppression should have been welcomed by the Church's leaders simultaneously; even stranger that the friars, especially the Dominicans, should have become the agents of the Inquisition. It is even possible that Dominic himself would have condoned such conduct, though it must be said that we have virtually no evidence on the matter – in spite of the ink which has been spilt in discussing it. But it is of such paradoxes that history is made. Peter Damian reckoned marriage, to take a single, piquant example, a doubtful legal cover

[30] The details are collected in Esser, *ubi supra*, pp. 225–64; see esp. pp. 239 ff.
[31] See below, pp. 222–9.

for sin. Wolfram von Eschenbach propounded a view in which romantic and religious elements could meet in harmony; the Church's theologians struggled through the nets of tradition to erect marriage into a sacrament;[32] but the society in which they all lived, by and large, regarded it as a union by which was determined something of greater consequence—the passage of landed property – and it is hard to say that the doctrines of romantic love, presented to us in serious and comic dress with great variety and sophistication by the poets of the late twelfth and thirteenth centuries, seriously impinged on the practice of marriage in high society before the seventeenth century. Here is a sample of the rich complexity, subtlety, and absurdity of this problem, which will occupy scholars for many years to come.

[32] Cf. above, pp. 48 ff.

8

Religious Sentiment and Church Design in the Later Middle Ages

A lecture delivered in the John Rylands Library, Manchester, on Wednesday, 14 December 1966.

MY interest in this subject was aroused by a famous paper by the greatest of English liturgical scholars, Edmund Bishop, 'On the history of the Christian altar'.[1] If precision of technique made Bishop a scholar, it was a rare combination of breadth and depth of vision, with a style which is fussy and Victorian in outward show, but which within reveals a philosopher's precision, that made him one of the immortals. The special gift of his finest essays was to reveal that major differences in liturgical practice or in church design reflected, among other things, profound differences in religious sentiment. 'One and single as may be the Christian Divine worship in its essence, the liturgical forms and formulae of the age with which we are now dealing [in this case the fifth century] are the genuine products of the native character, the proper and often very different religious feeling, of the various races, peoples, "churches", making up the one Church.'[2] And he went on to point out the way in which the fundamental difference in the tradition of east and west was reflected in the difference between the eastern altar hidden behind the iconostasis, and the

[1] *Liturgica Historica* (Oxford, 1918), pp. 20–38.
[2] Op. cit. p. 22.

western open to view. The roots of this difference he found in the earliest surviving liturgical books of east and west.

> 'In the Greek books a dominant note is this, the concern of the officiating priest, personally and individually, for his own unworthiness to offer the sacrifice; it is awe, fear, dread that speak to us in these Greek orders. This note may be said to be entirely absent from the Roman formulae, which may be counted by hundreds; whilst in its stead this dominant note may be discerned: that the sacrifice is the sacrifice of combined priest and people, *"et plebis et praesulis"*.'[3]

Bishop's doctrine that religious sentiment is a reflection of national character (to express it somewhat crudely), though deeply felt and subtly expressed, is not one which should appeal to scholars of the late twentieth century. But he showed in a profound and convincing way that major elements in liturgical practice and church design are not due to whims of taste and fashion, but also express widely felt sentiments and attitudes; or, as I should put it, in every substantial variety in church design one may find an attempt to solve a problem in a church's function, to follow this and that new or old fashion, and to reflect in an appropriate way some of the religious sentiments of the age. Re-reading Bishop's paper started me a little further along a line of speculation which had teased my mind in some measure for many years. Not far from Stratford-on-Avon there is a spot where, owing to the extreme confusion of county boundaries, four shires meet. My purpose is to pursue a line of thought, a string of problems; they are problems on the boundaries of five fields of study, of liturgy, theology, literature, archaeology, and *Kunstgeschichte*, and it would be absurd to pretend to have solved these.

The *Lay Folks' Mass Book*, a devotional manual probably composed in French by an archdeacon in the diocese of York between 1170 and 1189, and known to us from an English translation of about a hundred years later, lays it down that when the host and chalice are elevated in the canon of the mass, the lay worshipper, who is presumed at this stage to be kneeling, shall

[3] p. 23.

lift his eyes and look at God's body and blood re-created in his presence.[4] There is no doubt that elevation of the host – later followed by the chalice – was becoming a widespread practice in the late twelfth century, and that its purpose was to enable the faithful to see the host and the chalice. The way had already been prepared by a practice of the late eleventh century and later of raising the host during consecration. Elevation proper began to be a widespread practice in the time of Pope Innocent III (1198–1216), and the ambiguity which has covered the practice ever since was revealed by Innocent's successor, Honorius III, who ordered the faithful to bow their heads in reverence at the elevation.[5] It is tolerably clear (and quite explicit in some late copies of the *Lay Folks' Mass Book*)[6] that what was expected of the faithful was that they should both look and bow; and in the Catholic revival of Mary's reign this was made, in some places, a test of orthodoxy. There is a nice story in Fox's *Acts and Monuments* of a magistrate who hid in a rood loft so as to spy on the congregation, and punished those who failed to gaze on the consecrated host.[7]

This might naturally lead us to assume that every effort would be made to ensure that all the worshippers in a church could see the priest at the altar and the elevated host from a kneeling position. It is true that in southern Europe, and especially in Spain, some major churches were built in the later Middle Ages with remarkably open vistas; and this may be one of the reasons for the fashion for open churches which became so widespread in Catholic countries in the age of the Baroque. But in many parts of

[4] Ed. T. F. Simmons (*Early English Text Soc.*, 1879), p. 38, cf. 28; on its probable author, Jeremiah, Archdeacon of Cleveland, see Sir C. Clay, *Yorkshire Archaeological Journ.*, XXXVI (1944–7), pp. 412–15, cf. 427–8. Cf. A. Vallance, *English Church Screens* (London, 1936), p. 40.

[5] See *Dict. de Théologie Catholique*, art. Élévation (IV. ii. pp. 2320 ff.); *Decretales Greg. IX.* iii, 41, 10; cf. S. J. P. Van Dijk and J. H. Walker, *The Origins of the Modern Roman Liturgy* (London, 1960), pp. 360 ff.

[6] Cf. pp. 38–9.

[7] *Acts and Monuments* (ed. G. Townsend, London, 1843–9), VIII, p. 663; cited Vallance, p. 40. On screens in general, F. Bond, *Screens and Galleries in English Churches* (London, 1908) is still fundamental; on their later history, with valuable insights into the medieval background, see G. W. O. Addleshaw and F. Etchells, *The Architectural Setting of Anglican Worship* (London, 1948), esp. chap. II.

northern Europe, and nowhere more conspicuously than England, the late Middle Ages saw the construction of ever more formidable screens; and if the need of the laity to see the sacrament were the only consideration in church design (which, needless to say, it has never been) one could only marvel at the perverse ingenuity which provided every possible obstacle to the human gaze by planting a forest of marvellously carved woodwork, and then preserved a meagre view of the high altar by cutting squints and holes in walls and screens.[8] The screens of the later Middle Ages obliterated the vista in cathedral and abbey churches, and divided even parish churches into distinct compartments. In marked contrast, a Norman Archbishop of Canterbury or Bishop of Norwich had apparently been visible over screen and altar to worshippers in the far west of the nave. In recent times anyone sitting behind an altar has been liable to be obscured by cross and candlesticks. I think it is clear that at every period of the Middle Ages it was a common practice to have no permanent ornaments on the altar at all. One cannot say if this was the normal practice; we do not know, cannot know, the answer to that question. One of the constant difficulties of this whole topic, indeed, is that historians of architecture and religious sentiment have commonly failed to realize how great a variety of practice existed at all times and in many different regions. In early centuries only paten and chalice, gospel book and reliquaries were allowed on the altar at all; and there are many pictures of altars from every age, with only such things, or nothing at all, upon them.[9] In the mid and late middle ages one commonly finds a

[8] Vallance, pp. 40 ff. See Pl. III.

[9] For instance, an altar with a reliquary and hosts exposed on it, but nothing else, is shown in the scene of Harold's oath in the Bayeux Tapestry (the table under Harold's left hand is clearly an altar); to take another, much later example, the *Mass of St Giles* in the National Gallery (15th cent.) shows the altar of St Denis with retable and side curtains, and the great cross of St Eloi behind it, but with no crucifix or candles on the altar – nothing, in fact, save the missal. (On this picture cf. W. M. Hinkle in *Journal of the Warburg and Courtauld Institutes,* XXVIII (1965), pp. 110 ff. It is reproduced in *Flowering of the Middle Ages,* ed. J. Evans, London, 1966, p. 25). There is, of course, much variety in late medieval pictures of altars. On altars in general, see J. Braun, *Der Christliche Altar* (2 vols., Munich, 1924); cf. Bishop, loc. cit. and pp. 301–13.

single candle, or one candle and a cross, or two candles and a cross, portrayed on altars; but these were clearly not universally used, and may commonly have been there for service-time alone; and it was not until the thirteenth century that we first hear of six candles on the altar, and then only in the papal liturgy, and only during pontifical high mass.

But if the bishop is unlikely to have been hidden behind cross and candlesticks when he sat on his throne or came down from it to pronounce a blessing, may he not have been obscured from view by one or more screens? The whole question of the early history of screens is very obscure.[10] We may be sure that from the late thirteenth century onwards they tended to grow higher and more opaque; but so far as I know no recent study has been made of the very slender evidence as to the nature and height of eleventh- and twelfth-century screens. None survives in this country.*

[10] The discussion in Bond, pp. 1–11, is still useful, although not all his explanations are convincing. The early history of the rood, and its relation to the rood screen, particularly need investigating. On the Carolingian evidence, see E. Doberer in *Karl der Grosse*, III (Dusseldorf, 1965), pp. 203–33. The difficulty of precision at the point where precision is most needed – the problem of how much a worshipper could see, of how complete was the vista – is well illustrated by the case of the Cistercians. M. Aubert, in his great *L'architecture cistercienne en France* (2 vols., 2nd edn., Paris, 1947), I, p. 317, asserts that the lay brothers could not see the high altar in a Cistercian church. But the only texts he cites are of the thirteenth century, and while they show that in at least one Cistercian church the lay brothers' choir was a separate compartment, they reveal nothing about what could or could not be seen over the screens. It seems hard, however, to believe that Cistercian screens would have been more substantial or more draught proof than others of their day; and the onus of proof seems to be on those who would deny that lay brothers could observe conventual mass at the high altar in the twelfth century at least. In general, the problem is difficult because the evidence is fragmentary and what there is defies generalization: it is clear that as in so many aspects of medieval architectural history, there was much variety in every period. (Since this was written I have observed that rough patches on the nave piers at Buildwas Abbey (Salop) suggest screens round the lay brothers' choir about 5 ft high, with choir screens about 1 ft higher.)

*[Additional note. Reference should have been made to Sir William St John Hope's paper 'Quire Screens in English Churches . . .', *Archaeologia*, LXVIII (1916–17), pp. 43–110, and to his account of the lost twelfth-century screen at Ely, which was a wall 14 ft 6 in high (perhaps lower originally) pierced by three arches. See. esp. Pls. IX–X and pp. 86 ff.]

As far as my knowledge goes, twelfth-century screens on the continent are either very low or have very open arcades.[11] I have found nothing in the written sources to suggest that English screens in the first half of the twelfth century were more formidable than the screen of that period which still adorns San Clemente in Rome; and though I am fully aware of the danger of deducing architectural forms from isolated miniatures, I am inclined to suppose that the picture of St Æthelwold blessing in his famous Benedictional suggests that screens of dimensions similar to that in San Clemente were known in England in the tenth century at least.[12] I am inclined, too, to suppose that the practice of elevating host and chalice is likely to have grown up in churches in which it was a comparatively easy matter to see the priest, even when one was kneeling. By the same token, there are other elements in church design in the eleventh and twelfth centuries which seem nonsensical unless one presupposes a long and splendid vista. Abbot Suger tells us that women used to stand on their menfolk's heads on the great festivals of the saints of St-Denis in order to see mass celebrated and the relics presented, not because screens obscured the view, but simply because of the human throng.[13] The fact that a new cathedral could be planned in Norwich in the 1090s with the bishop sitting on a modest stone seat behind the high altar would be somewhat absurd if no one could see him – or even if no one in the nave could ever be expected to see him; and the same absurdity applies even more forcibly to the kind of plan Suger favoured by which the place taken by the bishop's seat in Norwich was occupied by the shrine

[11] M. Salmi, *Églises romanes de Toscane* (Paris, 1961), Pl. 70, shows a low twelfth-century stone screen; Pls. 35 (Pisa, Duomo), 63 (Carrara) also show low marble and stone screens. Pls. 133, 139 show sanctuaries, which could be paralleled, e.g. in Germany, raised above a low arcade and clearly visible to a distant worshipper.

[12] For San Clemente see *Atlas of the Early Christian World,* ed. F. Van der Meer and C. Mohrmann (London, 1959), Pl. 430 (and on its date, L. Boyle, O.P., in *Archivum Fratrum Praedicatorum,* XXX (1960), pp. 417–27); for Æthelwold, F. Wormald, *The Benedictional of St Ethelwold* (London, 1959), Pl. 8. See Pls. I, II.

[13] E. Panofsky, *Abbot Suger on the abbey church of St-Denis* (Princeton, 1946), pp. 42–3, 88–9, 134–5.

of the patron saint. This practice was known as early as the seventh century, but it flourished most conspicuously (so far as our observation goes) in the eleventh, twelfth, and thirteenth centuries.[14] One can be unusually confident about some of the aims of the Norman cathedral at Norwich, not only because its main fabric survives relatively complete, but also because we know how it contrasted with its pre-Conquest predecessor at North Elmham.[15] Norwich Cathedral took two generations to complete, but the essential plan seems to be that which was in the mind of Bishop Herbert Losinga when he finally moved the see of East Anglia there in the 1090s. He brought with him the synthronon from Elmham, that is, his own stone throne and the seats of his senior clergy which were apparently arranged in a semi-circle round the apse at Norwich as nearly as could be as they had been in his earlier cathedral. Otherwise the contrast was complete: Norwich is nearly four times the length of Elmham, and vaster in every proportion. It may be that Elmham was exceptionally small; and it is clear that the Normans brought fashions and styles with them that they had been accustomed to in Normandy; that were, as is well known, the local expression of a fashion which spread all over the north of France and had a close relationship to ideas of design and ornament for large Romanesque churches over a much wider area than that. None the less the contrast between old and new must have been very conspicuous in the diocese of East Anglia. If one had entered Elmham Cathedral in 1066 when the bishop was presiding at mass, one would have found oneself

[14] Braun, *Der Christliche Altar,* II, pp. 547 ff. (and cf. idem, *Die Reliquiaren,* Freiburg, 1940); M. Grabar, *Martyrium: recherches sur le culte des reliques et l'art chrétien antique*, I (Paris, 1946), ch. v, pp. 400–581. Grabar probably exaggerates the influence of relics on church design in the period.

[15] See plans in A. W. Clapham, *English Romanesque Architecture before the Conquest* (Oxford, 1930), p. 89, and *English Romanesque Architecture after the Conquest* (1934) (henceforth Clapham, I and II), Fig. 11; on Elmham, see H. M. and J. Taylor, *Anglo-Saxon Architecture* (2 vols., Cambridge, 1965), I, pp. 228 ff; S. E. Rigold in *Medieval Archaeology,* VI–VII (1962–3); on the bishop's throne and the history of the synthronon see C. A. Ralegh Radford in *Archaeological Journal,* CXVI (1959), pp. 115–32. S. E. Rigold, art. cit. p. 70 n., has suggested that the synthronon may have come from the old site of the see of Suffolk at Hoxne; but see my article in *Collectanea Stephan Kuttner,* ed. A. M. Stickler, *Studia Gratiana*, XII (1967), pp. 39–60, esp. 41–2.

face to face with Æthelmer, brother of Archbishop Stigand; if one had entered Norwich on a similar occasion when the great nave was complete, one would have found oneself similarly face to face with Bishop Everard or William Turba; but the difference would be analogous to the difference between seeing a great man across a drawing room and seeing him across the Albert Hall.

A similar story can be told, in certain respects with more precision, about the development of Canterbury Cathedral; and it enables us to spread our contrast more widely, to observe the development of medieval church design through three main phases: first, the church of the early Middle Ages, sometimes a single building, sometimes a group, but rarely provided with a single focus; next, the great open basilicas of the eleventh and twelfth centuries, designed above all to emphasize a single focus; and, finally, the divided structures of the late Middle Ages.

In Canterbury the plans of the two great churches, the Cathedral and St Augustine's Abbey, as they were on the eve of the Norman Conquest, are tolerably well-known – the cathedral from Eadmer's description, the abbey by excavation.[16] The abbey was one of the classic examples of a great church made up of several chapels loosely strung together, with no great central basilica for large gatherings or celebrations. On the eve of the Conquest Abbot Wulfric was engaged in building his rotunda, which would have tied the group of buildings together in a way reminiscent of St Benigne at Dijon, and (more remotely) St Riquier and other continental churches whose plans included circular, or otherwise centrally planned, chapels in imitation of the church of the Holy Sepulchre.[17]

The pre-Conquest cathedral was a more unified building, a basilica with an apse both to east and to west, like many ninth- and tenth-century churches, especially in Germany. As in these, the unity of design was broken by a variety of major altars; and in

[16] Cf. Clapham, I, pp. 85 ff., 149 ff.; H. M. and J. Taylor, I, pp. 134 ff.; R. W. Southern, *St Anselm and his biographer* (Cambridge, 1963), pp. 260 ff.

[17] Cf. C. Heitz, *Recherches sur les rapports entre architecture et liturgie à l'époque carolingienne* (Paris, 1963), esp. pp. 106 ff. for the influence of the Church of the Holy Sepulchre and the history of the centrally planned church; cf. R. Krautheimer, in *Journal of the Warburg and Courtauld Institutes*, V (1942), pp. 1 ff.

certain respects its liturgical arrangements seem to have been very similar to those at Fulda. The high altar in the midst of the eastern apse was dedicated to Christ: but the main celebrations took place in the western apse. On great festivals the Abbot of Fulda sat enthroned in a raised chapel at the west end, and came forward to celebrate (still facing east) over the altar and the tomb of St Boniface. In Canterbury Cathedral, Lanfranc's immediate predecessors also sat enthroned in a raised chapel to the west, and celebrated facing east over the heads of the people, who turned their faces to the east and their backs on the Archbishop.[18] The difference was that at Canterbury the western altar was St Mary's, and the great reliquaries lay in the eastward part of the church: St Dunstan's altar in the choir surmounted by a large 'pyramid', Sts Ælfheah, Oda, and Wilfrid in the apse, on either side of and behind the altar of Christ, raised up, like the western apse, above a crypt in which the relics were actually housed. This kind of combination of a unified architectural scheme with a church lacking any single central focus is very clearly revealed on the famous St Gall plan.[19] This shows, not only separate altars or groups of altars in the eastern and western apses, but the whole church broken up into boxes giving an effect somewhat analogous to the family box-pews of seventeenth- and eighteenth-century England. How high the screens were between such chapels is an insoluble problem. Surviving fragments of Carolingian screenwork suggest that they could be fairly substantial, and of stone, and obscure the view of a kneeling worshipper.[20] But only slight fragments survive, so far as I know, and those owe their survival partly to the strength and durability of the material. It is natural to suppose that Carolingian screens were normally of wood and comparatively slight affairs, and Eadmer clearly intends us to presume that St Dunstan's pyramid, the altars of Christ and of Wilfrid

[18] Eadmer in Gervase of Canterbury, *Hist. Works,* ed. W. Stubbs (Rolls Series, 1879), I, pp. 7–9; cf. Clapham, Taylor, loc. cit. For the somewhat scanty evidence on the orientation of celebrants in the early Middle Ages, see Braun, *Der Christliche Altar,* II, pp. 412 ff.

[19] H. Reinhardt, *Der St Galler Klosterplan* (St Gallen, 1952), esp. frontispiece.

[20] See *Karl der Grosse,* III, p. 221 (Abb. 1, 2).

were visible to the worshippers. The Archbishop was only invisible because the people turned their backs on him.

We can see behind these examples three forces clearly at work; and at work simultaneously, so that if we ignore any one of them the buildings of the ninth, tenth, and eleventh centuries become immediately unintelligible. The design of Fulda was a direct imitation of St Peter's Rome, and as characteristic a product of the Carolingian renaissance as the importation of St Benedict's *Rule* or the Gregorian Sacramentary in the same period; but a very striking event, because it was the first time (so far as we know) that a really large basilica had been built north of the Alps. Doubtless the Archbishop's position at Canterbury was also an imitation of Rome (as Eadmer hints) or of Fulda or of some other intermediary.[21] Medieval architecture was often imitative, and the idea that the spirit of the Gothic revival was somehow lacking in the Middle Ages is quite false. Thus when the University of Oxford commissioned a precise imitation of the Abbot's kitchen at Glastonbury and called it a chemical laboratory, they were doing very much what a German Cistercian community did in the early thirteenth century when they sent a lay brother to make precise drawings of the Abbey of Clairvaux so that he could reproduce it stone by stone and drain by drain for their own abbey.[22] Medieval architects in all periods could also be original and creative, as I need hardly say; and when they imitated their models could be surprisingly various, as various as the Church of the Holy Sepulchre and old St Peter's. In a recent book on Carolingian architecture, Carol Heitz has argued that some of the most striking features of Carolingian design (including the imitations of the Church of the Holy Sepulchre) reflect the liturgical prac-

[21] On Fulda see Heitz, pp. 65–7, emphasizing the liturgical background to this as to all church plans of the age; but not denying the evident influence of Rome (in this passage I owe much to an unpublished paper by Dr R. A. Markus). Eadmer (loc. cit.) indicates that the pre-Conquest cathedral at Canterbury was also an imitation of St Peter's. It could be argued that while in style and much else the two Cathedrals reflected northern tastes, the difference in design between Lanfranc's and its predecessor was also the difference between two types of basilica in Rome.

[22] M. Aubert, *L'architecture cistercienne en France*, I, pp. 97–8 (for the Oxford analogy, see *Victoria County History, Oxford*, III, p. 58).

tices of the age; and that features like Wulfric's rotunda were the setting for the rise of liturgical drama, especially for the representations of the visit to the tomb on Easter morning and the other liturgical and dramatic events of Holy Week.[23] As a single explanation of changes in design the thesis seems palpably inadequate; that such considerations played a part he would seem to have established in a thorough and ingenious manner. Liturgy apart, the multiplicity of altars in the St Gall plan very probably reflects the larger spread of relics, and almost certainly the increasing number of priests who could and would wish to celebrate mass. In the sixth century, when a monastery might expect to have only one priest, and some had none at all, so many altars would have collected the dust. The end of the process did not come till the twelfth century, when it came to be assumed that all choir monks would ultimately be priests, and daily celebration of mass became the norm; but the development which lay behind this goes much further back, and the multiplication of altars is a clear indication of it.

In the Cistercian plan and style one finds a close union of function, fashion, and religious sentiment: without any of these they are wholly unintelligible; and yet the result was buildings in many ways strikingly different from the other fashions of the age. The contrast between the austere and whitewashed churches built by St Bernard's disciples and Suger's lavish, richly coloured St-Denis clearly illustrates the divergent attitudes of twelfth-century designers.[24] It reveals the danger of taking one or another feature of an age and claiming it as in some sense characteristic or typical; much damage has been done to genuine historical enquiry by the romantic or idealist search for the 'climate' of an age. It is often in diversity, in the range of possibilities open to men, that one finds a truer key to understanding.

Canterbury Cathedral, as Lanfranc found it on his accession in 1070, had some resemblance to a great basilica (one must suppose) in that a vista opened from one end to the other. But the

[23] Heitz, esp. pp. 175 ff.

[24] See F. Bucher in *Comparative Studies in Society and History*, III (1960–1), pp. 89–105; Aubert, *passim*; and on Suger, Panofsky, op. cit. (some of Suger's gifts to St-Denis are illustrated in *The Flowering of the Middle Ages*, ed. J. Evans (London, 1966), p. 26).

lack of a single focus, and the multiplicity of altars and chapels, made it also resemble the divided church beloved of the Carolingians, of which the jumble of chapels in St Augustine's Abbey nearby was a striking example. Lanfranc swept the old cathedral away and within seven years[25] had built a new cathedral – a remarkably short time even by twentieth-century standards. It is hardly likely that Lanfranc's cathedral was substantially larger than its predecessor, and one must assume that its conception and plan appeared to Lanfranc sufficiently different to justify the enormous expense and energy involved. It is clear that it was an open basilica; in plan and design it was similar to the great churches of Normandy familiar to Lanfranc in his middle life, most notably to his own Abbey of St Étienne, Caen. St Dunstan's tomb ceased to be a central feature, or even a feature at all; and St Ælfheah was for a time altogether removed from the calendar.[26] This disappearance of the local saints at Canterbury is one of various pieces of evidence that when the Normans first came they doubted or despised the native English saints. In most churches the reaction was probably quite short-lived. There seems little doubt, however, that the absence of Dunstan and Ælfheah from Lanfranc's scheme, and their restoration to prominence in the new choir undertaken in the time of St Anselm, correctly reflect the much stronger sympathy with English saints and English traditions that one would expect in the man who so fully won the confidence and admiration of the English monk Eadmer that he dedicated his best energies to writing books in Anselm's honour.

Thus in Lanfranc's later life, a visitor to his cathedral who chanced to enter when the Archbishop was presiding at high mass would have found himself in a fine new church whose design encouraged him at once to turn his eyes to the main altar

[25] Eadmer, *Historia Novorum* (ed. M. Rule, *Rolls Series*, 1884), p. 13; the sources for our knowledge of Canterbury are laid out in O. Lehmann-Brockhaus, *Lateinische Schriftquellen zur Kunst in England* . . . , I (Munich, 1956), pp. 166–265; cf. Clapham, II, p. 21 and references. See Pl. IV (For 'c. 1171–78' in this Plate read 'c. 1071–78').

[26] F. A. Gasquet and E. Bishop, *The Bosworth Psalter* (London, 1908), pp. 32–3, 63–4. Other cases of Norman doubts or scepticism about English saints and relics are noted in D. Knowles, *Monastic Order in England* (Cambridge, 1940), pp. 118–19.

of the Saviour, and beyond it to the throne in the apse where he would see a formidable figure; the most eminent living exponent of the doctrine of the real presence presiding over the sacrament in which the body and blood of Christ were brought to Christ's altar.

If Anselm had lived to see the new choir finished, one might have witnessed, a generation later, a very different scene.[27] The Archbishop would still have presided from a throne behind the high altar according to a practice which one may think was by now rather old-fashioned in northern Europe – though practised in some Roman basilicas and Norwich Cathedral at least in this age. Anselm would have been much more distant than Lanfranc, as became that most remote and etherial of philosophers; but he would no longer have been the sole focus of attention. Dunstan and Ælfheah had been restored, and their altars, hiding their relics, lay before the Archbishop's throne, to right and left. Two generations later, shortly after the murder of Thomas Becket, the cathedral was gutted by fire – an event which conveniently provided the opportunity to recast the choir and extend it yet further, to provide a sumptuous setting for the shrine of Canterbury's most popular martyr. When this was complete, and Stephen Langton, the papal legate and the Archbishop of Rheims, had presided over Thomas's translation, on great occasions the Archbishop would be enthroned on the new stone chair, which still survives, and which was placed in what was now the traditional place for the Archbishop's throne, behind the high altar; so that a thirteenth-century Archbishop of Canterbury presided with St Thomas behind him and St Dunstan and St Ælfheah at his feet, surrounded by the saints whose earthly representative he was.

I have tried to reconstruct the relation between the Archbishop's throne and the altars and shrines of the saints as precisely and factually as one can. The deductions that one may draw from these arrangements, the purposes one may see in them, are matters for careful thought and delicate discrimination. But the story of the Archbishop's throne must be completed; for its somewhat absurd conclusion brings us back to the contrast with which I began.

It was probably normal at this date, when a great shrine rose behind the high altar of a cathedral, for the bishop to be moved to

[27] For what follows, see Ralegh Radford, art. cit.; cf. Southern, pp. 260 ff.

some other situation, so as not to obscure the saint or be obscured by him; commonly, throughout the mid and late Middle Ages, bishops' thrones were placed on the south side of choir or sanctuary.[28] In the course of the thirteenth century this seems to have happened at Canterbury. The traditional throne of the Archbishops, however, had now become part of the immemorial customs of the office, and so the stone chair was left in its place and new Archbishops solemnly enthroned in it. But in the course of the fourteenth century, as was common in that age, a large reredos rose behind the altar, thus drawing a curtain between the martyr and his flock. No doubt the pilgrims went in crocodile round the ambulatory to view him; one can hardly suppose that in any real sense the curtain was drawn over 'the holy blissful martyr' in the age of Chaucer. But the cathedral ceased to be a visual unity; the Carolingian conception of a jumble of rooms came back, much strengthened, and the Archbishop's chair disappeared from view along with his eminent predecessor. Oddly enough, however, the chair was left in place, and new Archbishops continued to be enthroned on it until the Reformation, though none of the congregation could witness the fact, so far as we know. To convince the witnesses that the task had really been accomplished, he was enthroned again in the normal chair to the south of the sanctuary. The whole process sounds comical to us; yet it can hardly have appeared so to contemporaries, or they would have abandoned the practice. It is interesting to reflect on the parallel between the Archbishop who was both invisible and visible and the elevation of the host and chalice in the late Middle Ages, visible to all,[29] yet behind a massive screen which made God's body seem distant and remote.

[28] On bishops' thrones see F. Bond, *Wood Carvings in English Churches: Stalls and Tabernacle Work* (London, 1910), ch. VII. On the siting of reliquaries, Braun, *Der Christliche Altar*, II, pp. 547 ff.

[29] In principle, that is: in practice, in a crowded parish church, the elevation cannot have been visible to all on all occasions; and in an abbey, collegiate, or cathedral church the screens were often opaque: in the late Middle Ages layfolk could only effectively attend mass in these when it was said at a nave altar. The provision of nave altars (with parclose screens), special aisles, and even parish churches close by the abbey church was increasingly common in the fourteenth and fifteenth centuries.

The changes of the late Middle Ages can be observed even more completely in my final witness, Winchester Cathedral. The position of the choir and the height of the screens before the late thirteenth century are obscure; there are some indications that when the central tower was rebuilt in the early twelfth century it was designed to accommodate a screen no higher than that in San Clemente.[30] By the end of the thirteenth century at least one lofty screen had been built, and by the mid fourteenth century two substantial screens of stone effectively blocked any view of the choir from the nave; a layman wishing to observe the elevation had to wait for a mass on one of the nave altars. The beautiful choir stalls which still survive are of about 1300; from then on the monks were enclosed on three sides by screens of considerable height. At the end of the fourteenth century the enormous reredos which also still survives (though much restored) rose behind the high altar, effectively hiding St Swithun and his shrine. Thus was completed a process which had begun when the retro-choir was first extended at the turn of the twelfth and thirteenth centuries. Step by step, culminating in the fourteenth century, St Swithun was swung round on his axis. No doubt his shrine had always been approachable from the ambulatory as well as from the choir; but in a real sense it had presumably faced west in earlier centuries, and dominated the vista in one of the longest naves ever built. By 1400 it was visible only from the east. The high altar itself was

[30] The top of the bases of the tower arches are higher within the choir than in the transepts, and seem higher than would be normal above the floor level (allowing for the difficulty of ascertaining with confidence the floor level in the twelfth century). This would be intelligible if the mouldings were meant to show over the top of a low screen similar in scale to that at San Clemente. The classical general study of Winchester Cathedral is still that of Willis in *Proceedings at the Annual Meeting of the Archaeological Institute of Gt Britain and Ireland, at Winchester, September 1845*. Of recent studies, N. Pevsner in *Archaeol. Journal,* CXVI (1959), pp. 133 ff., is of particular interest: he shows that the retro-choir was heightened soon after its first construction; the reasons for this are only briefly discussed, but one would suppose that in part at least it was to make the eastward approach to the shrine of St Swithun more dignified and effective. There has indeed been some dispute from time to time as to the site of Swithun's shrine, but the archaeological evidence, and analogy of similar arrangements, seem to leave little doubt that the chief shrine was in the 'feretory', immediately behind the high altar.

still visible, as in most great churches, from the choir aisles as well as from the choir. But in the early sixteenth century even this opening was screened for most of its length, so that by the time Bishop Fox's screen was complete, choir, sanctuary, and high altar were united in single box, entirely surrounded by screens of stone and wood; a rectangle lavishly carved and decorated, a church within a cathedral.

When Bishop Fox died in October 1528 a screen of stone and wood surrounded the monks of Winchester Cathedral on every side, cut them off in a physical sense from the world of pilgrims and blasphemers as they had never been cut off before; and – who shall say? – may even have helped to cut them off from the sense that their world was nearly at an end, that little more than a decade remained for the monastic community established by St Æthelwold. The monks have been gone these 400 years, yet the greater part of the screen still survives – and all of it survived till 100 years ago. This reflection must act as a check on any interpretation of its history which depends too closely on the comfort or the tastes of the monastic community. Yet it is clearly with them that one must start.

There is a curious analogy, significant if not stretched too far, between the history of church design and of the design of great houses in medieval England. The palaces of Yeavering and Cheddar were groups of separate halls and outbuildings, just as St Augustine's Canterbury or Glastonbury Abbeys had no great nucleated church but formed a group of ancient chapels which gradually tended to coalesce.[31] The greatest of the Norman palaces may have been similarly diverse, but their characteristic home was the large stone keep, which consisted essentially of two large rooms, and knew nothing of privacy. The great Norman churches were built in the golden age of the vista; nave and choir may in a sense have made them buildings of two rooms, though the link and the view between them was crucial. In the later Middle Ages the domestic buildings in castles and large houses became steadily less communal, less military; they set out on the slow path that

[31] Notes on the palaces as well as the abbeys will be found in H. M. and J. Taylor, I, pp. 134 ff., 154–5 (also P. Rahtz in *Medieval Archaeol.,* VI–VII (1962–3), pp. 53–66), pp. 250 ff., II, 696–7.

leads from William I's Tower of London, which was essentially a building with two rooms and a chapel, to Knole in Kent in its full seventeenth-century development, with 365 rooms. In part this reflects one of the most notable revolutions in our history: the development of the idea of privacy, of the notion that some parts of our life at least should not be exposed to public gaze, an idea entirely or almost entirely foreign to the early Middle Ages. It also reflects growing standards of comfort: more glass in the windows, more fireplaces, more wainscotting to hold draughts at bay; in a general way, more furniture, though the furniture of the late Middle Ages was hardly designed to suit present day conceptions of comfort. The relevance of these notions to our story is obvious enough. The wandering layman, the draught, the wild west wind, were excluded from the choir or the chancel of a church as they were excluded from a family's private apartments. The domestic buildings became less communal – dormitories were partitioned, and there seems to have been a general tendency for the dwindling monastic communities of the late Middle Ages to spend more and more of their time in cubicles and flatlets fitted up in the 'infirmary' and the abbot's or prior's lodging than in cloister, chapter house, and refectory. There are few finer examples of a late medieval manor house with many private rooms than the fifteenth-century infirmary and prior's lodging at Much Wenlock.[32]

Yet the domestic analogy will lead us to a superficial conclusion if we leave our problem at this point. Comfort and domestic privacy alone hardly explain the intricate richness of craftsmanship lavished on screens, roofs, altars, reredoses in late medieval choirs and chancels.[33] It is indeed helpful – it brings out some of the significance of the complete separation of nave and chancel in a parish church symbolized by the opaque tympanum which filled all the space behind the rood, above the screen and loft. But it cannot explain everything; it runs counter to the principle already established that major changes involve complex causes and it

[32] D. Knowles and J. K. S. St Joseph, *Monastic Sites from the Air* (Cambridge, 1952), pp. 54–5; D. H. S. Cranage, in *Archaeologia,* LXXII (1922), pp. 122 ff. (Much Wenlock).

[33] See especially Bond, Vallance, op. cit.; F. E. Howard and F. H. Crossley, *English Church Woodwork* (2nd edn., London, 1927).

throws no light at all on why the reredos has to fall (as it commonly does) between the high altar and the shrine: why St Swithun, St Thomas Becket, and the rest had to be excluded from the sanctuary along with the laymen.

This may have been partly due to their nefarious link with the laymen: that if one wished to exclude the gossiping throng from ear and eye one had to exclude also the shrine so many of them came to visit. But it is hard to believe that the shrine would have been hidden if the saints were still, as in some sense they had been in earlier centuries, the chief normal living occupants of their churches.

The domestic analogy contains within it the seed of its own dissolution. It prompts us to ask, for whom was the sanctuary enclosed and wainscotted?

High in the valley of the Rhône, where the spirits of Italy and the north may be supposed to mingle, there is still to be seen in the church of Münster in Goms a much restored reredos of the very early sixteenth century. It is a Liebfraukirche; and the various scenes from her life which adorn the reredos show that the Blessed Virgin was not excluded from the choir of her Church; the Madonna and Child which dominate its centre remind us that her son also came from time to time to live in her Church; and along the foot is a portrayal of the Last Supper which reflects the chief function of the altar on which it was meant to rest. The design presupposes – as do most reredoses and retables of the late Middle Ages – an altar normally bare, without cross or reliquary or tabernacle. Altar and sanctuary were dedicated essentially to the mass, to the active presence of the Lord, not to the reserved sacrament. The sacrament was indeed reserved. In the twelfth and thirteenth centuries, so far as we can tell, it was often left lying about, sometimes in a loose pyx, sometimes not enclosed at all. But as time passed it became common to enclose it in a hanging pyx or lock it in an aumbry in the wall; the tabernacle on the altar first appears in Germany in the late fourteenth century, and was known in most parts of Europe in the fifteenth, but the reserved sacrament was rarely a conspicuous object in the Middle Ages.[34]

[34] Braun, *Der Christliche Altar,* II, pp. 623 ff.; cf. pp. 574 ff., 599 ff. for the history of reservation, pyxes, etc.

It is clear, then, that once we have asked the question, for whose reception was the sanctuary enclosed, so that even Swithun was excluded, the answer must be, in its simplest terms, for God's presence in the sacrament of the altar. His presence there was reflected in many other relevant circumstances. Thus, St Francis of Assisi (unlike some of his followers) had an enormous respect for the humblest of priests, because they were the vehicles of divine grace which consecrated the blessed sacrament,[35] and one of the characteristic expressions of his own humility was his refusal to go beyond deacon's orders. This made it all the more appropriate that the clergy should have a separate compartment in a church, and provided the justification, in terms of religious sentiment, for their increasing domesticity inside as well as outside church. They were increasingly 'separated for the work', in a literal as well as a figurative sense.

Devotion to the Blessed Sacrament was one of the familiar aspects, and tendencies, of late medieval religion. Not everyone accepted the trend; where it was most strongly evidenced, there the reaction against it was powerful too. It may be more than a coincidence that the love of screens and wainscotting was most developed in the lands of Luther and of Wyclif and Cranmer – though one must remember that these screens also helped to keep the winds at bay in the same lands, which are the coldest in western Christendom.[36]

The trend, however, was clear enough. The tendency of late medieval sacramental theology and devotion was to emphasize the real presence to the exclusion of every other aspect of the sacrament, and especially to obscure its significance as the means whereby the faithful at large were united to the Mystical Body of Christ. No doubt this was reckoned implicit in the sacrament at all times, but in the late Middle Ages it was rarely emphasized.

[35] *Opuscula sancti Patris Francisci Assisiensis* (2nd edn., Quaracchi, 1941), passim, esp. p. 78 (*Testament*); the link between sacrament and priesthood is developed at length in *Epistola II*, pp. 99 ff.

[36] And also that it is partly because of the chances of survival that we reckon heavy screens especially characteristic of the north: the Anglican and Lutheran churches avoided the passion for destroying screens in the seventeenth century which was particularly marked in Catholic lands in the age of the Baroque (cf. Addleshaw and Etchells, pp. 15 ff., 37 ff.).

Instead the tradition stemming from Lanfranc and his predecessors urged the physical presence of Christ in the Eucharist; and the more sophisticated intellectual world of the thirteenth century saw Transubstantiation promulgated, a doctrine which emphasizes the depth and reality of a change not visible to the human eye. The great sacramental theologians of the late Middle Ages tended to emphasize, as did the architect who designed the Angel Choir at Lincoln, that the priest partakes in the life of heaven when he consecrates the bread and wine. Lanfranc's doctrine had been a natural counterpart of a visible consecration and led naturally to the elevation of host and chalice, to the realization throughout Christendom of the Roman tradition that the Eucharist was a visible event. The theology of later centuries tended to emphasize the personal nature of the Eucharist as an individual approach by the priest to the central mysteries of the Church, and it is this which helps to explain why the great mystics of the late Middle Ages tended to assume that the sacrament was an essential part of their mystical experience and not in any way separate from it. The natural counterpart of this way of approaching the Eucharist was the enclosed sanctuary, the remote, invisible choir of northern Europe in the late Middle Ages.

The story which lies behind this has never been fully told:[37] we obviously need a detailed study of late medieval religious devotions, which pays adequate notice to their variety and their peculiarities and to their profundity. Before this has been done it would be rash to make our analysis more precise than we have made it here. Yet I think I have said enough to explain why I think that the best commentary on the reredos of Winchester Cathedral is to be found in a famous passage in Thomas à Kempis's *De Imitatione Christi*.[38] Not that the builders of the reredos and Thomas had identical thoughts, but that both lived in the same world, a world of rich and varied experience, even if its own richness now seems inadequate to the central mysteries of the Christian faith.

[37] For an excellent introduction, with useful references, see C. W. Dugmore, *The Mass and the English Reformers* (London, 1958), Part I, esp. ch. IV; see also arts. 'Eucharistie' in *Dict. de Spiritualité* and *Dict. de Théologie Catholique*.

[38] III, i. 30–3, in ed. L. M. S. Delaissé, *Le manuscrit autographe de Thomas à Kempis et 'L'imitation de Jésus-Christ'* (Paris, etc., 1956), II, pp. 256–7.

'Many folk rush off to diverse places to visit the relics of the holy saints, and marvel to hear their deeds. They gape at the splendid buildings of churches and they kiss the saints' bones wrapped in silk and gold.

'And lo! You yourself are present, are with me, here, on the altar, my God, the holy of holies, creator of men, the Lord of the Angels.

'Often in viewing such things men show idle curiosity and a searching after novelty, and small fruit for betterment of life they pluck, especially when they go lightly hither and thither without true penitence.

'But here You are wholly present in the sacrament of the altar, God and man, Christ Jesus: here is taken bountiful fruit of eternal salvation as often as you are worthily and devoutly received.

'No light thoughts, nor idle curiosity, nor pandering to the senses, leads us to this, but strong faith, devout hope and pure charity.'

When we look at the churches of the late Middle Ages, we may often see reflected in them the selfish and material tastes and interests of the patrons and craftsmen who created them; but we may also see, if we look for it, a world of devotion and religious sentiment with a character of its own appropriate to the age which preceded Reformation and Counter-Reformation.

9

Innocent III and Gregory IX[1]

ON 28 September 1197, the Emperor Henry VI, King of Germany, Italy, and Sicily – very shortly to become (as he supposed) King of Jerusalem – suddenly died. The great empire which he had built up collapsed; and the Holy Roman Empire whose title he bore was disputed by rival claimants. On 8 January 1198, the elderly Pope, Celestine III, followed him to the grave, and on the same day the cardinals elected their youngest, most vigorous colleague, the Roman aristocrat Lotario dei Conti, as Innocent III. The Papacy had feared the ambitions of Henry VI, and Innocent seemed the man to grasp the opportunity afforded by his death. Soon after, on 6 April 1199, the other great dynastic

[1] The essential foundation for this chapter may be listed under three headings, corresponding to the three layers of papal activity in medieval Christendom.

(a) At the level of high theory, the precise position of Innocent III and his successors has been much disputed. See especially B. Tierney's bibliographical survey of canonist theory in *Traditio*, x (1954), pp. 594 ff. (supplemented in *Speculum*, xxxvii (1962), pp. 48 ff.), discussing W. Ullmann, *Medieval Papalism* (London, 1949); M. Maccarrone, *Chiesa e stato nella dottrina di papa Innocenzo III* (Rome, 1940); A. M. Stickler in *Traditio*, vii (1949–51), pp. 450 ff., and other studies; see now also J. A. Watt, *The Theory of Papal Monarchy in the Thirteenth Century* (London, 1966).

(b) For papal monarchy in practice over western Christendom, and for the range of papal activity, A. Luchaire, *Innocent III* (6 vols., i, ii, 3 ed., Paris, 1906–11; iii–vi, 1st ed., 1906–8) is still useful, though we should now want to add particularly to his account of curial and legal activity. See *Selected Letters of Innocent III concerning England,* ed. C. R. Cheney and W. H. Semple, (Nelson's Medieval Texts, 1953), and *The Letters of Pope Innocent III concerning*

figure of the 1190s, Richard I of England, also died. The stage was cleared; one of the most energetic, confident and high minded of the medieval Popes prepared to arrange a new scene.

It is worth dwelling for a moment on Henry and Richard, since what they represented was a foil, or a counter-poise, to the purposes of Pope Innocent. They were, like Innocent, international monarchs, entirely devoid of any deep sense of local or national loyalty. Henry was a German, the heir of the Hohenstaufen emperors. But most of his reign was spent planning and executing the conquest of Italy and Sicily; he raised his eyes to the world of the eastern Mediterranean and to Jerusalem; and the Byzantine Emperor was his brother-in-law. Richard was King of England; but he only spent a few months in England during his reign, and most of his reign was spent on the adventure of the Third Crusade, or in trying to establish and extend his dominions in France. In passing, so to speak, he rearranged the affairs of the kingdoms of Sicily, Cyprus, and Jerusalem – shortly to be disarranged again by Henry VI – and spent more time in each of these three kingdoms than in his own. These men were regarded as monarchs by divine grace (or divine oversight); they made capital of local loyalties to their family and their dynasty; and Henry and Richard were deadly enemies and rivals, who became friends shortly before Henry's death. Apart from the accidents of war and rivalry, these

England and Wales, ed. C. R. and M. G. Cheney (Oxford, 1967). On Gregory IX as Pope, H. K. Mann, *Lives of the Popes*, XIII (London, 1925); as Cardinal, E. Brem, *Papst Gregory IX bis zum Beginn seines Pontifikats* (Heidelberg, 1911); R. B. Brooke, *Early Franciscan Government* (Cambridge, 1959), pp. 59 ff. On relations with religious orders, see ibid. and Grundmann, *Religiöse Bewegungen. . . .* (2nd ed., Hildesheim, 1961). On the inquisition, Maisonneuve (above, p. 144 n.). The *Deliberation* is translated in B. Pullan, *Sources for the History of Medieval Europe* (Oxford, 1966), pp. 194–200. For relations between Gregory IX and St Francis, see *Scripta Leonis, Rufini et Angeli*, ed. R. B. Brooke (Oxford Medieval Texts, 1970), index, s.v. Gregory IX.

(c) For the Papacy as a city state, Luchaire, op. cit. I; D. P. Waley, *The Papal State in the Thirteenth Century* (London, 1961); and the forthcoming general survey by P. Partner.

On the possibility that the Papacy might have become an oligarchy, see W. Ullmann, *The Origins of the Great Schism* (London, 1948). On the origin of the conclave, K. Wenck, 'Das erste Konklave der Papstgeschichte', *Quellen und Forschungen aus Italienische Archiven*, XVIII (1926), pp. 101–70.

men were more at home in each other's courts than among lesser folk in their own countries. Richard's nephew, Henry III of England, was to imitate him: he allowed his brother to become Holy Roman Emperor (for a time), his son, very nearly, King of Sicily; he built Westminster Abbey on a French model and was happiest when staying with his brother-in-law, St Louis, King Louis IX of France. His dynastic dreams all ended in disaster, and the English nobility thought his Sicilian adventure as absurd as it seems to us. But it serves to remind us that almost all great monarchs from the twelfth to the nineteenth centuries, in a part of their mind at least, were cosmopolitan dynasts, more at home in each other's courts than among their own people; for them national aggrandisement, if they could have understood the term, was based on, or synonymous with, the grandeur of their families.

Pope Innocent was a man no less cosmopolitan in his outlook; but his was an intellectual and a religious vision: he was not unaware of his family, and the most outstanding of his cardinals, Hugolino dei Conti, the future Pope Gregory IX, was one of them; but unlike some later popes his ambitions were not clouded by the desire to endow his family. His father was of the nobility of Latium, his mother of Rome; he was a Roman born. To him, as to Gregory VII, there seemed nothing strange in seeing the whole of Christendom summarized, united, in one city, and all divine authority on earth in his own person. As a young man he had travelled to Paris and Bologna; he had made a distinguished name for himself as a professor of theology and canon law. But as Pope he never moved far from Rome; he ruled the Church by letter and messenger; he manipulated kings, princes, and bishops in every corner of Christendom. Most of them, most of the time, were not real people to him; he hardly met them unless they came to Rome. They were abstract visions, conjured in the brain of one of the most intellectual rulers the world has known. From the intensity of this intellectual vision springs the glory and the misery of Innocent's career.

After the death of Henry VI in 1197 two men disputed the succession to the kingdom of Germany and the western Roman Empire: Henry's brother, Philip of Swabia, and the head of the rival dynasty in Germany, Otto IV, who was nephew to Kings

Richard I and John of England. It was natural for Richard to support his nephew against Henry VI's brother. But he was more immediately concerned to dispute with the King of France, Philip II, for supremacy in the French kingdom; and it was therefore natural for Philip of France to support Philip of Swabia. The stage was set for an international conflict. When Otto IV's chances of success were finally destroyed at the battle of Bouvines in 1214 by Philip of France, the immediate consequence was that Otto's uncle and ally, John of England, was left at the mercy of his rebellious barons in England; it was the spark which set off the chain of events leading to Magna Carta in 1215.

Clearly Innocent could not ignore the events in Germany when he ascended the papal throne in 1198. But could he control them? He reckoned his authority supreme on earth, without superior under Christ, whose Vicar he was. He accepted, however, some limits in theory and practice. God had never intended Popes to intervene or hold sway over temporal rulers in the ordinary course of their government; nor could he in practice exert administrative control in every corner of Christendom when news travelled no faster than a galloping horse – and usually much slower – and decisions must commonly be taken when the essential circumstance had altered. A glance at Innocent's registers shows that he was not unduly hampered in his activities by these considerations. He sustained an enormous correspondence, dealing with matters grave and trivial, with every kingdom and almost every bishopric in western Europe. No Pope in the late Middle Ages could concentrate his whole energy on a single project: he was a juggler with many balls in the air.

Yet Innocent felt a special responsibility for the Empire, and he quickly arranged for his correspondence on this issue to be kept in a special register for speedy reference. A dispute of this kind, dividing the loftiest temporal authority God had set in Christendom, and bringing civil war and misery to three kingdoms, involved a moral issue which a Pope could not ignore; where moral issues were involved, Innocent saw no boundary to his authority in theory, and could therefore allow none in practice. But the Empire concerned him even more nearly. Was it not the Pope who had created the Holy Roman Empire by transferring it from Byzantium to Rome when Charlemagne was crowned on Christmas Day 800? Was it not the Pope who presided over the anointing and coronation of an emperor – and did not this mean that he had the obligation (and, of course, the right) to judge whether the candidate was suited to the office? No Pope could answer anything but yes; no German prince or emperor-elect could answer anything but no. To have agreed wholeheartedly to this formulation would have been to accept a degree of tutelage under the Pope which no emperor could risk. Neither Philip of Swabia nor Otto IV dared submit wholly to the Pope's judgement, much as they wanted his alliance, for fear of the damage this would do to their prestige in Germany.

Innocent waited, patiently at first, for one or other contestant to submit to his judgement. But as the months passed, and 1198 turned into 1199 and then into 1200, his patience wore thin. He was in a cruel predicament. He could only hope for a clear settlement if both parties submitted to his judgement; but if he did nothing, Christendom would think he had forgotten his duty; Christ and St Peter would feel that their work was left undone by their negligent deputy. Innocent was in his way an imaginative man, and even his able, energetic, and ardent temperament found the responsibility of his office almost crushing.

Late in 1200, at a secret Consistory, he discussed with the cardinals what the decision should be; which of the candidates should be emperor. Innocent was a firm believer in consulting the cardinals, so long as they agreed with him; and so far as we can tell he handled them adroitly. For there is little indication that they seriously resisted his dictatorial proposals. In this case, they accepted Innocent's *Deliberation*, a most elaborate scholastic argument about the rights and wrongs of the imperial dispute. Never has a great political issue been so finely analysed in relation to high principles. How does a Pope make a political decision? He must consider what is lawful, since the law to which he submits is an emanation of divine law. He must consider – for this is his special and supreme function in matters political – what is morally right, and which candidate is more suitable. And he must pay some attention too to political expediency; if he supports a candidate of the highest credentials who has no hope of success, for example, he will foment useless civil war, and this cannot be morally right. Innocent picked up each of these criteria, and applied them to Philip and Otto; and he felt bound also not to neglect a third candidate, Henry VI's infant son Frederick, the future Emperor Frederick II. Frederick had been two years old when his father died, and so was not reckoned a serious candidate in so dangerous a situation. But if one reckoned hereditary succession among the grounds for electing a man emperor, he had to be considered; the princes had sworn an oath to support him; and Henry on his deathbed had laid on the Pope himself the charge of caring for the boy, and made him his ward, and this gave Innocent a responsibility he could not overlook.

But the German monarchy was not reckoned by the Pope a hereditary monarchy. As with the Pope himself, what mattered most was how the formalities of election had been conducted; and in this regard the legal issue was nicely balanced between Philip and Otto. Morally, Otto was reckoned the better candidate, in effect because he was the more likely to listen to papal directives. Frederick, whose legal claim was slender, had a strong moral claim on the Pope. It was, however, wholly inexpedient that Frederick should be supported by the Pope: he had at that date no support in Germany, and his success would mean that Sicily and Germany would become a single kingdom, as Henry VI had planned; this the Papacy traditionally feared more than any other political alignment in Europe, for an Emperor who controlled Sicily had the papal states at his mercy, and a Pope at loggerheads with the Emperor could not call in the King of Sicily to protect him. At the end of the day, after a very fine investigation of all the issues, Innocent declared, as we might expect, for Otto.

One cannot help admiring the lofty aspiration, the pursuit of high principle, which inspired Innocent's *Deliberation*; nor lamenting how rapidly so well intentioned an exercise revealed the seeds of its own destruction – or perhaps we should say, as Christians of all denominations would probably now agree, that the Pope had somehow misconceived Christ's and St Peter's intentions. For it seems inherent in its nature that the *Deliberation* could never be repeated, if it was to carry due weight: it had to be a decision once for all. Yet all the circumstances could change: expediency might reveal Otto a weak or dangerous candidate; he might change his attitude to the Papacy and prove himself morally unsuitable. In point of fact, both these dangers came to pass. At first Otto had little success and one cannot acquit Innocent of fomenting civil war – little as he really wanted to – by his obstinacy in support of the weaker candidate. To say so much is not for a moment to say that might is right, but only that Innocent, sitting many hundred miles from the seat of conflict in Rome, could hardly appreciate the true circumstances in Germany. But as the years passed it became increasingly clear, even to Innocent, that Philip was winning, that there was little practical benefit to be gained by continuing support of Otto, and that Philip's case, on grounds of morals and expediency, was looking distinctly brighter. At this point, fate played Innocent a cruel trick. In 1208 Innocent finally gave way and recognized Philip as King of Germany and Emperor-elect; but within a few months Philip was dead, at the hand of an assassin. Innocent and the German princes joined in recognizing Otto. In 1200 this would have been a victory; but it had come too late, and proved hollow. Innocent had been compelled to abandon the basis of the *Deliberation*, and change sides twice; his growing disillusionment is shown by the fact that he and his chancery lost interest in the special register on the imperial dispute, and wound it up: he could no longer hope that it would be a creditable record of great achievements.

Hitherto, when Innocent smiled on Otto, Otto had been content to abase himself before the Pope, since he was his only powerful ally. Now he was acclaimed King by all the German princes (1208–9), and set off for Italy to be anointed and crowned Emperor. He was no longer dependent on the Pope; and his prestige would be bound to suffer if he continued to show any subservience. In the following months Pope and Emperor quarrelled; and Innocent found to his horror that whoever was King of Germany was liable to feel himself heir to the ambitions of Henry VI and try to unite Germany and Sicily. In the world of politics, this was what the Pope most feared. He hesitated long before fomenting civil war again; he hesitated longer still before facing squarely the alternative, the young Frederick II, the son and heir of Henry VI, and of all his ambitions. In the end he gave way, and helped the German princes to rebel against Otto, to declare him deposed, and finally to replace him by the man who was to prove the most dangerous enemy to the Papacy of them all, Frederick II of Hohenstaufen.

Throughout his reign, this crucial affair was only one of Innocent's many preoccupations. He was an expert lawyer, and the re-organization of the papal court of appeal, and the vast structure of canon law which supported it, was near his heart; he had his finger on every aspect of papal administration – temporal administration in the papal states, and spiritual administration everywhere – through the law courts and the very numerous letters which issued from his Chancery. He allowed himself to be talked into launching two Crusades – the first, of a traditional kind, towards the Holy Land; the second against enemies within, the heretical Cathars or Albigensians in the south of France. The first, usually known as the Fourth Crusade (1204), turned out to consist in the Conquest of the Byzantine Empire and the capture of Constantinople; that the Crusade proved only a destructive attack on another Christian power was damaging to Innocent's prestige and self-esteem; but he was a resilient man, and in his last years summoned the Fourth Lateran Council of 1215, intended to launch a movement of reform in all spheres of the Church's life, and to set in motion another Crusade for the recovery of Jerusalem.

It would be unfair to judge Innocent by the Albigensian Crusade, though he cannot be acquitted of conniving in it. The very rapid growth of heresy in western Europe, especially in southern France and northern Italy, represented the greatest threat to the Catholic monopoly before the Reformation. Responsible churchmen reacted in two ways. They argued that it was a temporary crisis, and merited crisis measures: they began to devise a machinery of religious persecution such as western Europe had never known since the conversion of the Roman Empire. They argued too that the crisis was a punishment, at the human and the divine level, for the sins and inadequacies of the Church: that a movement of regeneration, a great missionary effort, was needed, rather than brutal punishment. In the long run the most powerful heresy of the day, that of the Cathars, was killed; though the story of the Reformation shows that heresy itself was far from killed. The measure of success that the Catholic monopoly achieved in the thirteenth and fourteenth centuries seems due to two causes: to persecution on the one hand, and the effective counter of a new kind of preaching on the other. The former was to lead, under Pope Gregory IX (1227–41) to the formation of the Holy Inquisition – a system of enquiry and legal investigation which could end in obdurate heretics being passed over to the secular arm; what the lay rulers might do was not officially the Church's business – though if the rulers burnt the obdurate, their aspect in the hierarchy's eyes was the more blessed.[2]

At the centre of the new kind of preaching were the founders of the new Orders of Friars, men who took the vows of monks, but were allowed, indeed instructed, to wander, to set a new kind of example, and to preach. This seems to us the exact opposite of the Inquisition; by a tragic irony Gregory IX was to unite the two by making the Friars the instrument of the Inquisition.

Yet both Innocent and Gregory were happier giving patronage to the friars for their own proper work. Innocent came under a volley of criticism in his own lifetime for his patronage of little informal groups of dedicated men, sometimes ex-heretics, who could preach and set a good example; the bishops who bore the burden and heat of the day in the heretical areas thought these groups a nuisance and liable to lapse into heresy themselves. They passed a decree at the Lateran Council forbidding the formation of new orders (or at least the compilation of new Rules). St Francis escaped the closure this might have meant, since he had already had a verbal confirmation of the Franciscan Rule in 1210; and the other chief founder of the Orders of Friars, St Dominic, escaped it by taking an existing Rule as the basis of the way of life of the Dominican Order. But both Orders were little developed when Innocent died in 1216; both owed their survival and growth in a measure to the friendship, as Cardinal and Pope, of Gregory IX.

Innocent's was a more subtle mind than Gregory VII's had been, and his temperament, though authoritarian, was much more diplomatic. Yet in a measure he shares one of Gregory's most notable weaknesses: the tendency to judge distant potentates by

[2] See pp. 141, 154.

their external actions. King John of England refused to accept the Archbishop of Canterbury legally elected after a long dispute in 1205–6. Innocent launched his strongest weapon, an interdict which closed virtually all the churches in the country – a fearful weapon, as it proved, since almost all Englishmen were forbidden the sacraments for seven years. Finally, John gave way, and received the Archbishop elect, the eminent, high-minded Stephen Langton, an old friend of Innocent's at Paris University and in the Roman Curia. When John surrendered, he went the whole way: he even surrendered his kingdom to the Pope and received it back from Innocent as a papal 'fief' – that is, he accepted that the Pope was henceforth his temporal as well as his spiritual overlord. Innocent was enchanted, and completely taken in: hitherto John had been an obdurate and disobedient tyrant; from now on he could do no wrong. When the English barons rebelled and forced John (with Langton acting as mediator) to give his consent to Magna Carta, Innocent was scandalized. To rebel against a king without just cause was a serious infringement of the moral law – and to rebel against so good a king was even worse. Magna Carta was condemned, and Langton suspended. The consequences of this absurd *démarche* soon after died with John and Innocent, but it bears striking witness to the difficulty that even so shrewd a man as Innocent must have, in medieval circumstances, to take a sensible view of personalities and events in distant England.

Innocent died in 1216; and from 1216 to 1227 the Papacy was ruled by an elderly, respected, and attractive Curial official, who took the name of Honorius III. In 1227, in his turn, Innocent's relative, Cardinal Hugolino, became Pope as Gregory IX. So far as we know, he did not have Gregory VII in mind when he chose the name; but it was curiously appropriate, for in him was combined the spirit of Innocent III and the spirit of Gregory VII.

Gregory IX is remembered above all for three things: for the bitterness of his fight against the Emperor Frederick II, for founding the Inquisition, and for his friendship with St Francis and St Dominic. They were a part of a complex, multifarious, multitudinous activity similar to Innocent's; but they provide between them a fair summary of his personality and deeds. He was a trained lawyer and an immensely experienced Curial judge and administrator. He was an impulsive, warm-hearted man with strong spiritual feeling; yet in part of his nature he seems one of the most ruthless of thirteenth-century potentates.

It is impossible to pick out one aspect of his work and say 'this is the true man': several men lived under his skin, as is common with ambitious and powerful men who have to quell and channel a sensitive current in their temperament. But it is fair to say that in his handling of the Inquisition, in his bitter fight with Frederick II, and in one side of his work for the friars, it is the needs of his office and the mantle that had fallen on him which dictated his acts – only the extravagance and formality which sometimes appear reveal the man under the cloak. The office was regarded as something far greater than the person who occupied it. Gregory VII had felt overwhelmed and desperately lonely when he became Pope – even though his promotion answered to an ambitious element in his make-up. Innocent III had worn himself out in eighteen years, while still under 60, seeking to do nothing St Peter would take amiss, to surrender nothing his predecessors had claimed, to live up to the immense obligations of his office.

From the last years of Gregory VII's reign on, the Popes had been accustomed to look to the Norman rulers of South Italy and Sicily for protection against an over-mighty Emperor. For all Innocent III's ability, energy, and persistence, he had in the end left Frederick II in possession both of Sicily and of Germany: by the time of Gregory IX's accession any pretence that they would presently be divided once again was wearing very thin, and Frederick had revealed himself as a brilliant ruler, with ambitions which knew no limit save the circumstances in which he lived, and with no scrap of respect for the Papacy. If he died leaving the Holy See a pawn in Frederick's hands, he would have failed in the first responsibility that St Peter – and Gregory VII and Innocent III and all the rest of the line – had laid upon him. This fear became an obsession.

Frederick had announced some years before that he would go on Crusade; but the date of departure unaccountably kept being postponed. On his accession Gregory called loudly on the Emperor to go. Then the Crusade set forth, leaving Frederick behind, lying ill in bed; an illness which Gregory viewed with scepticism. Gregory excommunicated him twice for this delay; then excommunicated him for setting off while still under the ban; and renewed the ban again when he returned having triumphed by diplomacy not by war. One can admit that Frederick was deliberately provoking the old man; one can admit that he went east not out of any religious zeal but to add Jerusalem to his many crowns, and for this reason made a treaty instead of fighting, a treaty to suit himself, not the sponsors of the Crusade. But when all allowances are made, the story remains absurd: it seems a farce to us, and it seemed preposterous at the time to many Roman citizens and some even of his cardinals. For a time Rome herself closed its gates to Gregory.

But he was not entirely without allies: Christendom at large was inclined to judge Frederick's proceedings as severely as posterity has judged Gregory's: and if the Romans found the Pope a tyrant and a nuisance, the free cities of northern Italy found Frederick equally obnoxious when he claimed their allegiance to him, as Emperor. For a time, peace was patched up; then the Pope became increasingly alarmed, as the 1230s went on, at Frederick's successes in north Italy – his own subjugation would obviously come next. In November 1237 Frederick caught and routed the army of the Lombard League of cities at Cortenuova. But he made the mistake of demanding total surrender from their leader, Milan, and this the Milanese refused. Frederick made the most formidable preparations to besiege the city, but meanwhile was losing time. In October 1238 he abandoned the siege of Brescia, which had been intended as a minor rehearsal for the major act. On Palm Sunday 1239, Pope Gregory, exasperated once again by a series of irritants, and convinced that his own cause was closely tied to the fortune of these northern battlefields, once again excommunicated Frederick. Two years of indecisive war followed – and gradually the Emperor drew nearer to Rome; yet Gregory had a measure of success in rousing the opinion of the rest of Europe, though his despotic temperament alienated some of those close to him, even the cardinals. On 22 August 1241, the Pope died; the struggle continued; but in the end Gregory triumphed from the grave, and after Frederick's death in 1250 the power of the Hohenstaufen Emperors crumbled away.

Meanwhile, in Assisi, a happier monument of Gregory's cares was rising: the Basilica of the saint whom he had loved and canonized, Francis of Assisi. In some ways they had been worlds apart. When Gregory as Cardinal had entertained the saint, and he had refused to eat at the great man's table, but sat on the floor, dining off scraps he had begged from door to door, the Cardinal was embarrassed, even though his guests were evidently much edified. When he took Francis to the papal Curia to preach before the cardinals, he was in a cold sweat lest the saint's simplicity make him a laughing stock. Of this Francis was perfectly well aware and he did nothing to assuage the Cardinal's fears: he abandoned his prepared speech and danced a jig before their Eminences to reveal his joy in God's love – and so, to his friend's intense astonishment, carried all before him. But their friendship was real; they told each other home truths; the Cardinal prevented Francis from some of his more foolish schemes, and Francis in return refused to allow the Cardinal to abandon his great responsibilities and become a friar. As Cardinal and later as Pope, Gregory showed a curious mixture of real intuitive understanding and the hierarch's blind concern for practical usefulness. He made it possible for Francis to follow his own very personal inspiration; yet he also encouraged everything which made the Order more obviously useful, including (after Francis's death) involving some Franciscans in the Inquisition.

From his grave Gregory won a victory over the Emperor which was in his lifetime always beyond his grasp; a victory in some ways more dangerous than defeat, for it confirmed the tradition that the Pope must try to control the political scene in Italy – and so helped to lead to the situation in the late Middle Ages that the Papacy seemed just another petty Italian principality. Perhaps in a measure Gregory might have foreseen this danger; but he was himself an Italian aristocrat by birth, and the relationship of his office to Italian politics seemed natural to him, as well as being part of the inheritance his office laid upon him.

In any event this was a problem for the generations ahead. When he died, he was obsessed with a much closer, more immediate vision. He saw a small college of cardinals divided among themselves; some indeed either in Frederick's camp or in his prisons. He knew that some thought his own measures had been too extreme; he felt to the full the lonely responsibility his office laid upon him. His fear was that the cardinals might refuse or fail to elect a Pope, and that Frederick would divide the Roman Church and rule it. At this moment, it seems, there came into his mind the suggestion made by an eminent English professor of canon law a generation earlier, that if the cardinals failed to elect a Pope, they should be imprisoned until they had come to a common mind. So Gregory sent for his close friend, the lay leader of the Roman officials, the Senator Orsini, and discussed the future with him. When Gregory died, the Senator grabbed as many cardinals as he could lay hands on and imprisoned them in one of the palaces of Rome, where they were subjected to every kind of discomfort, starved, and abused, to speed them to a suitable election. One cardinal complained that the soldiers poked their weapons up through his mattress to give him a sleepless night. But the Senator's reply to all complaints was to lay in their midst the coffin containing the unburied body of the dead Pope. One of the cardinals fell ill and died; and this gave his colleagues an inspiration. They hastily chose another of their number, who was also reckoned not long for this world; he survived his promotion a fortnight only, but it was long enough for the rest of the cardinals to escape to a safe distance from Rome, where they stayed, defying the Senator, and failing to elect a successor, for nearly two years. Finally they elected a well known moderate cardinal as Innocent IV; and Gregory's mantle descended on him so successfully that he became, as Pope, fully as intransigent as his predecessor, but with more practical success. In these ironical circumstances the idea of the papal conclave was born. In the end it was to prove (though much modified) a sound instrument for ensuring a true election, and may be reckoned, along with the Orders of St Francis and St Dominic, among the happier legacies of the stormy career of Pope Gregory IX.

10

Paul Sabatier and St Francis of Assisi[1]

A lecture composed in 1957–8. See p. 9, Preface.

NO medieval saint has been as popular in the last two generations as St Francis; and popular, not only with Roman Catholics, but with men and women of every denomination and of none. It is natural that it should be so, but this general enthusiasm is nonetheless no ancient thing. A variety of circumstances gave it birth; but if we had to pin-point a single date or single event of particularly spectacular importance in its growth, by general consent it would be the publication of Sabatier's *Vie de S. François d'Assise* in 1893. It caused an excitement comparable to the publication thirty years before by Sabatier's master, Renan, of his *Life of Jesus*; it was translated into many languages and remained for many years a best seller. It was warmly commended by the Pope and then put upon the Index. It aroused bitter antagonism from with-

[1] My knowledge of Sabatier is based on A. G. Little's memoir in *Franciscan Papers, Lists and Documents* (Manchester, 1943), pp. 179–88. The relation of Sabatier's to current views of Franciscan origins is discussed in R. B. Brooke, *Early Franciscan Government* (Cambridge, 1959), pp. 1 ff.; for a general conspectus of the sources for Francis's life see her article in *Latin Biography*, ed. T. A. Dorey (London, 1967), pp. 177–98; for the history of Sabatier's interpretation of the *Speculum Perfectionis*, see *Scripta Leonis*, ed. R. B. Brooke (Oxford Medieval Texts, 1970), pp. 5 ff. Citations from the *Vie de S. François d'Assise* are given both from the French edition (first publ. 1893, 1894 on title-page – cf. Little, p. 179) and the English translation (L. S. Houghton, London, 1926 ed.) – and quotations are from this translation (slightly adapted) unless otherwise stated.

in the Franciscan Order and from some Italian Catholics. But in the course of time this passed; Sabatier was too great and too saintly a man, too much of a peacemaker, to arouse lasting antagonism; his subject was too precious to all the protagonists not to make much strife unseemly. By the time of his death in 1928, Sabatier was universally recognized as the father of modern Franciscan studies; scholars of every faith agreed that his faults as a historian were many, but his best work inspired. I shall have much to say of the weaknesses of Sabatier; so let me say at once that his *Life* is one of the masterpieces of historical literature. There are sounder accounts of St Francis: Sabatier himself regarded Father Cuthbert's *Life* as the best of all, and although there have been some good lives since his death, I should be inclined to agree. But Sabatier remains the indispensable introduction; it provides the breath of inspiration as no other work, medieval or modern; we shall hardly touch St Francis unless we read it – although, equally, we shall get a strange focus on him if we read nothing else. But Sabatier's *Life* is more than just a bottle of champagne to brace us for sterner things; it is a masterpiece of history as well as of literature. It is a unique expression of historical method; and no historian can come away from reading it without being the better for it.

The vogue of St Francis was the product of the romantic movement; but it was remarkably slow to mature. It came by many routes. The Catholic revival proliferated pious books and pamphlets; the passion for Italy and Italian literature made the *Fioretti* (The Little Flowers) widely known, and Assisi attracted the tourist; above all, the study of Italian art led Ruskin and his disciples to search behind Giotto and Cimabue for the saint whose story was told in their splendid frescoes. In the end they found him; and the nineteenth-century romantics found (or thought they found) a man after their own heart, a lover of mankind, a lover of animals, an apostle of liberty – a liberal romantic in the thirteenth century.

When the *Life of St Francis* was published in 1893 its author was thirty-five. He devoted the rest of his life very largely to Franciscan studies, and at the time of his death he was Professor of Ecclesiastical History in the Faculty of Protestant Theology at

Strasbourg, after a career divided between lecturing at Strasbourg and pastoral work in the Cevennes. And yet he never revised his *Life*, and never wrote another comparable book; most of his later work is in the shape of technical studies and editions of texts. Almost none of them are popular works, though they are never dull. He was an artist in everything he did, and there was nothing austere about his scholarship; he is one of the few scholars ever to describe in the footnote to a learned text, without incongruity, a fête organized by the leading citizens of Assisi in his own honour. The great Theodor Mommsen sowed his wild oats as a young man in his *History of Rome*, and devoted a substantial part of a long career to technical studies refuting it in detail. In a similar way Sabatier contributed innumerable lectures and studies in his later years, but the synthesis of his work, so to speak, came first.

As we should expect, the *Life* is the inspired utterance of a young enthusiast, not the product of mature reflection, and it owed a great deal to Sabatier's masters. The greatest of these was Renan, and by Sabatier's own account, it was Renan himself who enjoined him to devote himself to the study of St Francis. Renan's influence is very evident in Sabatier. It was the feeling for scenery, for the genius of countryside, which inspired Sabatier to write much of his *Life* in Assisi, just as Renan's *Life of Jesus* had been planned in Palestine; a romantic glow suffuses every page of both books; both reveal the capacity to fudge the edges of harsh intellectual problems, at its worst, the grotesque subjectivism which aroused Albert Schweitzer's anger against Renan; yet they combined these qualities with a penetration into character and situation and an intellectual vitality which amounted to genius. Perhaps Sabatier's most obvious debt to Renan lies in the critical study of the sources with which, like Renan's, his book opens; for in this, above all, is revealed the spirit which saved critical scholarship from being buried under the heap of sawdust with which the scientific historians of Sabatier's day wished to envelop it. It combines scholarly acumen and accurate marshalling of evidence with high imagination – the imagination to organize the material into a coherent and lucid argument, and the imaginative insight and sympathy which penetrates to the heart of each source, and sees its author as a person, in his historical setting.

As a pure historian Sabatier probably surpassed his master. Partly this was because he lived in a time of rapid progress in historical studies, and began where Renan left off; partly because of their subjects. To penetrate into the mind of a historical source has some meaning when one is dealing with the biographers and chroniclers of St Francis, who reveal their aims and characters in their writings; but the gospels require an altogether sharper and tougher instrument than the romantic historians possessed. Sabatier passed the limits which divide reconstruction from fantasy, but not so gravely as his master.

In the introduction, at the very outset of his work, Sabatier revealed his attitude to history. He reveals himself, first, as the subjective, imaginative historian.

> 'When I began this page the sun was disappearing behind the ruins of the Castle of Crussol and the splendours of the sunset gave it a shining aureola; the light flooded everything, and you no longer saw anywhere the damage which wars have inflicted upon the old feudal manor. I looked, almost thinking I could perceive at the window the figure of the chatelaine.... Twilight has come, and now there is nothing up there but crumbling walls, a discrowned tower, nothing but ruins and rubbish, which seem to beg for pity.
>
> 'It is the same with the landscapes of history. Narrow minds cannot accommodate themselves to these perpetual transformations: they want an objective history in which the author will study the people as a chemist studies a body....
>
> 'Objective history is ... a utopia. We create God in our own image, and we impress the mark of our personality in places where we least expect to find it again.
>
> 'But by dint of talking about the tribunal of history we have made most authors think that they owe to themselves and their readers definitive and irrevocable judgements....
>
> 'But perhaps below the Areopagites, obliged by their functions to pronounce sentence, there is place at the famous tribunal for a simple spectator who has come in by accident. He has made out a brief, and would like very simply to tell his neighbours his opinion. This ... is not a history *ad probandum*....

'Francis's official historians . . . have done him in general ill-service. Their embellishments have hidden the real St Francis, who was, in fact, infinitely nobler than they have made him out to be. Ecclesiastical writers appear to make a great mistake in thus adorning the lives of their heroes, and only mentioning their edifying features. . . .

'By such means the saints, perhaps, gain something in the respect of the superstitious; but their lives lose something of virtue and of communicable strength. Forgetting that they were men like ourselves, we no longer hear in our conscience the command, "Go and do thou likewise".

'It is, then, a work of piety to seek behind the legend for the history. Is it presumptuous to ask our readers to try to understand the thirteenth century and love St Francis? They will be amply rewarded for the effort, and will soon find an unexpected charm in these too meagre landscapes, these souls without bodies, these sick imaginations which will pass before their eyes. Love is the true key to history.'[2]

There you have the faith of a romantic: we must see things from the inside, see them as the individual expressions of the things which make the world what it is – liberty, the beauty of nature, the love of man, and (for Sabatier, the liberal protestant) the love of God. After this expression of romantic faith, we pass to the critical study of the sources; we become for a while scientific investigators. It may be that the two elements are not always in perfect harmony; but the historian's faith that his activity is both impersonal and personal, that history is both a science and an art, has rarely been so sublimely stated; and this was crucial to the development of historical studies, threatened in their prime by a divorce between romantic journalism and learned dust.

The weapon Sabatier fashioned was wonderfully suited to his theme. St Francis was not made to be revealed to pedants. Subtlety, penetration, and imaginative sympathy are needed to fit a man to study the career of this most brilliant, mercurial, imaginative, and sympathetic of men; and these were just the qualities with which Sabatier was most abundantly endowed. The effect

[2] *Vie*, pp. xxiv–xxviii; *Life*, pp. xxxi–iv.

was to breathe life at every point into the story of the saint, and at many points to alter the whole perspective of the tale.

The skeleton was already familiar to pious Catholics and pious romantics: first the conversion of the lively merchant's son of Assisi, who loved the colour of life and hated squalor and disease, to the leper's friend, the servant of the poor, the repairer of churches; then the search for a vocation, the discovery in the words of the Gospel that he was called to follow the first disciples of Jesus, to go and preach, and take nothing for the way; then the gathering of the first group of disciples, the first preaching tours, the first visit to the Pope; gradually followed by the expansion of the Order, by the growing fame of its founder, by his recognition as a force in the Church's life; and finally the establishment of the Franciscan Rule and the prolonged illness of the saint, the mysterious reception of the Stigmata – the imprint on his body of the wounds of the Crucified – and his death two years later, in 1226 at the early age of forty-four.

It would be futile to try to summarize the rich detail of Sabatier's portrait of the saint and of his career. It is brilliantly done. The author's prejudices are evident at every turn, but they are so obvious as not seriously to mislead us. Sabatier was a Protestant pastor, but he had no use for organized churches. His account of the Church and the Papacy is coloured by his own views, although from time to time, as one reads his diatribes, one is astonished at his capacity for self-criticism, and for being fair-minded in the most unlikely places. But he held to the idea that the tragedy of the Franciscan Order was its rapid conversion into a great ecclesiastical machine which lacked the sparkle and the fervour of the founder. No generalization so broad could be wholly true, and there have been many returns, many new beginnings; there has never been a lack of friars of deep fervour. But every modern scholar worth the name would accept the fact of the change at least in part. Sabatier, naturally enough, exaggerated it: he saw the history of the Order, not as a natural falling off from a great ideal or as its gradual transformation, but as the perversion of an ideal by the blind folly of scheming hierarchs; the villains are Hugolino, the Cardinal Protector, later Pope Gregory IX, and Brother Elias, St Francis's second in command, whom Sabatier portrayed as

Hugolino's tool. That St Francis's ideal was capable of surviving, that any attempt to tamper with the saint's wishes in the unholy cause of common sense or ecclesiastical policy was criminal, it never entered his mind to doubt. Still less did he consider that some of the changes might themselves have value. It is strange that a historian who makes a special claim to have broken with the tradition of hagiography should have shown himself so little inclined to criticize his hero. Sabatier's Francis has life and vigour and charm, but no faults; his biographer had swallowed him whole.

Sabatier's romanticism was intellectually consistent: St Francis was an individual with a message; anything which tampered with his individuality or stood between him and the lonely path of self-expression was a shade of the prison house. Francis and his idea were all of a piece: a sacrament of joy and love. Sabatier professed a great dislike of iconoclasts; and to break the spell of his creation often seems a fearful iconoclasm. In truth, too harsh a break would serve no useful purpose, because in some respects Sabatier surely came very near the truth: nearer, perhaps, in the splendid lecture he gave in 1908 on 'The Originality of St Francis' than in the *Life*. Sabatier, the protestant, startled the learned world by pronouncing that the originality of St Francis lay in his catholicism. He had been reproached with making Francis a precursor of the Reformation.

> 'If I deserved the charge, I regret it, and will strive to make amends. Let us hope that the simplicity of my *mea culpa* will lead my honourable critics to show an equal good will, and that one day they will cease to believe that they do honour to St Francis in portraying him as a sort of passive instrument in the hands of the hierarchy.'[3]

Then he proceeded to sketch his view of Francis's catholicism – submission to the Church, but a joyful, positive submission,

> 'adhesion rather, the adhesion of the son who knows in advance that his father is right, but who never thinks of obeying without

[3] Sabatier, *et al.*, *Franciscan Essays*, I (British Soc., of Franciscan Studies, 1912), pp. 9, 11, 17.

understanding, still less of regarding as normal obedience in the dark'.

Sabatier is sketching the paradox of the service which is perfect freedom; and that Francis joyfully accepted the authority of the Church, rejoiced in submission to the priests who administered the sacrament, and yet felt himself to be perfectly free to pursue his own courses can hardly be denied. The admirable Crichton left the butler's pantry to become the leader of the shipwrecked family circle; but Francis did not need to leave the pantry to become a leader – the humbler his life, the more men followed him. Sabatier concluded his analysis by quoting in Latin St Francis's words on obedience – he would not translate them, for fear of even seeming to make the saint whom he worshipped in his own image.

> 'Holy obedience makes a man subject to all the men of this world and not only to men, but also to the beasts and wild animals so that they can do with him what they would – so far as is given to them by the Lord from on high.'

Submission to priests and the holiness of the sacrament are the central theme of St Francis's own writings; and though Sabatier (with a singular fairmindedness) accepted the fact, and although he has some fine pages on the sacrament in his *Life*, one would hardly realize their importance from a cursory reading of it. This passage in the lecture of 1908 is the first hint that obedience plays a far larger part in Francis's writings than poverty (poverty, indeed, is hardly mentioned outside the rules); and I doubt if Sabatier ever fully realized the fact. There was some truth in the charge that in his book he saw St Francis as a liberal protestant; he felt his inspiration too closely not to associate him with himself. But essentially the fault (if such it was) was the product of the romantic attitude to psychology and to literary criticism. It was dogma to many romantics that great art and great living were the product of spontaneous and exuberant genius: Francis was always simple, natural, direct, uncomplicated. And it was also a dogma that a literary text must be appreciated whole: if a first reading of St Francis's last *Testament* gave him an impression that it was the *cri-de-cœur* of a dying man, trapped in the toils of authority, then that is how he would see every line of it. No one doubts that Francis was anxious at the end lest his Order become just another ecclesiastical organ and lose its simplicity; and the *Testament* contains a stern warning against altering his plans. He is, as always, very dictatorial: he would obey all mankind, so long as all mankind obeyed him in return. There is, at the end, the urgency of a last message from a dying man. But most of the *Testament* is a reiteration of Francis's normal theme, firm but undisturbed; I cannot see it, as Sabatier saw it, as the dying outcry of a tragic hero.

Nor was Francis uncomplicated. His originality lay in his perception that to preach to the poor one must be poorer than they are, to serve the simple one must be simpler than they are. The ordinary poor people of Italy might listen respectfully to a sound theologian with a University degree, but it meant nothing to them. And so Francis made himself poorer than the poor, simpler than the simple. It did not come naturally or easily to him: his spontaneity was the product of a long training. The tricks, the pranks, the strange charades by which he bewildered his followers are surely in part a reflection of a deeper irony. The clever and brilliant son of wealthy parents could not throw off his nature and his background without occasionally remembering that in an age in which social distinctions counted for so much, he had surrendered the rank of wealthy burgher in order to be received in the hovels of the poor – and also in the palaces of princes and cardinals and popes – where his father would never have been seen.

At the beginning of the *Life*, in the critical study of the sources, Sabatier enunciated principles of criticism distinctly superior to his own practice; and many scholars who thought to revise Sabatier have had the uncomfortable experience of finding here their best ideas anticipated. He saw, first of all, that the basic evidence was the saint's own writings, the few that survive. He then worked through the biographers, giving a sympathetic appreciation of each; and very properly giving a first thought to the *Vita Prima* of Thomas of Celano, in spite of its rhetorical style, which revolted Sabatier's romantic temperament. He found some fault with it, but rightly took it to be the most reliable and the earliest of the lives which have survived *in toto*. But he gave more sympathetic attention to the so-called *Legend of the Three Companions*, a strange, confused narrative, which Sabatier showed to be at least incomplete, if not a compilation. In the main, however, he set a high value by the legend, on the ground that it evoked the atmosphere of primitive joy and simplicity. It is doubtful if it is as primitive or as simple as Sabatier thought and its place in the genealogy of Franciscan sources is still a puzzle.

The Legend of the Three Companions opens with a letter purporting to have been written by three of St Francis's companions, Leo, Angelo, and Rufino, in 1246, as the introduction to a final collection of stories about the saint gathered from their own experience and that of their friends. Sabatier correctly perceived that the *Legend* as we have it hardly fits the summary in the letter; in particular that it has nothing to say of the middle and later years of the saint's career, about which the companions ought to have been particularly well informed. This set him on the track of what was missing.

It was the beginning of what is surely one of the strangest stories in the history of medieval scholarship.[4] By the time Sabatier came to write the *Life*, he had taken the first step in pursuit of Brother Leo and his associates; a daring and brilliant step; and, as events were to show, he was almost entirely right. Sabatier analysed a confused jumble of matter called the *Speculum Vitae*, put together in the fourteenth century, which he knew at the time only from garbled printed editions of the sixteenth and seventeenth centuries; and he came to the conclusion that there was in it a nucleus of 118 chapters which had the sniff of the primitive about them, which he was able to use in his *Life*. He was deeply sensitive to atmosphere, and for the most part his instinct was right; nor was it all instinct, because he was able to produce internal evidence of the homogeneous nature of these stories, and external evidence to show that a certain number of them were attributed to Brother Leo at the beginning of the fourteenth century. It is now universally accepted that the bulk of these stories was the work of Brother Leo and his associates, although they had been altered quite a bit before they entered the *Speculum*

[4] See n. 1; Little, pp. 183–5.

Vitae. So far, Sabatier's intuitive criticism had been entirely vindicated.

When the *Life* was complete, Sabatier set to work in pursuit of manuscripts. In due course he discovered the book he was looking for; in a number of libraries scattered about Europe there survived a tract of 124 chapters bearing the title of *Speculum Perfectionis*, 'The Mirror of Perfection'. All but eight of these chapters corresponded with all but two of the collection he had previously analysed. His guess had proved itself triumphantly; and, as so often, the overwhelming psychological effect of a prophecy fulfilled convinced him that his search was at an end, that he had found the authentic writings of Brother Leo. As luck would have it, one of his manuscripts bore a colophon which seemed to mean that the book was written in 1227 – within a year of St Francis's death. In 1898 he published the *Speculum Perfectionis* with the subtitle 'the most ancient legend of St Francis of Assisi, written by Brother Leo'. It is a portentous edition; a lavish work of scholarship; a mixture of technical detail, brilliantly conceived argument, and barely concealed excitement. With characteristic humility he obviously regarded the publication of Brother Leo's life in 1898 as of far greater moment than the publication of Paul Sabatier's in 1893.

> 'It is not without a lively sense of pleasure that I offer to the public today the biography of St Francis by Brother Leo. . . . If this splendid legend is at last recovered, we owe it entirely to scientific criticism, and to the perseverance with which its principles have been applied to the study of the Franciscan documents. Many folk see in criticism only the hammer of destruction and demolition. That is very unjust, for when the moment comes, it can also take the mason's trowel and raise above the ruins constructions built to last.'

'It was a cruel irony of fate', wrote A. G. Little, 'that when Sabatier relied on his own intuition he was right, when he relied on manuscript authority he went wrong: it is the reverse of the experience of most historians.'[5] It has since been shown that the

[5] Little, p. 184.

date on the colophon in the manuscript known to Sabatier, 1227, was a mere scribal error for 1318; that 1318 is the true date of the *Speculum Perfectionis*, and that it contains a certain amount of material definitely not derived from Brother Leo and a certain amount copied from the *Vita secunda* of Thomas of Celano. The essential point of Sabatier's case, that the bulk of the *Speculum* was Leonine, is now established; but the proof has come in the shape of earlier documents from which something like the original form of the stories can be reconstructed. There is still plenty of room for dispute about details; but the main lines are clear. They were already laid down in Sabatier's lifetime, most firmly and brilliantly by F. C. Burkitt in 1926;[6] but Sabatier alone remained unconvinced. He clung to the theory that the *Speculum Perfectionis* was composed in 1227, in pathetic isolation. He was too honest not to see the arguments against him and the weakness of some of his evidence; and there are hints that he felt more doubt than he ever revealed. But he maintained at the end, as he had maintained in 1898, that although the evidence was perplexing the balance was in his favour. Some of the arguments he developed in later life were not meant to be taken very seriously. Among other objections raised by his tormentors was a passage in which Brother Leo is mentioned in terms of glowing compliment. How could Leo write such things about himself? 'The weakness of this argument . . . has been shown by the conduct of the very man who most actively pressed it,' wrote Sabatier in the second edition of the *Speculum*, published by the British Society of Franciscan Studies after his death. 'In the month of May 1898 . . . Mgr Faloci-Pulignani attached five exclamation marks to a quotation of this passage; and added "Oh the rare modesty of Brother Leo who speaks thus of himself". He deduced therefrom that he could not be the author of these pages; but in 1906 Mgr Faloci himself was led to an identical act.' He proceeds to tell with delightful irony the sad story of Faloci's pamphlet. Faloci-Pulignani was Dean and Vicar-General of Foligno; and when trouble arose at Rome in 1905 he was forced to prepare a pamphlet in his own defence which he published the next year. In it he printed a brief from the

[6] In *St Francis of Assisi: 1226–1926: Essays in Commemoration* (London, 1926), pp. 15–61.

Vatican and a testimonial from the mayor extolling the virtues of the Dean and Vicar-General of Foligno. If Brother Leo cannot have published his own praise, these documents, said Sabatier, must be forged.[7]

But whether Faloci-Pulignani's testimonials were forged or not, the nucleus of the stories in the *Speculum Perfectionis* was, in fact, closely based on the writings of Brother Leo. They were originally written some twenty years after St Francis's death by men with a strong nostalgia for their younger days; there is a certain *tendance* about them; but they provide nonetheless the freshest and most attractive approach to St Francis which we have – the most exciting of all the 'intimate biographies' of the Middle Ages. In any ordinary sense they do not form a biography – therein lies their value. They are stories about the saint; and he was the sort of man whose personality could only have been revealed to us in stories. The *Fioretti* have something of their charm, but they are legendary; these are the personal reminiscences of Francis's closest friends. There have been many great teachers and preachers; but the secret of their magnetism is usually lost. We cannot hear the voice of St Bernard or Luther, nor fully understand what drew the crowds to Abelard. But thanks to these stories we know quite a lot about Francis's technique. A contemporary said of him 'He had not the manner of a preacher, his ways were rather those of conversation.'[8] So close was his imitation of Jesus that he even taught by parables; but his parables are as individual in their way as his Master's. In the recorded parables of Jesus the effect is produced by speech, by a spoken imagery; the characteristic story about St Francis may include a little speech, but more often takes the form of a charade. A novice received permission from his minister to have a psalter, but having a scruple about it, he went to see St Francis. He approached him one day (not for the first time) as he was sitting warming himself by a fire and asked his question. Francis looked at him with a twinkle and said: 'After you have a psalter, you will want . . . a breviary'; then 'you will sit in an armchair, like a great prelate, saying to your brother,

[7] *Speculum Perfectionis*, ed. 2 (Brit. Society of Franciscan Studies, 1928–31), II, 152–3.

[8] *Vie*, p. 274; *Life*, p. 241.

"Bring me the breviary".' 'Thus saying, with great fervour of spirit he took some ashes from the fire', and as it were washed his hair with them, murmuring to himself over and over again ' "I a breviary, I a breviary" '. Later on the unfortunate novice plucked up courage to ask him again, and this time Francis shrugged his shoulders and told him to do as the minister had said. Then Francis stood and watched the friar walking off, and in a moment called after him, 'Wait, wait', ran to him, and asked him to show him the exact spot where he had given his permission. When they were there, Francis fell at his feet and begged his pardon – 'Mea culpa' – for he had given him leave to break the strictness of the Rule.[9]

From stories such as this we can obtain a real insight into the way Francis worked. We must not deduce from them too rigid principles; Francis, like his Master, gave personal answers to personal questions more often than enunciating principles; the strictness of his treatment of the novice was due partly to his intuition into the novice's mind, his sense of what was right for *him*; partly, too, to his feeling that as founder of a large and growing Order, he must himself set an unswerving example. Some of the harsher sayings of his later days grew from his knowledge that every word and act might be taken by his followers as a precedent and a law.

Not all the stories are as delightful as this – and some, like his treatment of the brother who hankered to use money and was made to carry a coin in his teeth and put it in a pile of dung, are more effective than pleasant. But they do help us to understand why Francis in his own day was intensely loved, and they help us too to catch the infectious gaiety of the man who devised the Christmas crib (with real straw and real animals), who preached to the birds, and upset the stately dignity of the College of Cardinals by coming among them in his dirty old habit and dancing a jig.

In the end, like Sabatier, we must submit to the spell; and, if we are human, revel in the spectacle of this most astonishing of mortal men. We owe our perception of the joy of St Francis above all to Sabatier. That was his essential contribution. It was not the

[9] *Scripta Leonis*, pp. 209 ff. (nos. 70 ff.).

product of the imagination alone, nor of scholarship alone, as I hope I have made clear; but of something like an inspired mingling of the two.

There is a great deal of nonsense in Sabatier's work; it is remarkable how little he contributed to our understanding of the later history of the Order or to any other historical topic. He lived and died with two great illusions. Of one of them I have said sufficient; the other (to some extent) is with us still. Sabatier was always on the search for intimate historical material, and never afraid to look for it in seemingly unlikely places. The greater part of Angelo Clareno's *History of the Seven Tribulations of the Order of Friars Minor*, written about 1320, had recently been published by the Jesuit scholar Father Ehrle, to whom Sabatier and all medievalists owe a very great debt.[10] In it Sabatier found a history of the Order after his own heart, a history written by a friar with a devotion to the saint equal to his own, who saw the saint and his true successors as individuals battling against the forces of human wickedness and clerical chicanery. Sabatier was too good a scholar not to realize that Clareno's diatribes were a reflection of his own sorrows – of the bitter triangular conflict between the Spiritual and Conventual Franciscans and the papal Curia in the late thirteenth and early fourteenth centuries. But Sabatier accepted the general interpretation, and he and many of his successors were led to attribute the origin of this later conflict to the saint's own lifetime.

It was his conviction that deep and violent conflict was already in existence before 1226 that enabled Sabatier to believe that a tract so evidently reflecting 'Spiritual' tendencies as the *Speculum Perfectionis* could have been written in 1227; and it was this belief which made him think that Leo in 1226 and 1227 was under the same unfortunate necessity which afflicted Mgr Faloci in 1905 and 1906. We owe much to Sabatier positively, for the things on which he was right, for his inspiration; much too, for his mistakes. I am sure that all those who have contributed to revising his errors

[10] In *Archiv für Litteratur- und Kirchengeschichte des Mittelalters* (Berlin und Freiburg-im-Br., 1885–1900), II, pp. 106–55, 249–327 (for the rest, see reference in *Scripta Leonis*, p. xiii: a complete ed. by Professor R. Manselli is in preparation).

would admit that they often saw the truth reflected in the mirror of Sabatier's errors. And that is no bad definition of a great scholar.

It is true that the brilliance and lucidity of Sabatier's writing have sometimes bewitched us; but this is no argument against his weapons. When he is right, he is inspiring; when he is wrong, he fascinates us as Euclid fascinated Hobbes: 'By God, this is impossible.' His special talent was his appreciative sympathy of his subject. 'It is in such cases,' as he himself said, 'that criticism needs to be delicate, to mingle a little divination with the heavy artillery of scientific argument.'[11]

It was characteristic of Sabatier that he should be a peacemaker. A. G. Little tells a delightful story of Sabatier's efforts to subdue the religious feuds of his home in the Cevennes, and of how he found him one day after shopping at both the two bakeries in the village, with two loaves under his arms, which he described as 'pain catholique' and 'pain protestant'.[12] In the years following the first edition of the *Speculum Perfectionis* societies and periodicals grew under his hand – the *Collection d'études*, the *Opuscules de critique historique*, the International Society of Franciscan Studies, the British Society of Franciscan Studies. Among the contributors to the collections, edited by this French patriot whom the Germans had ejected from Strasbourg and Renan's pupil whose book had been placed on the Index, were leading German and Catholic scholars, in particular the German Professor Boehmer and the Catholic Père Mandonnet. It was characteristic of him, too, that when the seventh centenary of the coming of the Friars was celebrated in Canterbury Cathedral in 1924, and Little gave an address on 'Some recent researches in Franciscan history', Sabatier spoke on the message of St Francis for today.[13] There was no vulgar separation between Sabatier the historian and Sabatier the man.

'In one of the frescoes of the upper church at Assisi, Giotto has represented St Clare and her companions coming out from

[11] *Vie*, p. 241; *Life*, p. 212.

[12] Little, pp. 179 f.

[13] F. C. Burkitt *et al.*, *Franciscan Essays*, II (Brit. Soc. of Franciscan Studies, 1932), p. ix.

San Damiano all in tears, to kiss their spiritual father's corpse as it is being carried to its last home. With an artist's liberty he has made the chapel a rich church built of precious marbles.

'Happily the real San Damiano is still there, nestling under some olive-trees like a lark under the heather; it still has its ill-made walls of irregular stones, like those which bound the neighbouring fields. Which is the more beautiful, the ideal temple of the artist's fancy, or the poor chapel of reality? No heart will be in doubt.'[14]

At the very end, about the Basilica which houses Giotto's frescoes:

'Built under the inspiration of Gregory IX and the direction of Brother Elias, this marvellous Basilica is also one of the documents of this history, and perhaps I have been wrong in neglecting it.

'Go and look upon it, proud, rich, powerful, then go down to the Portiuncula, pass over to San Damiano, hasten to the Carceri, and you will understand the abyss that separates the ideal of Francis from that of the pontiff who canonized him.'[15]

Sabatier was less than fair to Gregory IX, and the Basilica is marvellous indeed; but no one who has seen San Damiano and the Carceri could fail to understand the inspiration Sabatier felt.

[14] *Vie*, p. xxvii; *Life*, p. xxxiii.
[15] *Vie*, p. 399; *Life*, p. 345.

11

St Dominic and his First Biographer[1]

A lecture read 12 March 1966, and published in Transactions of the Royal Historical Society, *Vol. 17, 1967.*

THE Order of Preachers was created under the skilled direction of two great men: Dominic of Caleruega and Jordan of Saxony. Whatever else they may have been, both were brilliant organizers; they sketched between them the most sophisticated constitutional organization known to the Middle Ages; for good or ill, they created for us the idea and technique of committee government. Both, it is clear, had tidy and lucid minds. We know that Jordan wrote excellent Latin, was capable of making plain in a few words

[1] The magisterial study by M.-H. Vicaire, O.P., *Histoire de S. Dominique* (2 vols., Paris, 1957), cited here, as Vicaire (1964), from the English translation by K. Pond (London, 1964), makes extensive reference to modern literature on St Dominic unnecessary; Professor Vicaire gives a full bibliography on pp. 436–44. The book was accompanied by *S. Dominique de Caleruega d'après les documents du XIIIe siècle* (Paris, 1955), French translations of the major sources with a useful introduction, cited as Vicaire (1955); and had as its chief predecessor P. Mandonnet and M.-H. Vicaire, *Saint Dominique, l'idée, l'homme et l'oeuvre* (2 vols., Paris, 1937), cited as Mandonnet-Vicaire. Vicaire (1964) treats exhaustively most aspects of Dominic's life; the majority of the numerous modern lives are of substantially less value. Among English studies, the interpretations of R. F. Bennett, *The Early Dominicans* (Cambridge, 1937) and D. Knowles, *Religious Orders in England*, I (Cambridge, 1948), pp. 146 ff. are of particular interest; Professor Knowles has discussed Vicaire (1964) at length in *Blackfriars*, XXXIX (1958), pp. 147–55.

In preparing this lecture I owe particular help to the guidance and inspiration of Professor David Knowles and of my wife, Dr R. B. Brooke.

the nature of the casting vote in general chapter, and equally capable of communicating to his friend Diana Dandalo, and to us, the inwardness of spiritual friendship and the delight of missionary work among the students of Bologna and Paris, many of whom he gathered into the Dominican Order. In addition, Jordan was Dominic's first biographer and one might well expect a biography of great authority, like the first life of St Bernard, or even of great intimacy, like Eadmer's *Life of St Anselm*.[2] Jordan's book is a very singular work; to me it seems full of surprises, surprising above all for its dullness; and it is this quality which I shall investigate here.

Needless to say, this quality has not escaped the attention of scholars. There are some who have not noticed, or not admitted it; but sooner or later it tends to be reflected in what they write. It has been particularly observed how sharp is the contrast between Jordan's book and the early lives of St Francis – a contrast which is a constant and legitimate source of complaint to students and disciples of Dominic. Three lines of explanation have been offered. It has been pointed out that Jordan did not know Dominic very well. Dominic was born about 1172, and was already well past forty when he began to found the Order; and he only spread it beyond the confines of Provence four years before his death. Jordan of Saxony became a Dominican in 1219; although we know they met before this, it cannot have been much more than a chance encounter; and they appear never to have been together for more than a few days, and that only two or three times, between 1219 and Dominic's death in 1221.[3] It is indeed somewhat surprising that Jordan should have become Dominic's successor as Master General of the Order, and even more surprising that he should have written the first life of the saint.

[2]Cf. R. W. Southern, *St Anselm and his Biographer* (Cambridge, 1963), esp. ch. IX.

[3] Cf. B. Altaner, *Der hl. Dominikus, Untersuchungen und Texte* (Breslau, 1922), pp. 6–7, 13–14; Bennett, *Early Dominicans*, p. 20 n. For Jordan's entry into the order and later career see esp. E. Mortier, *Histoire des maîtres généraux de l'Ordre des Frères Prêcheurs*, I (Paris, 1903), pp. 137–253; H. C. Scheeben, *Beiträge zur Geschichte Jordans von Sachsen* (*Q*[*uellen und*] *F*[*orschungen zur Geschichte des Dominikanerordens in*] *D*[*eutschland*], XXXV, 1938), pp. 36 ff.; *idem*, *Jordan von Sachsen* (Vechta, 1937).

The second line of explanation is, however, that his book is not a life at all, but a history of the foundation of the Order, and that Dominic as a person is therefore not central to its theme.[4] This too is true, but it is only a half truth, and looked at more closely adds to the puzzle rather than helps to solve it.

The third line of explanation is that Dominic was perhaps, after all, rather a dull man, and that Jordan was therefore in some sense making the best of a bad job. This has been the view of many historians, and it was given classic expression when H. C. Lea observed of Dominic 'he made less impression upon his contemporaries than his followers would have us believe'.[5]

Neither alone nor together do I find these explanations wholly satisfactory; and I take comfort at the outset by observing that some of the most eminent modern scholars who have worked on Dominic find him anything but dull.

Jordan's preface makes it clear that some of the friars had been grumbling that memory of the Order's early days and of Dominic was growing dim, and it was this which stirred him to write his book, in 1232 or 1233, a dozen years or so after the saint's death.[6] Since it was soon followed by Dominic's translation and canonization, we may reasonably suppose that one of its objects was to foster the cult. Like Celano's first life of St Francis, it was in some sense a *pièce justificative* for his canonization at the hands of his old friend and patron, Hugolino, Pope Gregory IX; though Celano's book was written after, whereas Jordan's preceded the canoniza-

[4] Cf. H. C. Scheeben's introduction to his edition of the Libellus (*M[onumenta] O[rdinis Fratrum] P[raedicatorum] H[istorica]* XVI, Rome, 1935), pp. 20–1 (cited as Jordan). Vicaire (1955), p. 16, emphasizes the positive qualities of Jordan: 'Il est maître de sa plume et sait conter avec agrément, brièveté, précision, bonhomie et humour'. This I do not deny: nor his capacity to give vivid personal impressions. What I find profoundly puzzling is his failure to make Dominic a living figure, a failure (noted by Vicaire, p. 18; and see below) made all the more striking by these qualities.

[5] H. C. Lea, *History of the Inquisition in the Middle Ages* (2nd edn.), (New York, 1908), I, p. 256, cited Bennett, *Early Dominicans*, p. 28.

[6] Between Christmas 1231 and May 1233: Scheeben in Jordan, p. 22; Vicaire (1955), p. 17. The account of the translation was added before 1235, probably in 1233–4; possibly as an addition to the *Libellus*, possibly as an encyclical letter (Vicaire (1955), pp. 16–17).

tion.[7] Yet it is not a biography or a saint's life in the ordinary sense. 'It seemed good to me,' writes Jordan in the preface, '– who, though I was not among the first, none the less have conversed with the first brothers and saw the blessed Dominic himself both when I was outside the Order and after I had joined it, and knew him well (*familiariter*); I made confession to him and took the order of deacon at his wish, and put on the habit four years after the Order was first founded; it seemed good to me, I say, to put in writing everything in order, which I saw myself and heard, and knew from the description of the first brothers, of the beginnings of the Order, of the life and miracles of our blessed father Dominic, and of some other brothers, as they came to my mind, so that his sons who will be born and arise in the future, shall not be ignorant of the first beginnings of this Order, and wish to know in vain, since passage of time may make it impossible to discover anything sure about those beginnings.'[8]

I have quoted this passage in full, because it makes abundantly clear, I think, two of the puzzles with which we are at grips. When St Bonaventure, like Jordan the head of his Order, and one of the great writers of the western world, set to work to write St Francis's life in the 1260s, he claimed that nothing would have induced him to do anything so presumptuous if the fervent wish of the brothers and the insistence of the whole General Chapter had not compelled him.[9] Thomas of Celano protests somewhat less, but his first life was written, he says, by Pope Gregory's order, and his second, composed in the name of Francis's intimate companions, was written on the instructions of the General Chapter and the Minister General.[10] This was the normal convention:

[7] Celano's two 'lives' (cited as 1 Cel., 2 Cel.) are in *Analecta Franciscana,* x (Quaracchi, 1926–41); for 1 Cel., see c.1 and note in MS. P, c. 151 (*ed. cit.*, p. 115 n.): I would accept the date, 25 Feb. 1229, in MS. P for the approval of 1 Cel., in spite of the doubts of J. R. H. Moorman, *Sources for the life of S. Francis of Assisi* (Manchester, 1940), pp. 67–8; cf. M. Bihl in *Archivum Franciscanum Historicum*, XXXIX (1946), p. 21 ff.

[8] Jordan, c. 3. 'Visum est mihi' is an echo of Luke 1, 3; the opening of Luke may have influenced other passages in Jordan (as Dr T. M. Parker has suggested to me), but it is not easy to establish any precise influence.

[9] *Legenda maior*, c. 3 (in *Analecta Franciscana*, x, p. 558).

[10] 2 Cel., cc. 1, 223.

to write a great man's life was presumptuous; one professed one's inadequacy and laid the blame on authority or on the insistence of friends.[11] Jordan of Saxony makes no such excuse: 'It seemed good to me,' he says, and he says it twice, making the best meanwhile of his own knowledge. This was at least a breach of convention, and is surprising; and it underlines the major problem: if Jordan did not really know Dominic well enough, why did he write at all? The prologue at least, if we may accept what it says, seems to make clear that no one forced him to write.

The second point is the ambiguity of purpose which is revealed. Jordan has confused two genres. Normally, one either wrote a life of a saint (or candidate for sainthood), or a history of the Order, like the various Cistercian *Exordia*.[12] It has commonly been supposed that Jordan really intended to write one or the other: in former times most scholars reckoned it was a life of the saint; in recent times it has been fashionable to call it a history of the Order. One of the manuscripts supports this view by referring to it as 'De initio ordinis', another as 'liber principii ordinis';[13] and its most recent editor, Dr Scheeben, reasonably entitled it 'Libellus de principiis', echoing Jordan's words. But the titles in the manuscripts have no authority, and Jordan's words suggest strongly that his purpose was twofold, if not frankly ambiguous. This is confirmed by the book itself. Most of the time Dominic is in the background. Several early brothers are sketched more vividly than he. One is prepared for this at the outset. 'There was a man in the land of Uz', runs the opening of the book of Job, 'whose name was Job'; Celano's first life of Francis echoes it thus: 'There was a man in the city of Assisi (which is situated on the confines of the valley of Spoleto) whose name was Francis.' But Jordan opens: 'There was a man in the parts of Spain of venerable life whose name was – Diego'[14] and in many early passages the initiative and

[11] The convention is not governed by anything like a rigid rule: but Jordan's breach of it is none the less striking.

[12] See esp. *Exordium Magnum Cisterciensis*, ed. B. Griesser (Rome, 1961); for the controversies on the earlier Cistercian documents, see D. Knowles, *Great Historical Enterprises* (London, 1963), pp. 197 ff.

[13] Jordan, ed. Scheeben, p. 25, n.a.

[14] 1 Cel., c. 1; Jordan, c. 4.

holiness of Diego, Bishop of Osma, Dominic's first patron, are stressed far more than Dominic's own work. This was not imposed on Jordan by his material, for after the first chapter on Diego, we are carried back to Dominic's family and birth and given a conventional hagiographical narrative until Dominic arrives at Osma. It almost seems as if Jordan dragged Diego in at the outset to put Dominic in his place. And so it goes on: as one reads, from time to time one thinks that the book is tending clearly in one direction; then in another. Down to Diego's death in chapter 30, the Bishop is the central figure; then Dominic takes over and one is rapidly transported through the early stages to the key moment, in the brief chapters 53–5, when the brothers first settled in Paris, Orléans, and Bologna. At this stage the excitement is mounting, and one might expect, from any point of view, an exposition of Dominic's own work and plans as the Order at last took shape. But chapters 56–85 are (with very brief interludes) concerned with two other friars, Reginald and Henry, and with Jordan's own entry into the Order. In chapters 86–7 Jordan and Dominic meet briefly at the General Chapter in Bologna in 1221, the last of Dominic's life, but in chapter 88 Jordan sets off for Lombardy; 89–91 are an interlude on brother Everard, and in chapter 92 Dominic takes to his bed for the last time. This is not the end: his death, burial, and miracles occupy some space, and there is an account at the end of his manner of life and holy character, followed, characteristically, by a passage on another friar. Down to the death of Dominic, an impartial reader is bound to feel that it is primarily the Order, not the saint, which interested Jordan. But this is not the final impression; for one cannot help but observe that Dominic's life provides the framework of the whole. It opens, in effect, with his birth, and it closes with his death – to which his translation was later added as an afterthought.[15] There is not a word on the Order's affairs between 1221 and 1232; perhaps Jordan felt it was unbecoming to describe his own generalate, and perhaps it was too recent to need any description. But one cannot help noticing the contrast between Jordan's readiness to describe the history of the Order before he knew it and his silence on most of what he knew really well. If he

[15] See Jordan, pp. 4 ff.; Vicaire (1955), pp. 16 ff.

was more concerned to tell the history of the Order than of the saint, it is hard to see why the book should culminate in what purports to be a characterization of the founder, and why its author should regard an isolated event in the 1230s (the saint's translation) as a suitable addition all on its own.

Unintelligible, that is, unless we decide, in the end, that Jordan was simply incapable of writing a sensible book or of sticking to his purpose. This is a possible view, and it cannot be convincingly refuted, since we have no other work of his comparable in scale or design. Yet two things tell against it. First, clarity of purpose is most decisively revealed in Jordan's work as Master General.[16] Throughout the years when first St Francis and then Brother Elias were reducing the Order of Friars Minor to chaos, Jordan of Saxony was forming and establishing the tiny plant which he, scarcely out of his novitiate, had taken over from the founder, and seeing it grow into a great Order. It is perfectly true that successful men of action often fumble when they take to the pen; but our second difficulty in believing Jordan to be merely incompetent is the contrast between the *De principiis* and his letters. They are not long or elaborate enough for us to judge their author as an exponent of literary form; but they reveal a man who knew the conventions of writing in his age – and so presumably knew the conventions which he has broken in his book; they show a singular adroitness in adapting tone and style to a particular situation, and he asks for and gives consolation with a skill reminiscent of St Bernard. Here is his Christmas card to Sister Diana: 'I have had no time to write you a letter on the ample scale I would wish, but I am writing and sending you one word – one small word enclosed in a manger, which was made flesh for us, the Word of grace and health, of sweetness and glory, good and soothing: Christ Jesus and Him crucified, lifted up on the cross, raised up to the right hand of the Father. Raise your soul to Him

[16] See above, p. 215, n.; H. C. Scheeben, *Die Konstitutionen des Predigerordens unter Jordan von Sachsen* (*QFD*, XXXVIII, 1939); the early recension of the constitutions is also ed. Denifle, in *Archiv für Litteratur- und Kirchengeschicht edes Mittelalters*, I (1885), pp. 165–227; French transl. in Vicaire (1955), pp. 137 ff.; for their historical development, see Mandonnet-Vicaire, II, pp. 203 ff., 273 ff.; Vicaire (1955), pp. 113–21; G. R. Galbraith, *The Constitution of the Dominican Order, 1216–1360* (Manchester, 1925).

and may rest be yours in Him for ever. . . . And there is another short and modest word, your affection and your heart, which will speak up for me and make amends for me in your heart to your loving self. . . .'[17] Jordan can be economical in his use of language: when he describes the students he has recruited to the Order one is left to assume much of the excitement of his fishing; but he handles the theme of human affection with a firm, deft hand, though always in the context of divine love and eternity. It is the quality most strikingly developed, sometimes quite passionately developed, in the letters, and it is the quality most difficult to grasp in the *De principiis*. However unwillingly, we must face the possibility that the dullness of Jordan's book, and the ambiguity of its purpose, were in some sense and some measure deliberate.

At a casual reading, the *De principiis* gives the impression that Dominic's purpose unfolded inexorably, that he was a man of deep reflection who (however affable to his friars) kept his own counsel and made his own, carefully reflected, plans. Yet there is evidence from a variety of sources that Dominic could be extremely impulsive; and this has sometimes been noticed by modern scholars, at least as an occasional intrusion into a calm life.[18] Let us pause for a moment to consider three striking pieces of evidence of his impulsiveness.

On 13 August 1233, twelve years after Dominic's death, Brother Stephen, prior provincial of Lombardy, was called to give evidence at the process for Dominic's canonization – the records of which form the only substantial body of early evidence about the saint apart from Jordan's *De principiis*.[19] 'He also said that when he himself, the witness, was studying at Bologna, Master Dominic came to Bologna and preached to the scholars and other good men, and he himself confessed his sins to him, and it seemed to him that Dominic was attracted to him. One evening, when the witness was sitting down to dinner in his hostel with his fellow-students, brother Dominic sent two friars to him, saying: "Brother Dominic commands that you come instantly to him."

[17] *Beati Iordani de Saxonia Epistulae*, ed. A. Walz (*MOPH*, XXIII, 1951), no. xli.

[18] Cf. esp. Knowles, *Religious Orders*, I, p. 149 and n. 5.

[19] *MOPH*, XVI (1935), pp. 153–54.

And he replied: "When I have had my dinner, I will come to him." And they said: "No! Come at once." And so he got up, left them all, and went to Dominic; and he found him with a crowd of friars in St Nicholas' church. And brother Dominic said to the friars: "Show him how to ask forgiveness." When he had asked pardon, he put his hands in Dominic's – and before he let him go, Dominic put the habit of the Friars Preachers on him saying, "I will give you arms, with which you may fight against the devil the whole of your life." And the witness was mightily astonished, then and later, how Dominic came to call him and clothe him in the habit of the Friars Preacher, since they had had no previous conversation on his entering religion. He believes he did it by divine inspiration or revelation.'

The second piece of evidence comes from Franciscan sources, and is perhaps the most celebrated, and certainly the most disputed event in Dominic's life. It is the familiar story of how Francis and Dominic met in Rome in the palace of Cardinal Hugolino, patron of both Orders.[20] It tells how, after a highly edifying exchange of humility, Dominic asked Francis to give him his girdle, and suggested that the two Orders should be merged. The story comes from Celano's second life of St Francis and although it is not one of those whose source can still be found in the writings of Brother Leo and his fellow-companions of the saint, Celano was usually careful to collect his information from friars who had known Francis well.

This is the only one of the many stories of meetings between Francis and Dominic which is generally accepted by modern scholars as having an authentic nucleus. Most recent accounts of their relations depend on a penetrating study by Berthold Altaner, who dated this meeting to the early months of 1221.[21] By this date

[20] 2 Cel. cc. 148–50.

[21] 'Die Beziehungen des hl. Dominikus zum hl. Franziskus von Assisi', *Franziskanische Studien* IX (1922), pp. 1–28. Altaner argued in favour of 1221, though he reckoned a meeting in 1216 (using Gerard of Fracheto – see below) a possibility. His argument for 1221 depended on the assumption that Francis and Hugolino first met in 1218, a view no longer held; but Altaner's date for the meeting of the two saints has survived the removal of its main prop: cf. Vicaire (1964), pp. 494, 515, 521 (Vicaire is even more sceptical than Altaner about Gerard of Fracheto's narrative, and says in general (p. 515): 'the

Dominic's work for his Order was nearly complete, and his death not many months away. However impulsive he was, it is really incredible that he should seriously have proposed a merger at that date, especially as the Franciscans were only just beginning to recover from some months of disarray due to the founder's absence in the east. It has therefore become the custom to accept the story of the saints' meeting, but deny its content, or assume that in practice all that took place was a friendly exchange of good feeling. But if it could be placed some four or five years earlier, as some scholars have held,[22] one might take Dominic's scheme quite seriously, so long as one is prepared to accept him as a man of unusual humility and impulsiveness.

In his first life Celano describes a crucial meeting between Francis and Hugolino in Florence. Before this meeting, he tells us, they were not intimately acquainted, but linked in mutual charity by repute of holiness alone – 'sola fama beate vite'. It has sometimes been supposed that they were now meeting for the first time; but if so, one would hardly trouble to say they were not 'intimately acquainted', and it is for various reasons difficult to believe that this was indeed their first meeting. Since, however, the work in which it is described was commissioned by Hugolino himself (as Pope Gregory IX), the impression it gives, that Hugolino and Francis had not met often before, is likely to be correct. This meeting probably took place in 1217, certainly not later than 1218.[23] It was Dominic's practice to visit Rome in the winter and

meeting of the two saints remains hypothetical'). It has sometimes been argued that mendicant hagiographers would naturally have invented meetings of the two saints. They are, however, remarkably rare in the early legends (apart from the two discussed here, there seems nothing till the much later story in the *Actus-Fioretti*, and Altaner, p. 8, shrewdly observed that St Bonaventure had succeeded in reproducing the gist of the passage from 2 Cel. while quietly dropping Dominic from it).

[22] See H. Grundmann, *Die religiöse Bewegungen im Mittelalter* (2nd edn., Hildesheim, 1961), pp. 145 f.

[23] 1 Cel. cc. 74–5; cf. A. Callebaut in *Archivum Franciscanum Historicum*, XIX (1926), pp. 530–58; R. B. Brooke, *Early Franciscan Government* (Cambridge, 1959), pp. 286–7. 1218 is much less likely than 1217, since in 1218 Hugolino did not reach Florence until August at the earliest, and possibly October. For the evidence that Hugolino and Francis met before 1217, see Grundmann, *op. cit.*, p. 146 n.

this meeting with Francis in Hugolino's presence could have taken place at the turn of any year between late 1215 and early 1218 or at the turn of 1220 and 1221.[24] If we are to place any credence in the passage which describes how Dominic suggested a union, we should look for as early a date as possible, before Dominic's Order and its un-Franciscan features were formed. 1216, 1217, or the opening months of 1218 would meet these conditions.

The other early version of the meeting of the two saints is in some ways even better authenticated. It occurs in the collection of stories about the early Dominicans gathered by Gerard of Fracheto in the late 1250s, a book which has earned a bad reputation owing to the extreme credulity of its author.[25] Yet there are copious indications that he did not invent the tales he recounts, but faithfully passed on what he was told. For our purpose, the naïve scribe Fracheto is in some ways preferable to the more sophisticated Celano. Fracheto, moreover, is quite specific about his source: 'A certain Friar Minor, observant and reliable, a man who had been for long a companion of St Francis told (the story) to several friars, one of whom put it in writing for the Master of the Order.' He goes on to tell how Dominic was in Rome, appealing to God and the Pope 'for the Order's confirmation'; and how he had a dream in which he saw the Blessed Virgin present Dominic and Francis to Christ as two men who would bring the world back to Him. Francis was then a stranger to Dominic; but when he met him next day in a church, Dominic recognized him as the colleague of his dream, embraced him, and said: ' "you are my colleague, you and I will run the race together; we will stand as one man and no adversary will prevail against us". Then he told his vision, and they were from that moment "one heart and one soul"[26] in God.'

[24] For Dominic's visits to Rome, see Vicaire (1964), pp. 191, 202, 216, 240, 277, 330, 336 and notes. In 1218–19 he wintered in Spain, and in 1219–20 St Francis was in the east.

[25] Gerard de Fracheto, *Vitae Fratrum*, i, 1, 4, ed. B. M. Reichert, *MOPH*, 1 (Louvain, 1896), pp. 9–11.

[26] Cf. Acts, iv, 32, also quoted by the prologue to the early Dominican Constitutions, from the Rule of St Augustine (*QFD*, XXXVIII (1939), p. 49).

In spite of its credentials, this story has commonly been disbelieved; largely, perhaps, because it was first printed from a manuscript which ascribed the event to the time of the Fourth Lateran Council of 1215; and it is doubtful if Francis attended the Council. But the reference to the Order's confirmation, which is all that the best manuscripts give as an indication of date,[27] more naturally refers to Dominic's visit to Rome at the end of 1216, when he succeeded in obtaining his Order's confirmation. And if it be true that this was their first meeting, the meeting in Celano's second *Life* cannot be earlier than the arrival of Dominic in Rome in November 1216.

It sits on the surface of these stories, however, that they describe the same meeting. The purpose of the story in Celano is to emphasize that the two Orders should imitate their founders, who were so close in spirit they even thought of uniting the Orders. Doubtless the same intention underlay the transmission of Fracheto's narrative, although he gave it its place in his book as evidence of the part the Blessed Virgin played in the foundation of the Order of Preachers. One is the more inclined, therefore, to give credence to the part of the story irrelevant to this purpose – namely the meeting with Francis, and Dominic's initiative in suggesting that they should work together – which is probably as near as a Dominican source could ever get to the suggestion for a union. One might argue, indeed, that the Franciscans were only too likely to invent such a suggestion. But Celano's narrative reveals some embarrassment. The tale in general is intended to show the two saints' friendly rivalry in humility; it is implied that

[27] Only MS C (and later sources) attribute it to the Lateran Council; since this is one of the two surviving MSS of Gerard's second recension, it could be, as Reichert seems to have supposed, that this was Gerard's own second thought. But if his apparatus correctly states that C alone (which Reichert knew only at second hand), and not A, the other MS of the second recension, has this change, it seems more likely to be a later gloss. The other MSS read 'pro ordinis confirmacione'; 'confirmatio ordinis' is the phrase used by Jordan, c. 45, for the confirmation by Honorius III in 1216. Grundmann, *Die religiöse Bewegungen*, pp. 146 ff., shows that it is on the whole probable that Francis visited Rome in 1215, so that 1215 is a possible date for the meeting of the saints; but the indications seem clearly to favour 1216.

neither obtained a decisive advantage in the competition over the other. But this effect can only be sustained by a slight stratagem. When Dominic makes his offer, Francis's reply is not recorded. One is left to assume that he said no rather firmly; but to admit as much would have given Dominic a clear advantage. To believe this story a Franciscan invention is not without its difficulties;[28] and the more closely one looks at the two stories, the more probable it becomes, I would think, that they represent two different versions, separately transmitted by early companions of St Francis, of the same incident. If we accept this, then Dominic offered Francis an amalgamation at the turn of 1216 and 1217; whether we accept it or not, Fracheto's story is clear evidence that the two saints met and that Dominic took the initiative in expressing their unity of purpose, at this date.

In 1216 Dominic had about sixteen friars, and in that year they were first recognized as an Order following the rule of St Augustine, that is to say, as canons regular, but with a special instruction to preach. They were still a very local Order, living all together in Toulouse. But in 1217 their lay protector, Simon de Montfort, lost his grip on Toulouse, and Jordan of Saxony himself provides us with our third piece of evidence for Dominic's impulsiveness.[29] Dominic foresaw, he tells us, Count Simon's death. 'Then he called on the Holy Spirit and gathered the brothers, and said to them that this was his heart's intention, that he should send them throughout the world, few though they were, and that they should live together there no more. They were all astonished at this pronouncement of so sudden a decision; but the clear authority of sainthood in him inspired them, and they readily acquiesced, hoping that it would all turn out for the best.' The tiny band was sent to Spain, France, and Italy, and soon afterwards Paris and Bologna, the university cities, became their headquarters, and the whole of Christendom their parish. At the same time Dominic set up another friar as abbot of the congregation, though retaining ultimate direction himself.

[28] See above, pp. 222–3 n. 21.

[29] Jordan, cc. 46–8. For the background to these events, see Vicaire (1964), ch. XII, and esp. pp. 229–30 for evidence that Dominic had some special experience in Rome in 1216–17.

If I may for a moment simplify somewhat crudely the picture of Dominic with which we have commonly been presented, I might say that he appears as the type of the calm administrator, the man with a clear purpose, the model of medieval constitutional theory in practice, the man to whom we owe the principle of representative government.[30] For all these propositions there is a good deal to be said; they cannot tell the whole truth, but they are near enough to it to make Jordan's story as astonishing to us as it was to his brothers – and even more astonishing, as I would think, the lack of surprise with which most modern historians have greeted it. Dominic had toiled among the Cathars for many years, in spite of every discouragement, with little to show in the way of outward success; suddenly he threw his cap over the moon; the apostle of representative government turned his Order upside down without any sort of consultation or referendum. Jordan tells the story in his cool, matter-of-fact, deadpan way, and gives no clue what lay behind it – save that it followed the collapse of Simon de Montfort's authority. This is a reasonable explanation of the timing of the move, but inadequate to explain the cataclysmic nature of the move itself. If a lay patron fails, it is sensible to look for a safer refuge; Dominic's solution was (from a worldly point of view) the supreme gamble of his life. In the main, he turned his back on the heretics; he turned to the Church at large, to recruiting in student centres, to organizing a peripatetic order, to preaching everywhere and to everyone.

The universities were a new goldmine. But in turning his back on the heretics, in looking to the world at large, in sending the

[30] Vicaire, loc. cit., cites evidence for a mysterious illumination about this period, and observes how little we know of the saint's inner spiritual life. This is very true, and it may be held that the discussion in the text proceeds at a somewhat superficial level. But Dominic was evidently a man profoundly influenced by the world around him. Constantine of Orvieto (c. 25, *MOPH*, XVI, p. 304), writing in 1246–7, adds a vision in Rome to Jordan's narrative and makes this the explanation of his *démarche*; a witness at the canonization (*MOPH*, XVI, p. 185) attributed the dispersal to 'spiritus propheticus', which does not, however, suggest any special knowledge of the matter. Another witness noted that Dominic acted against the will of Simon de Montfort, the Archbishop of Narbonne, the Bishop of Toulouse, 'et quorumdam aliorum prelatorum' (*MOPH*, XVI, pp. 143–4).

friars on long tours – and in appointing someone else to be disciplinary head of the Order – Dominic was doing what Francis had done. If it is true that Dominic and Francis had met a few months before this event, and that Dominic had been so gripped by Francis's inspiration that he offered to submerge his Order in Francis's, then something of the strangeness of Jordan's story is made plain. No doubt visions of a new vocation for his Order had been in Dominic's mind before, but the very suddenness of his resolution suggests a recent, overwhelming experience of the kind men suffered at the hands of Francis of Assisi. That Francis influenced Dominic is so obvious an idea that scholars have been competing with one another for two generations to find ever more ingenious proofs that it did not or need not have happened.[31] It is perhaps true to say that those who approach the problem through the study of Francis have generally assumed that Francis influenced Dominic, as (they usually feel) he must influence any sensitive person who comes in contact with him. Those whose first interest lies in Dominic have generally denied all influence or at least been minimizers. I am a *Franciscanisant* by marriage, and so, it may be thought, inclined to maximize his influence. It may be so. The precise nature of Francis's influence on Dominic can never be fully demonstrated; and the issue has been somewhat confused by a concentration in most discussions on the subject on the issue of poverty. Students of St Francis will always feel, no doubt, that the marked development in Dominic's idea of poverty in his later years owed something to Francis.[32] But strict ideas of poverty lay in the atmosphere they breathed, and Dominic never went further than the Waldensians or the Cathar *perfecti* with whom he had so long disputed. The idea that the right way to deal with the heretics was to ignore them, to walk all over Christendom – and beyond – and that the right way to run an Order was to abdicate: these were much more original notions, and in their pursuit Dominic (consciously or unconsciously) was imitating

[31] Cf. the wise comment of Professor Knowles in *Blackfriars*, XXXIX (1958), pp. 153–4.

[32] Cf. Knowles, *Religious Orders in England*, I, p. 149 and n. For a judicious statement of the argument for Dominican independence, see R. F. Bennett, *Early Dominicans*, pp. 33 ff.

Francis. That much is certain; the rest each student will decide for himself.

A leader among the early Franciscans once observed that the Friars Minor should love the Preachers very much, because they owed much to them and had occasionally been shown by them what not to do.[33] There are reasons for thinking that Dominic may have returned the compliment by deliberately avoiding some of the most striking characteristics of the Franciscan movement. The Order of Friars Minor was the personal creation of its founder: 'After the Lord had given me brothers, no man showed me what I ought to do; but the Most High Himself revealed to me that I ought to live according to the teachings of the Holy Gospel. And I dictated a simple Rule in a few words, and the Lord Pope confirmed it for me.'[34] Obedience was as central to Francis's ideal as poverty – obedience to the Pope, to the bishops, to the poorest priest: 'Holy obedience makes a man subject to all the men of this world, and not only to men but also to all beasts and wild animals, to do with him what they will – so far as is granted them by the Lord on high.'[35] But he remained the sole guiding spirit of his Order; the Rule, however much he might rewrite it, was the same Rule dictated to him by God; he repudiated papal privileges and relied until 1223 on purely verbal assent to his Rule.[36]

Francis's vision and his Rule were the sole stable authorities in his Order while he was alive. He was an unquiet man to live with, unpredictable, arbitrary, sometimes absurd;[37] he had a talent for

[33] 'occasionaliter instruxerunt nos ad futura pericula precavenda' (Albert of Pisa in Thomas of Eccleston, *De adventu Fratrum Minorum in Angliam*, ed. A. G. Little, Manchester, 1951, p. 82).

[34] *Testament,* in *Opuscula S. Patris Francisci Assisiensis* (2nd edn., Quaracchi 1941), p. 79.

[35] *Salutatio virtutum, Opuscula*, p. 21, see above, p. 204.

[36] In the *Testament*, Francis passes from the first to the last Rule without any indication that there was any difference between them: to him there was none, since both expressed in words God's revelation to him. For Innocent III's assent to the Rule, see H. Grundmann, *Die religiöse Bewegungen im Mittelalter,* 2nd. edn., pp. 127 ff.

[37] As when he wandered into the woods when his cell was about to catch fire to avoid having to harm 'brother fire'; this story comes from an excellent source: *La 'Legenda antiqua S. Francisci'*, ed. F. M. Delorme, *La France franciscaine*, II (Paris, 1926), nos. 49–50 (=*Scripta Leonis*, c. 50).

anarchy which he used with all the inspiration and the guile of a great teacher to instruct his followers that they must learn to live according to the gospel, and not enjoy the comforts of the Law. The effect of this was to make his Order noted for its disorderliness, its tendency to fall apart; and to encourage his followers, like the followers of Mohammed, to support their various theories as to how the Order should be governed by telling stories about the founder. In Dominic's Order this was neither necessary nor possible – at least to the extent that it occurred among the Minors. When a Dominican General Chapter issued an admonition suppressing a passage in the legend of the saint, the friars were hardly doing even on a small scale what Bonaventure did on the grand scale; they were not plastering the cracks, but merely attempting to suppress a tale about the founder which they reckoned unedifying.[38] There was little danger of his becoming the centre of controversies in the Order. His intentions were too little known and he had never attempted, after the revolution of 1217, to dictate to his followers in the way St Francis did. Strictly speaking, there was no rule save the rule of St Augustine; and even the constitutions which Dominic composed and promulgated in general chapters could have been changed, so far as we can tell, by any general chapter down to 1228.[39] It was in that year that Jordan of Saxony held the first *generalissimum* chapter, a grand affair (though even that was a remarkably compact body compared with the Franciscan General Chapter), which laid down that certain clauses in the constitutions were entrenched and unalterable, and that none of the others could be changed except by the approving votes of three consecutive General Chapters. It seems clear that the Order in the early 1220s had been too free to change its rules and constitutions; and this emphasizes how completely, at the end of his

[38] Cf. *Acta Capitulorum Generalium O.P.*, I, *MOPH*, III, p. 24; Moorman, *Sources for the life of St Francis*, pp. 141 ff., 148 and n.

[39] For the early constitutions, see above, p. 220 n 16.: I accept the general lines of Prof. Vicaire's reconstruction, though the evidence is not sufficient to make every detail secure, and we cannot tell what early canons were dropped before 1228. But Humbert de Romans specifically states that each individual chapter could make or abolish constitutions before 1228 (cited Mandonnet-Vicaire, II, p. 207 n.). The first part of the Constitutions, detailing the internal life of the Order, was sometimes referred to, however, as a 'rule'.

life, the founder had submerged his own views and methods in those of his brothers. Dominic and Jordan could afford a representative system of government with much wider powers than those enjoyed by the Franciscan General Chapter because they had no such sense of basic authority as Francis enjoyed. The Franciscans were blessed because God had spoken to Francis; the Dominicans reckoned that the Holy Spirit worked, in the long run, in the small committee of priors or elected representatives they called their General Chapter. As Dominic had taken upon himself to spread the friars by an arbitrary decision, so by an act less dramatic but in a way equally revealing an impulsive faith, he abdicated his authority in his last two years more completely than ever Francis did. Once again, one cannot fail to observe his extraordinary humility.

Dominic, then, submerged his personality in the Order. So effective was this that it would seem that he was in danger of being forgotten. If these inferences have any force, we are compelled to suppose that in the early 1230s Jordan of Saxony was faced by a dilemma. As a faithful servant of Dominic he must have known that the saint had repudiated what would nowadays be called a 'personality cult'. At the same time he and Hugolino, now Pope Gregory IX, doubtless wished to do due honour to his memory and have him canonized; and for this a revival of interest, a decorous propaganda of his sanctity was needed. The older friars, furthermore, could not fail to observe that Thomas of Celano had done honour to Francis, while Dominic's memory was fading; so they made entreaty that something should be committed to writing while there was yet time. In the Order of Friars Minor the 1220s and even more the 1230s were an era of conflict, all the more confused because no clear parties existed at this date.[40] So far as we know conflicts in the Order of Preachers were stifled at birth; and when one considers how free they were to criticize their General, how powerful, in theory, was the General Chapter, one can only marvel at the diplomatic skill of the first two Masters General, Dominic and Jordan. My own view is that Jordan's *De principiis* is an illustration of this: that he wished to do honour to the saint without departing from Dominic's own wish to be sub-

[40] See R. B. Brooke, *op. cit.* (p. 223 n.).

merged in the Order. This would at least explain why Jordan took all the responsibility for the book: he took the initiative out of the friars' hands so that he could give them the kind of book he felt was right for the circumstances. When Jordan wrote, Francis was vividly remembered as a human saint; several generations had to pass before he could become the ghostly thaumaturge of the *Fioretti* or the remote mystic of renaissance art. There were men alive in 1232–3 to whom Dominic was as vivid a memory as was Francis to his friends – and some of them gave witness in the canonization process, which for all its formal purpose is often a more lively document than Jordan's *De principiis*. Yet Jordan's Dominic is a man of conventional saintly virtues, whose intense humanity is already largely hidden. Jordan's successors added very little to his story, though Gerard of Fracheto and his helpers added to the number of his miracles, and the tradition that Dominic should appear as unlike Francis as could be was finally consummated in the revolting story of how he plucked a sparrow alive because it had the devil in it.[41]

In the end Dominic remains largely hidden from us. We can lift the curtain, but Dominic and Jordan swiftly and peremptorily lower it again. Yet this has the curious effect, not of diminishing, but of enhancing our sense of what the Dominicans owe to their founder. Lea thought that Dominic 'made less impression upon his contemporaries than his followers would have us believe'. I have tried to make clear why I think this may be the opposite of the truth.

[41] *Miracula b. Dominici*, by Sister Cecilia, c. 10, ed. A. Walz, *Misc. Pio Paschini*, 1 (Rome, 1949), pp. 306 ff. (this claims to be an eyewitness account; but the historicity of these *Miracula* is very doubtful).

12

The Merchant of Prato

A lecture given in the University of Newcastle-upon-Tyne (then King's College of the University of Durham) in March 1960. It is in the main a meditation based on Iris Origo, The Merchant of Prato *(London, 1957; the quotations are from the Peregrine Books ed., Harmondsworth, 1963).*

I want to take you in imagination back nearly 600 years – to meet an exceptionally wealthy, but otherwise very ordinary fourteenth-century merchant, to see reflected in him and his associates what the Christian religion and the Catholic Church meant to ordinary folk in the late Middle Ages. The doors are usually shut on the ordinary lives and assumptions of medieval people, and rather particularly of merchants, before the fifteenth century. Private letters of merchants are rare enough then; but if we go back to the twelfth and thirteenth centuries, even to Italy, the chief scene of merchant enterprise, there is virtually nothing comparable to the letters of the Celys and the Stonors of fifteenth-century England. Yet suddenly, in the second half of the fourteenth century, the windows of a merchant's house in Prato in north Italy, not far from Florence, are thrown wide open, and the personality and concerns of a wealthy merchant are revealed to us more precisely and more fully even than those of the Celys and the Pastons. The great riches of the *Archivio Datini* have been pillaged by a succession of Italian economic historians, and have provided crucial evidence for the techniques of commerce and banking in the fourteenth and early fifteenth centuries; they have also been used, less fully, by students of life and thought. Some years ago, a vivid biography of the Merchant of Prato was published in English by Iris Origo, which has made available for us, in summary, the whole picture of the merchant's family and business life.

Francesco di Marco Datini was born in or about 1335, and died in 1410. He was not born to poverty, but his parents died of the plague when he was young, and he was brought up by a guardian of somewhat straitened means. At the mature age of fifteen, Francesco set off with a small sum of money to the great city of opportunity of the day, the crowded and stuffy capital of the western Church and of western finance, Avignon, where the Popes lived for most of the fourteenth century. The Hundred Years War between England and France was at its height, and Avignon proved a convenient centre from which to engage in the armaments trade, on which Francesco's fortune was firmly based. From the start, however, he seems to have grasped three essential principles on which his prosperity was built: first, that a man could not prosper alone, but must enter into partnership with trustworthy associates; second, that trade was an uncertain and fluctuating business, and that it was unwise to put all one's eggs in one basket (all his life he sought for new outlets, new ways of investing his money so that his wealth should not depend on a single type of business or a single fleet of ships); and thirdly, he learned that moderate wealth was more secure than a sensational fortune. Although by the fourteenth century the Italian merchant bankers had devised a very elaborate system of credit instruments and most of the machinery of a banking system, currency was still inflexible, and credit was none too clearly related to silver and gold. The large banking houses achieved their positions by acting as agents for the Courts of Europe, above all for the papal Court, which from the late twelfth and thirteenth centuries on was involved in collecting vast sums in taxation from every corner of Europe. But the great banking houses came to depend on the Courts of Europe for their position: political favour was the key to their power and wealth, and they could not afford to dispense with royal favour as well as papal. Thus in the mid fourteenth century the English King Edward III discovered that he could force extravagant loans from the Florentine companies of the Bardi and the Peruzzi, until he eventually drove them to bankruptcy, involving in their destruction a great number of Florentines rich and poor. Francesco di Marco attempted, on the whole successfully, to keep out of politics; and so he never became one of the very great, and never went bankrupt. But he did everything else: he traded in armour and salt and cloth and Heaven knows what; he dealt in currency exchange. Gradually he entered partnerships and established agents over a wide area, especially in Italy and Spain; and eventually, in 1383, after over thirty years at Avignon, he returned to Prato a man of wealth.

He brought with him a young Florentine wife whom he had recently married in Avignon, and they set up a house together in Prato, though in the middle years of their married life they lived apart, he most often in Florence, she in Prato, and to this curious circumstance the historian owes a unique family correspondence. Both partners were strong-willed and efficient, and Marco was evidently a very able man of business. But neither was particularly well educated – the wife learned to write only after they were married; nor had they any special literary talents. But there emerges from the correspondence a pair of very striking characters, a vision of a marriage which was by no means a happy one, and yet far from a total failure; and from their letters and those of Francesco's Florentine attorney, Ser Lapo Mazzei, the merchant's one really intimate friend, a picture of the conventional setting of life which helps us, if we read the letters imaginatively, to answer a number of otherwise unanswerable questions.

Francesco, then, was a man of a strongly conventional turn of mind. He made his pile, intending to marry, rear a family to enjoy his wealth, then gradually withdraw from business and do his share of good works before he died. None of these schemes turned out quite as he expected. The marriage was childless, and not all the best and the worst medical advice of the period could help the couple to legitimate offspring. Francesco had children, though not many; and after a while one of them was brought up as his own, with his wife's grudging consent. As an old man he was able to console himself by getting a cardinal (the celebrated Pierre d'Ailly) to baptize one of his grandchildren – in his old age his prudence and avoidance of politics became somewhat eclipsed.

Margherita's failure to have children set up a barrier between husband and wife, and is clearly one of the chief reasons why he stayed away from home for such long periods. His letters to her are domineering, fussy, suspicious, and full of urgent repetition; in return she gave as good as she got in swift repartee, down-to-earth comment, explanation, and complaint. She was quick-tempered without malice; he full of care, suspicious of everyone, determined to rule his household in every detail, even though he visited it so rarely.

The correspondence provides us with a very remarkable commentary on medieval marriage. There is no hint of romance about it, though a pleasant hint of imprudence in the fact that Margherita had no dowry – but she 'came of good family'. There was certainly nothing else imprudent about it. The husband expected to be the director of all family concerns, to subject his wife, children, servants, and slaves (for slaves were not uncommon in fourteenth-century Italy) to a moral discipline distinctly more strict than he himself adhered to. The wife was expected to bear children and to run the home: she was the housekeeper, her husband's bailiff; but she also had the privilege of intimacy with him, and if she managed him in the boudoir, that was his affair, so long as she did not parade her dominance in public. Margherita's letters are often shrewish; but it seems clear that she played her part in public very well.

They had no children, nor did they live together for many years; and these were plainly the purposes for which Francesco had married her. But for all that there seems to have been a respect and a deep affection between them which matured in the last nine years of his life, when they were together more or less continuously; and although neither partner had conspicuously softened with age their relationship was definitely more mellow. At the least, it had survived the crisis at which Francesco's attorney had written to him: 'Let not the many, many letters you write, to increase your bodily welfare and your riches in this world, make you lose your charity and love for the person to whom you are bound by God's laws. For your rough soul and your frozen heart need to be comforted.'[1]

[1] Origo, p. 177.

The religious beliefs of the merchant of Prato were of the most conventional and orthodox kind: in a word he accepted the normal beliefs of his age without question; he had little time in early life for religious observance, but in his heart tried to treat God with the respect due to one's most powerful creditor; like many men of affairs he was superstitious and quickly swayed by a striking sermon; as with most sermon-goers the effect rapidly faded. He took great pains to avoid open usury; he took even greater pains to become rich; he admired and respected all the material symbols of wealth and power; invisible forces of good and evil he feared; he courted cardinals, but subscribed to the conventional anti-clericalism of his more earnest friend the attorney; he left all his goods to feed and clothe the poor.

The merchant's attitude to Church and religion appears in two ways: in the way in which the Church impinged on his work as a merchant, and in the expressions of his piety. The attitude of the medieval Church to wealth and its problems was a good deal more coherent and instructed than is often supposed. It is true that it started with a rigid law against usury which made illegal any open investment of money at interest, and so invited every kind of evasion and prevarication; and every responsible churchman, in reflecting on wealth, was bound to start by saying that 'it is easier for a camel to go through the eye of a needle, than for a rich man to enter the Kingdom of God'. But it was also part of the general social assumptions of medieval man that a wise man lived up to his wealth. The worst crime of the man of wealth was avarice; it was worse than mere greed. Francesco was often balanced on a knife-edge, as it were, between his fear of being thought too miserly and his fear of being thought too rich. Most men preferred the latter to the former. It was the Church's business to care for the well-being of poor and rich alike; and the medieval Church had taken on itself the task of distributing charity so as to meet the needs of the poor. It was one of the main duties of a rich man's confessor to direct his spending towards charity; to make sure that sufficient was spent to help alleviate local poverty and to prepare the rich man's soul for its encounter with the needle.

All this provided an outlet for wealth once acquired; but the attitude of the Church to its acquiring seems to have been purely negative. It suspected (quite correctly) hidden usury in most processes; but it is fair to say that many of the best minds who attended to the problems of usury and just price and excessive profit, began, from the thirteenth century on, to realize that mercantile profit was not just making something out of nothing, that the poor abused middleman was performing some function in society; though they hardly realized how much their own society was based on the rise of money economy since the eighth and ninth centuries, on the operations of money and markets in the eleventh and twelfth centuries and later, and on the extraordinary enterprise of medieval merchants. But a Pope could not be unaware that the finances of the papal monarchy would have been inconceivable without the developing techniques of exchange and banking. It is a notorious fact that this led to much winking at illegality; but it could equally be said that it led to a broader understanding by the Church of economic problems.

Usury was not only contrary to canon law; it was not respectable. When Francesco opened a house for money-changing a friend wrote to him, 'Several men have said to me, Francesco di Marco will lose his reputation as the greatest merchant in Florence, by becoming a money-changer; for there is not one of them' who practises no usury in his contracts;[2] and much more in the same vein. The nice story of the Bolognese professors who lent money at a high rate to their students to buy their books, and then bought them in again cheap when the books had to be pawned, is typical of many: the story shows that extremes of usury were indulged, the fact that it circulated how sensitive men were about it.

A precise definition of usury was always very difficult, because the Church had come reluctantly to concede the principle that though money should not breed money, a man might be paid for incurring danger or the threat of loss; and since any medieval investor took a substantial risk, it was exceedingly difficult to find a living compromise between these principles. But it would be a great mistake to suppose that the Church's law disappeared under

[2] See Origo, p. 150; for what follows see p. 152 (Bolognese professors), pp. 153 ff. (Spanish partners).

a welter of casuistry and evasion. The very fact that all the problems of the thirteenth-century Church were still in evidence and remarkably little altered in the days of the Reformation should warn us not to take the issue too lightly. The problem of usury was forgotten only in the eighteenth century; it is questionable whether the Reformation had any effect on it at all.

Certainly Francesco's letters do not support the view that usury was a purely academic problem. He made money as he could; usury and its problems affected him by setting a limit to his operations; he had little positive vision of the benefit to society that might accrue from his wealth. But he accepted the limit and stuck proudly to it. Some of his transactions seem usurious in the strict sense; but the medieval definitions have little meaning for us in any case. To Francesco, however, the definitions were clear: when it was brought to his notice that his Spanish partners were engaging in border-line transactions (including a modest form of hire purchase), he fell on them. His doubts were made vocal by the moral scruples of his attorney, by rumours that the King of Aragon was taking legal action against 'those who sell with deferred payments', and by his own awareness of the economic risks involved.

Francesco's attitude to usury was largely negative: he eschewed it as he eschewed everything illegal and dangerous. The pursuit of wealth was an end in itself: it gave him many things he valued – a fine house, the possibility of comfort, and a good position – but the habit of anxious profit-making was too strong for him to retire until the very end of his life. 'I ruled myself ill and did not what I could and should have done', he wrote when in his mid fifties, and 'in all this Lent I have heard only six sermons: that is a fine and good life, for one of my standing'.[3] And he often spoke of retirement; but little came of it. None the less, as the years passed, he spent more time and energy preparing for the next world and preparing for the disposal of his fortune.

Ser Lapo Mazzei, Francesco's attorney, though a younger man, began his preparations sooner, and his letters are a remarkable witness to the effect of private reading and long meditation on a pious, but practical minded and anti-clerical layman. He spent

[3] Origo, p. 156.

most of his time looking after the affairs of a Florentine hospital; he was thus able to provide for his own living and look after the poor at the same time. He was as assiduous as the friars who acted as rich men's confessors in pressing on Francesco and his like the duty of alms-giving, and he not infrequently drew Francesco's or Margherita's attention to a good cause. He read the letters of St Jerome and St Gregory, found comfort in the mystical poetry of Jacopone da Todi, and also kept a copy of the *Fioretti*, the Little Flowers of St Francis, to remind him of the sanctity of holy poverty. It is an interesting irony that the *Fioretti* was also one of the few books which Margherita, the merchant's wife, is known to have read. Ser Lapo and his like had a philosophy of wealth, of a kind; but they lived in a world in which the value of poverty was far more clearly defined and appreciated. But these folk were not sentimental about it; they knew its horrors too. And so the attorney came to feel, and on occasions won his friend the merchant to the view that it was the function of the rich to provide for the poor. Nor was Ser Lapo's attitude that so often (and on the whole falsely) described as 'typically medieval', that charity was for the giver, not for the receiver, that it was preached and performed for the soul of the rich man, not to meet the real needs of the poor. Ser Lapo was fully as much concerned with the poor as he was with his rich clients; he often found it convenient that Francesco had a soul, which could be unearthed and ministered to by alms-giving.

But for that soul, too, he cared deeply; and the friendship between the practical, yet spiritually-minded and gentle attorney, and the harsh, grasping merchant is one of the strangest and most attractive of the revelations of the *Archivio Datini*.

'Francesco, I have considered your state a hundred times, on my walks, and in bed, and in my study, when I was most alone. And charity constrains me to tell you the truth, which I think a most precious thing among friends . . . I have already known, from your letters, of your tribulations and the hindrances caused to you by the things of this world; but now that I have seen them with my own eyes, they are far greater than I believed. When I think of the cares of the house you are building, of your branches in far-off lands, your banquets and your accounts, and of many other matters, they seem to me so far beyond what is needful that I realize it is not possible for you to seize an hour from the world and its snares. Yet God has granted you an abundance of earthly goods, and has given you, too, a thousand warnings; and now you are nearly sixty, and free from the cares of children – and are you to wait until your death-bed, when the door-latch of death is lifted, to change your heart?

'In short, I would you should wind up many of your matters, which you yourself say are in order, and desist at once from any more building, and give away some of your riches in alms with your own hands, and value them at their true worth, that is, own them as if they were not yours. . . . I do not ask you to become a priest or a monk, but I do say unto you: put some order into your life.'

About fifteen years later, when Francesco was over seventy, Ser Lapo wrote to Margherita in similar vein.

'Tell Francesco that no man would be more greatly mocked than one who, already on the high seas with his ships, and the wind blowing in his sails, did not steer towards some port. Our port is God. He made us; He calls for us; He returns our gifts to use a hundred-fold. . . . Every man is evil, avaricious, proud, faithless, envious, self-loving; and if he shows some love, it is but a merchant's: "You did good to me, and so will I to you." But beseech your husband, who is your master, to have little to do with such evil men. Let him put an end, if he can, to his vile and worldly dealings; all things are possible in God. Let him use the little time left to us, at the end, for God; let us strive at least to die in peace. For it would be too late to enter your horse, when the race is already run.'[4]

Francesco perfectly accepted the assumptions on which this was based; it was only putting it into practice which was difficult for him. But even to this he made some concession at the very end

[4] Origo, pp. 221, 223.

of his life. Like many active men of strong constitution, death seemed infinitely remote to him until it came very close; but when it was close it was a vivid and horrible reality. His parents had been carried off by the Black Death; he lived through more than one visitation of plague; in later life he himself joined one of those strange processions of penitents who marched, humiliating and flogging themselves, hoping thus to avert God's anger. The popular piety of the time still retained a fairly simple notion of retribution: religious observance was not merely the natural Christian mode of worship, what was owed to God, but a definite payment on which the Christian's credit in the divine bank depended. Ser Lapo would have regarded this as too crude; but Francesco's attitude, so far as we can reconstruct it, was a conventional mingling of conventional (and therefore often inconsistent) assumptions. Religious observance was a normal part of life and a necessary part, both in the eyes of the world and in the eyes of God; the duty of alms-giving must be performed regularly and precisely, and if possible in person; the most important moment in a man's life was the moment of death, and this must be carefully prepared for.

The long dispute on the relations between Protestantism and the rise of Capitalism was in many ways misconceived, because the techniques and qualities which interested Weber and his followers, and even Professor Tawney,[5] existed some centuries before the Reformation. But this is not to say that the problem is not a deeply interesting one, nor that the pursuit of it has been wholly fruitless. The idea that there is an inherent connection between 'Protestantism' and 'Capitalism' seems to me absurd; but if one believes that Puritan principles, extreme anti-clericalism, and the commercial spirit commonly went together in seventeenth-century England, it is interesting to observe how frequently they appeared together in various parts of Europe in the Middle Ages. It is a widely accepted generalization that heresy appeared in France and eastern Germany in the twelfth century, chiefly in centres of trade and along well-defined trade routes; and that this was partly because the heretical tenets travelled with the merchant, and partly because it was the aspiring, half-educated, but

[5] See esp. R. H. Tawney, *Religion and the Rise of Capitalism* (London, 1926).

intelligent mind of the lay merchant which found least satisfaction in a clerically organized orthodoxy, and turned most naturally to new ideas and heretical notions.[6]

Neither Francesco nor Ser Lapo were ever tempted by any of the more open kinds of heresy known in fourteenth-century Europe; nor indeed were they active at this date in Italy. Francesco would have regarded heresy, like usury, as dangerous, and avoided it as he tried to avoid the plague. Ser Lapo liked to hear preachers who were mildly heretical. But what was characteristic of both of them, and of the society in which they lived, was a mild puritanism and a not-so-mild anti-clericalism. The statutes of the Florentine gilds regulated (in theory at least) the private lives of their members with minute precision: a member of the *Arte di Calimala* might not take a concubine (save from among his household slaves, who were excepted from all the rules), nor play a game of chance. The definition of a game of chance was drawn, however, much as it was drawn for the Victorian Sunday; and chess was permitted.

In 1375 and 1376 a great revolt had taken place against the temporal power of the Papacy in central Italy. In 1376 Florence was laid under papal interdict: a papal decree said that her citizens were to be regarded as heretics, her merchants were to be expelled from the territories of all Christian rulers, and their property confiscated; it was legal to steal the goods of a Florentine. 'This is what one gains by going against God and the Church', as a contemporary observed.[7] But there were also plenty of observers, especially among the Florentines themselves, who felt that the Papacy was abdicating its function by behaving in this way; and like so many of the acts of the fourteenth-century Papacy, it fostered existing shoots of anti-clericalism. It was in this period, for instance, that the English William Langland, author of *Piers Plowman*, was expressing his contempt for the Pope and his lack of interest in ecclesiastical organization in a country rejoicing in the anti-papal Statutes of Provisors and Praemunire. Langland was no heretic, at least in intention; he simply felt that the formal organization of the Church was functioning badly and was in

[6] But see pp. 146–7.

[7] Origo, pp. 51–2.

any event irrelevant. On the whole, Ser Lapo would have agreed with him.

Plague and the fervent preaching of a celebrated friar of great fervour (if dubious orthodoxy) eventually determined Francesco to make his will. He had already made up his mind to leave his fortune to the poor, and had had a draft made in which the disposal of the fortune, for pious purposes, was put in the hands of the Bishop of Pistoia. Ser Lapo was deeply shocked. The idea that a cleric should be trusted by a prudent lay merchant of Francesco's experience with the disposal of very large sums of money was, to the pious attorney, inconceivable. His list of the scandals which had come to light when clerics set to work to mismanage, embezzle, or merely enjoy benefactions intended for the poor is reminiscent of the choicest of medieval satire, such as Walter Map's on the Cistercians. Under continued pressure from Ser Lapo, and inspired by the warnings of the fervent friar, Francesco eventually set his will in order in 1400, and left the administration of his effects in the hands of a body which was to be 'in no respect under the authority of the Church or of officials or prelates, or any other member of the clergy'.[8] Nor was any altar or oratory to be set up in the house by reason of which the foundation could be regarded as an ecclesiastical benefice. It is interesting to note that Francesco's foundation is still in existence, and his name still remembered by the poor of Prato 560 years after his death.

This anti-clericalism might well have made central and northern Italy fertile ground for heresy, as it had done in the late twelfth century. But it must not be taken too seriously. So far as Francesco was concerned, it was combined with a meticulous attention to the formal observance of religion. Anti-clericalism was natural to him; he spoke his mind freely and often about clerics and monks; but he fasted and went to mass and to confession regularly; his ledgers were inscribed with the Ten Commandments, and many pages have the words 'In the name of God and of profit' at their head; a strange mixture, perhaps, but wholly characteristic of Francesco and his age. Material prosperity and its pursuit occupied most of his waking hours, and he needed a Ser Lapo at his elbow to remind him of God. But yet he was

[8] See Origo, pp. 326–8, 342 ff., 379–80.

extremely reluctant to exclude the Church from his will, for fear lest he lose valuable prayers. In the end, he accepted by implication Ser Lapo's view that to give everything to the poor mattered more than masses and ceremonies. But these things were not simple in Francesco's mind: he wanted the masses too. And so we take leave of the merchant of Prato, excluding the Church from the administration of his fortune, but calling no less than five Franciscan friars to help him in his sickness; a strange mixture of conflicting assumptions, as most men are.

It was not my intention to deduce from the letters of Francesco and Ser Lapo a composite picture of the medieval Church in the late Middle Ages; but rather to discover what light they had to throw on it, how they viewed it, how they lived in it, how it impinged on them. The outcome, inevitably, is a fair scatter of loosely connected themes; and, I hope, some concrete notion of what it was like to live in the medieval Church, of what were its real problems. At every point we are confronted by the barriers of our knowledge: the first lesson of medieval history is that the fields of our ignorance are boundless. It is a painful lesson, but we must go on learning it. I have not scrupled to walk on delicate grounds of historical reconstruction, and talk about the ideas, intentions, and wishes of men long dead and buried. In a sense these are beyond recovery, and I am aware of the danger of reading oneself into the past. But within limits the task is possible, and all the more worth trying for being dangerous. Many historians prefer to stick to more soluble and external problems; but this is never quite possible to the medievalist. Human nature changes, and unless we try and penetrate its changing nature, medieval man and his activities are closed to us. The medieval Church, among other things, was a state, a monarchy under an autocrat, the Pope. The attitude men had to the Pope and the Papacy, however elusive it may be, was one of the basic elements in medieval history, political and intellectual as well as ecclesiastical.

Two questions I have, however, definitely shirked, for the simple reason that our witnesses do not help us to answer them. But they are relevant none the less, because they are bound to be in anyone's mind as he studies the Church in the later Middle Ages. The first is, what signs are there of a reformation, or, more simply, why was there no reformation in the fourteenth century? And the second, did the enormous growth in European wealth between the eleventh and the fourteenth century lead to a corresponding decline of interest in spiritual concerns; or in other words, did material prosperity lead to growing materialism, and so to a decline of interest in the Christian faith? We can never expect to have precise answers to questions of this kind: the first is a might-have-been, and the historian, in the end, is confined by the narrow boundaries of what actually happened; the second hides behind a simple face a host of complex and puzzling problems.

The merchant of Prato was anti-clerical, and anti-clericalism was clearly fashionable. He and his like cared little for the official hierarchy of the Church, until they became so grand that they could correspond with cardinals. It is not clear that Francesco would have resisted a reformation or that Ser Lapo would have objected to one; but neither was likely to set one in motion. Francesco lived through most of the Great Schism when there were two, eventually three, rival Popes, and knew the eminent Cardinal d'Ailly; but there is no evidence that he knew or cared much for the issues involved. He was, indeed, immersed, most of the time, in his own affairs; and there can be no question that wealth and its outward symbols had a more precise and pervading significance for the men of the fourteenth century than they had for those of the eleventh. This was natural: many of the symbols had simply not existed in the eleventh century. But it is not the same thing to stigmatize the age as materialistic. The rise of living standards in the Church and the world in the eleventh and twelfth centuries had stimulated the new emphasis on and new popularity of asceticism in the monastic orders, and especially among the Cistercians. Growing mercantile wealth stirred St Francis, the merchant's son of Assisi, to found the cult of holy poverty, a cult which was to be the subject of violent controversy in the Church of the fourteenth century. It worked, in fact, both ways. But if we keep the merchant of Prato in mind, we shall save ourselves from falling into a number of traps which are set by questions of this kind.

The Reformation is often attributed, in part, to a crescendo of criticism of the Papacy and of every aspect of the medieval Church; we are told that it happened in the sixteenth century because the moment of maximum criticism happened to coincide with the advent of Luther. But it is, at the very least, worth reflecting, that the only comment of Walter Map, a not wholly uncharacteristic author of the twelfth century, on the Papacy is highly critical – like Luther, he accuses Rome of extreme corruption; that Walter Map's pages have more to tell us of heresy and heretics (however garbled) than Francesco di Marco Datini's; that the French and north Italian heretics of the twelfth and early thirteenth centuries caused as much panic in the Church as the Lollards and the Hussites – and that one sect of them, the Waldensians, still exists. If we regard the insouciance of a great part of the population as an essential element in the success of the sixteenth-century reformation, it is hard not to feel that Ser Lapo was more anti-clerical than many sixteenth-century Englishmen. There were many unexpected nooks and crannies in the medieval Church; and its history was anything but inevitable.

Index